Lived Islam in Africa and its Missiological Implications for Pentecostals

Nuekpe Dieudonne Komla

© 2023 Dieudonne Komla Nuekpe

Published 2023 by Langham Monographs
An imprint of Langham Publishing
www.langhampublishing.org

Langham Publishing and its imprints are a ministry of Langham Partnership

Langham Partnership
PO Box 296, Carlisle, Cumbria, CA3 9WZ, UK
www.langham.org

ISBNs:
978-1-83973-746-6 Print
978-1-83973-949-1 ePub
978-1-83973-950-7 PDF

Dieudonne Komla Nuekpe has asserted his right under the Copyright, Designs and Patents Act, 1988 to be identified as the Author of this work.

All rights reserved. No part of this publication may be reproduced, stored in a retrieval system or transmitted, in any form or by any means, electronic, mechanical, photocopying, recording or otherwise, without the prior written permission of the publisher or the Copyright Licensing Agency.

Requests to reuse content from Langham Publishing are processed through PLSclear. Please visit www.plsclear.com to complete your request.

All scripture quotations, unless otherwise indicated, are from The Holy Bible, English Standard Version® (ESV®), copyright © 2001 by Crossway, a publishing ministry of Good News Publishers. Used by permission. All rights reserved.

Scripture quotations marked (NIV) are taken from the Holy Bible, New International Version®, Anglicised, NIV®. Copyright © 1979, 1984, 2011 by Biblica, Inc®. Used by permission. All rights reserved worldwide.

Scripture quotations marked (RSV) are from Revised Standard Version of the Bible, copyright © 1946, 1952, and 1971 National Council of the Churches of Christ in the United States of America. Used by permission. All rights reserved.

Scripture quotations marked (NRSV) are from the New Revised Standard Version Bible, copyright © 1989 National Council of the Churches of Christ in the United States of America. Used by permission. All rights reserved.

Scripture quotations marked (NASB) taken from the New American Standard Bible®, Copyright © 1960, 1962, 1963, 1968, 1971, 1972, 1973, 1975, 1977, 1995 by The Lockman Foundation. Used by permission.

Scripture quotations marked (HCSB) are taken from the Holman Christian Standard Bible®, Copyright © 1999, 2000, 2002, 2003, 2009 by Holman Bible Publishers. Used by permission. Holman Christian Standard Bible®, Holman CSB®, and HCSB® are federally registered trademarks of Holman Bible Publishers.

British Library Cataloguing-in-Publication Data
A catalogue record for this book is available from the British Library

ISBN: 978-1-83973-746-6

Cover & Book Design: projectluz.com

Langham Partnership actively supports theological dialogue and an author's right to publish but does not necessarily endorse the views and opinions set forth here or in works referenced within this publication, nor can we guarantee technical and grammatical correctness. Langham Partnership does not accept any responsibility or liability to persons or property as a consequence of the reading, use or interpretation of its published content.

This work by Dieudonne Komla Nuekpe on Islam in Ghana from a Pentecostal perspective is very welcome for a number of reasons. First, the work identifies a strong bridge between Ghanaian Muslims and Christians in the common heritage of African Traditional Religions. Pentecostal/Charismatic Christianity's focus on the supernatural and spiritual encounters, including dreams, visions, and faith healing, resonates with many Ghanaian Muslims who the writer identifies as "folk Muslims." The missional approach adopted by the author will also resonate with Pentecostals. Both Islam and Christianity are missionary religions, and the discussion about engaging Muslims with the gospel will not come as a surprise to Ghanaian Muslims or Christians. What makes this work stand out, however, is the spirit of mutual respect and less confrontational approach the writer recommends. This makes the work a very valuable contribution to Christian understanding of Islam and engagement with Muslims in Ghana and beyond.

John Azumah, PhD
Executive Director, The Sanneh Institute
Visiting Professor, Yale Divinity School, Connecticut, USA

Dr. Komla begins this book by providing comprehensive information about the Islamic faith, which is essential for gospel workers among Muslims to comprehend. Then he takes the readers further, opening their missional eyes to see the needs of ordinary adherents called "folk Muslims" in the Ghanaian context. The book not only helps the readers with extensive knowledge about folk Muslims but also furnishes practical guidelines for holistically sharing the gospel among them in a loving, wise, peaceful, and effective way. The feat of his discussions culminates in his emphasis on the "power encounter" ministry considering the power-oriented worldview of Ghanaian Muslims. His passionate suggestions from his African Pentecostal perspective are spurring enough to make the readers revisit and review missional approaches to the so-called folk Muslims. This book is a must-read for those sincerely seeking an efficacious method for evangelism and discipleship among Ghanaian Muslims and other Muslims worldwide.

Caleb Kim, PhD
Director of PhD in Interreligious Studies,
Program Coordinator of the Center for the Study of Religions,
Africa International University, Kenya

With the awareness of the power-oriented religious context of Ghanaian Christianity, Dr. Nuekpe, with emic perspective, critically raises the significance of the gifts of the Holy Spirit for evangelizing the people of other religions who share the similar spiritual heritage. Ghanaian mission history demonstrates the effectiveness of evangelism with the power of the Holy Spirit. Today, considering those people who are in existential need due to lack of resources to cope with the pandemic, Christians have great opportunity to engage them with the gospel. While Dr. Nuekpe regards experiential aspects as an important factor affecting conversion of the people, he emphasizes the importance of worldview change through continuous study of the Scripture. This is a timely study giving great insight into effectively evangelizing the people not only in Ghana, but also around the world.

Chang Seop Kang, PhD
Adjunct Professor of Missiology,
Torch Trinity Graduate University, South Korea
Senior Pastor, Incheon Chinese Christian Church

I have been pointedly informed after reading through the pages of this masterpiece of work, and I trust it will bridge the gap between the Christian community and the Muslim community. Reaching out to the Muslim world with the gospel of Christ has been made easier and simpler by Dr. Dieudonne Komla Nuekpe.

Paul Frimpong-Manso, PhD
Former General Superintendent, Assemblies of God Ghana
President, Ghana Pentecostal and Charismatic Council
Chairman, Ghana Evangelism Committee

Dr. Nuekpe's approach to this subject of Christian-Muslim relations in Ghana is interesting and truly Pentecostal. While many scholars have taken the historical, doctrinal, dialogical, or political approaches to Islam and Muslims in Ghana, the author approaches the subject from a purely spiritual and conversion angle saying, "this study demonstrates that Ghanaian Muslims are predominantly folk Muslims, a group of Muslims who did not fully abandon the practices of African Traditional Religions (ATRs) when they adopted Islam. As such, folk Muslims are power-oriented people like Pentecostals, and both groups share the Ghanaian spiritual heritage of ATRs' practices. This paper proposes how this shared heritage can provide bridges for Pentecostals to engage Muslims with the gospel." His identification of the predominance of "folk" life among Ghanaian Muslims makes the work worth reading, particularly for people interested in sharing the gospel with Muslims. The book is a must-read for all Christians who seek to understand Islam in Ghana.

Nathan Iddrisu Samwini, PhD
Senior Lecturer in Islam and Christian-Muslim Relations, KNUST, Ghana
Previously Bishop of the Methodist Church Ghana, Tamale Diocese

Dr. Dieudonne Komla Nuekpe's *Lived Islam in Africa and Its Missiological Implications for Pentecostals* provides deep inspirations for missionaries around the world. The core theme of the book is how to effectively evangelize Ghana's folk Muslims. The author offers a concise and clear explanation of the history and characteristics of Ghana's indigenous religions, emphasizing their supernatural and spiritual aspects. Furthermore, the book delves into folk Islam in Ghana that is syncretized with these beliefs, and explores Ghanaian Christianity, particularly Pentecostalism. Then it analyzes the evangelistic strategies of existing churches and concludes that Pentecostalism is a powerful answer. The book demonstrates that God's supremacy provides a different level of dominance than other spiritual forces. This lesson leads to helping folk Muslim followers in Ghana to experience the power of the Holy Spirit. At the same time, the author emphasizes the need to have understanding of sound theological principles and cautions against an exclusive focus on supernatural abilities. That is, this book highlights the importance of harmony between the word of God and the power of the Holy Spirit.

While reading this book, I recalled an anecdote from the early days of Yoido Full Gospel Church, in which Pastor David Yong-gi Cho won a confrontation with a shaman regarding the healing of a sick woman. From the early church to the present day, being filled with the Holy Spirit has been the most effective way to preach the gospel throughout the ages. This book is an invaluable work that not only explains the strategies and methods of evangelization in Ghana and beyond but also provides deep insight into the essence of the gospel, the right missionary strategies, and the direction to follow.

Rev. Younghoon Lee, Ph.D
Senior Pastor,
Yoido Full Gospel Church, Seoul, South Korea
President, the Christian Council of Korea

Although Pentecostals and Muslims live peacefully in Ghana, the exclusivist stance of Ghanaian Christianity and the evangelistic zeal of Pentecostals to preach the gospel to Muslims result in occasional clashes and tension between them. In this excellent and well-written book, *Lived Islam in Africa and Its Missiological Implications for Pentecostals*, Dieudonne Komla Nuekpe has discovered the nexus of shared heritage that provide bridges for Pentecostals in Ghana to share their faith with folk Muslims in a peaceful atmosphere. The book is timely and thought-provoking; it will serve as a textbook for theological institutions and a resource book for all Christians who are concerned with Christian-Muslim relations in Ghana and beyond. Dieudonne is to be congratulated on making a valuable contribution to the important literature on Ghanaian Christianity.

Christian Tsekpoe, PhD
Head of Ministerial Formation and Training, Pentecost University, Ghana
Chairman, Home & Urban Missions Committee of the Church of Pentecost, Ghana

To Apostle Eric Nyamekye,
the Chairman of The Church of Pentecost, for peaceful
coexistence with Muslims for national development.

Contents

Foreword xiii

Abstract xvii

Abbreviations xix

Acknowledgments xxi

Introduction 1
    Statement of the Research Problem 1
    Background of the Study 4
        The Growth of Islam and Its Implications for Pentecostals 4
        The Rise of African Pentecostalism 6
        The Growth of the Church of Pentecost as Local African
            Pentecostalism 7
        Folk Muslims in Ghana 8
        Christians' Engagement with Muslims in Ghana 11
        The Approach of the Roman Catholic Church 12
    Statement of Purpose 14
    Problem 15
    Assumptions 15
    Methodology 16
    Limitations 18
    Thesis Statement 18
    Research Questions 18
        Central Research Question 18
        Subquestions 18
    Importance of the Research 19
    Definition of Terms 19
    Structure of the Study 20

Chapter 1 21
*The Historical Development of Christianity in Ghana and the
Impact of Pentecostalism*
    Indigenous Religion in Ghana 21
    The Arrival of Christianity 25
        Catholic Missions in Ghana 25
        Protestant Missions in Ghana 27
        The Impact of Western Missions 28

Origins of Global Pentecostalism	30
Pentecostalism in Ghana	34
The Precursor to Pentecostalism: Spiritual Churches	34
The Emergence of Pentecostalism	37
The First Phase of Pentecostalism	38
The Second Phase: Neo-Pentecostalism	39
The Impact of Pentecostalism on Ghanaian Christianity	41
Summary	44

Chapter 2 45
The Development of Islam and the Nature of the Christian–Muslim Relationship in Ghana

Islam in West Africa	45
History of Islam in Ghana	46
The Characteristics and Spread of Islam in Ghana	49
The Emergence and Expansion of Islam Since the Mid-Twentieth Century	52
Islamic Reformist Movements in Ghana	52
Emergence of Ghana's Islamic Groups	55
The Sufi Order: Tariqa Tijaniyya	56
The Mahdi Movement	59
The Ahmadiyya Movement	59
The Ahmadiyya Mission in Ghana	60
The Impact of the Ahmadiyya Mission	61
Shi'ism	63
Understanding the Christian-Muslim Relationship in Ghana	66
Inter-Muslim Groups	66
Islamic Violence Based on Socioeconomic and Political Dynamics	67
Doctrinal and Interpretational Differences	67
Christian-Muslim Relations	71
Historical Development of the Church of Pentecost's Missions to Muslims	73
The Converted Muslim Christian Ministries	77
Summary	83

Chapter 3 85
The Influence of Animism on the Beliefs and Practices of Ghanaian Folk Muslims

Core Beliefs	85
Arkan: The Five Pillars	88

  Shahada: Declaration of Faith 88
  Salat: Ritual Prayer 89
  Zakat: Almsgiving 91
  Sawm: Fasting 93
  Hajj: Pilgrimage 93
 The Everyday Life of Folk Muslims in Ghana 95
  Folk Muslims' World of Spirits 95
  Jinn and Spiritual Forces 96
  Religiomagical Practices 100
  The Evil Eye 105
  Divination or Pathfinding 106
  Veneration of Saints 107
  Ancestral Worship 108
  Rites of Passage 109
 Summary 112

Chapter 4 115
Existing Methods of Sharing the Gospel with Folk Muslims
 The Direct Approach 115
 The Indirect or Fulfillment Approach 117
 The Dialogical Model 118
 Interreligious Dialogue 119
 Muslims' Understanding of Jesus 120
  God's Self Revelation and Oneness 120
  The Birth and Life of Jesus 123
  The Crucifixion and Death of Jesus 125
  The Nature and Sonship of Jesus 127
  Jesus's Return 130
 Pentecostals' Theological Medium to Approach Folk Muslims 131
  Jesus as an Ancestor in the Ghanaian Folk Context 131
  The Holy Spirit as a Bridge to Folk Muslims 135
  The Power of Lifestyle and Character 137
  The Power of Oral Word Proclamation 138
  The Grace, Love, and Truth of Jesus to Folk Muslims 140
 Pentecostals and the Existential Needs of Folk Islam 147
 Summary 148

Chapter 5 151
Pentecostals' Engagement with Folk Muslims in Ghana
 Power Encounters and the Experiential Needs of Folk Muslims 151
 Understanding Power Encounters 152

    Power Encounters in the Former Scriptures..155
    Power Encounters in Jesus's Ministry 157
    Releasing Power Encounters through Prayer..159
    Pentecostalism as Folk Christianity 161
    Pentecostal Practices of Healing and Deliverance................................163
    Power Encounters as Continuous Phenomena....................................164
    Power Encounters in Missions to Folk Muslims Today......................170
    Muslims in the Postpandemic Era...172
    Summary...174

Conclusion 177
    Research Contributions 181
    Recommendations for Further Study 184

Bibliography... 185

Foreword

As the world enters the fourth year of the COVID-19 pandemic, it is cautiously attempting a return to the "old normal." While this is welcome news, the collective memory of illness and death – and the indignity of it all – will be difficult to forsake. Amidst an unending pandemic, many have been brought to acknowledge the helplessness of human beings in the face of disease and death, leading to contemplations on the world that follows death. While the natural result of such contemplation is often conversion to established religion, distorted results have varied from indiscriminate dependence on heresies to blind reliance on unhealthy spiritual practices.

Simultaneously, the pandemic has created new circumstances for forging solidarity across religious differences, united against discrimination and death. For instance, in the most recent issue of *Muslim World*, an article on "A Pandemic within a Pandemic"[1] has garnered attention for discussing Black Muslims and Black Christians in the United States standing in solidarity against the reality of medical injustice, in which systemic racism gives rise to the marginalization of minorities in vaccine distribution and expert care.

Published against this backdrop, *Lived Islam in Africa and Its Missiological Implications for Pentecostals*, by Dr. Nuekpe Dieudonne Komla presents timely and applicable missiological reflections on the role of Pentecostal Christianity in sowing cross-religious solidarity and healing in Ghana.

Christians and Muslims in Ghana have enjoyed a mostly cordial relationship in which until recently, Ghanaian Christians did not engage Muslims in evangelism. Specifically, Dr. Komla analyzes that three key facets of Ghanian

---

1. Grafton, "Muslim-Christian Relations," 563–72.

society have maintained peace among Christians and Muslims: "cultural community, cooperative education, and political alliance."

For most Ghanaians, one's ethnic or tribal identity precedes one's religious identity in importance: Ghanaians will view one another as brothers and sisters of one nation before recognizing them as belonging to a specific religion. Thus, this Ghanaian prioritization of communal identity constantly reinforced in and integrated throughout the public sphere – at the market, farms, funerals, cultural festivities – creates a foundation for Christians to forge healthy relationships with Muslims within the community. In an institutional dimension, the cooperative education system in Ghana invites Muslim and Christian students to attend the same high schools where all are exposed to African Traditional Religions (ATR), Christianity, and Islam. By creating a space conducive to building shared understanding, it consequently contributes to relieving interreligious tensions. Finally, Dr. Komla assesses that the practice of integrating both Muslims and Christians into elite government positions has contributed enormously to the peaceful coexistence of believers in Ghana by safeguarding against conflict caused by one religious group wielding political force upon the other.

Despite the generally peaceful atmosphere sustained by these societal mechanisms, Christian-Muslim conflict continues to arise in Ghana when both faiths strive to create converts. The emergence of some Christian groups that attempt to convert Muslims into Christianity without adequate knowledge of the appropriate means of engaging Muslims has led to fierce anti-Christian polemics by Muslims, marring the peaceful relationship between the two faiths. As Dr. Komla observes, the same applies to Pentecostal Christians in Ghana.

Although they once played a leading role in the growth of Christianity in Ghana, Dr. Komla evaluates that Pentecostal Christians now lack the proper understanding and approaches to engage Muslims with the gospel. To address these needs, this book highlights areas of misunderstanding and ignorance that can be reduced among Ghanaian Christians, beginning with the observation that Ghanaian Muslims are folk Muslims who share a common spiritual heritage of ATR practices with Pentecostals. Founded on his mastery of various texts as well as insightful reflections from his own ministry, the author posits that such ATR practices can serve as bridges for Pentecostal engagement with Muslims through the gospel, further proposing ways in which Pentecostals can engage Muslims while preserving the peaceful coexistence of faiths in Ghana.

The revitalization of Pentecostal engagement with Muslims in Ghana is especially crucial as the country struggles to recover from the pandemic and the challenges it posed to the truth claims and doctrines of many religious communities. With its emphasis on the physical healing and the sustaining power of the Holy Spirit in the midst of affliction, the Pentecostal community was positioned to respond effectively and innovatively to the COVID-19 pandemic. Indeed, Dr. Komla writes that such themes of healing, deliverance, and restoration that constitute the most essential commodities on the African Pentecostal market are the most felt needs of Ghanaian Muslims in the pandemic and postpandemic period, highlighting the potential that Pentecostal Christianity holds for Ghanaian Muslims. In this sense, Dr. Komla redefines Pentecostalism as "a reconstructed religion that responds to the daily needs and experiences of spiritual and physical insecurity that confront many Africans," irrespective of their religious affiliations.

Crafted by Dr. Komla with a deep understanding of Ghanaian Christianity and Islam, as well as insight into African Traditional Religion that encompasses the two, I hope and pray that this book will become a driving force for Ghana, known as the resistant belt to Islam in Africa, in becoming a resistant belt against the history of Muslim-Christian conflict.

Ah Young Kim, PhD
Professor of Mission
Torch Trinity Graduate University, Seoul (South Korea)
Director and Editor-in-Chief of Torch Trinity Centre for Islamic Studies

Abstract

This study describes folk Muslims' presence in Ghana and analyzes the missiological implications for Pentecostals. Ghana was once known as a resistant belt to Islam in Africa. Unfortunately, this resistance belt has collapsed, evidenced by an unignorable presence of Islam in Ghana. While Christian-Muslim relationships in Ghana are generally cordial, there can be tension, misunderstandings, and religious clashes among them when Christians share the gospel with Muslims or make efforts to proselytize using local mission models.

This research creates awareness of Muslims' presence in Ghana and highlights these areas of misunderstanding or ignorance to show how Pentecostals, the fastest-growing group of Christians in Ghana, can peacefully engage Ghanaian Muslims with the gospel. To do so, this study integrated research from intercultural and Islamic studies, Pentecostal missiology, church history, cultural anthropology, and biblical theology. Through a descriptive and analytic examination of such literature, this study demonstrates that Ghanaian Muslims are predominantly folk Muslims, a group of Muslims who did not fully abandon the practices of African Traditional Religions (ATRs) when they adopted Islam. As such, folk Muslims are power-oriented people like Pentecostals, and both groups share the Ghanaian spiritual heritage of ATRs' practices. This paper proposes how this shared heritage can provide bridges for Pentecostals to engage Muslims with the gospel. Specifically, four engagements are detailed: engagement with theology (truth encounters) through gentleness and respect, engagement through loving services that meet existential needs, engagement through power encounters that meet experiential needs, and engagement through discipleship and the sustaining power of the Holy Spirit.

Abbreviations

AECAWA-IRDC	Association of Episcopal Conferences of Anglophone West Africa Inter-Religious Dialogue Commission
AFMI	Action Faith Ministries International
ATRs	African Traditional Religions
BC	Bishops Conference
CCG	Christian Council of Ghana
CMA	Coalition of Muslim Associations
CMCM	Converted Muslim Christian Ministries
COP	The Church of Pentecost
GPCC	Ghana Pentecostal and Charismatic Council
ICGC	International Central Gospel Church
PhD	Doctor of Philosophy
PNDC	Provisional National Defense Council
PROCMURA	Program for Christian-Muslim Relationships in Africa
TTGU	Torch Trinity Graduate University
WHO	World Health Organization

Acknowledgments

Thanks be to God for his abundant grace, protection, and divine guidance that navigated me to Torch Trinity Graduate University (TTGU). As a Ghanaian proverb says, "Knowledge is like a Baobab tree, one person's arms cannot encompass it."[1] I acknowledge that my journey toward a doctor of philosophy degree could never have materialized without the tireless efforts of the people who devoted their time, knowledge, prayer, and financial support to it. This is a standing tribute to those valuable contributors too numerous to mention each by name.

Particularly meriting my profound gratitude is my supervisor Dr. Ah Young Kim, my lecturer and mentor par excellence, who has significantly impacted me and positively changed my perception about Muslims through her doctoral seminar on Islamic studies. This paradigm shift eventually birthed in me the decision to take on the current task. Dr. Kim provided expert guidance and unwavering encouragement, painstakingly leading me through the academic rigor from the initial proposal to the completion of this paper. I am truly grateful. I am grateful also to Dr. Hyung Jin Park for enthusiastically providing valuable research ideas, encouragement, and corrections. I thank Dr. Jeongmo Yoo for serving as an interdisciplinary reader and Dr. Chang Seop Kang for his constructive criticism, prayers, and contributions. I sincerely thank Dr. Seung Hyun Chung (external reader) for participating in my academic journey and spending precious time to read my work.

I would also like to express my heartfelt appreciation to the past and present presidents of TTGU, Dr. Jung-Sook Lee and Dr. Yoon Hee Kim, for their leadership and institutional support. I am grateful to all the professors who

---

1. "Baobab: How One Tree Gives Life Mystery and Hope," 28 July 2017, https://storytimeedu.org/stories/2017/7/26/tree-of-life-the-baobab.

have taught me and encouraged me during my entire time at TTGU. I thank the TTGU administrative staff and the librarians.

I would like to express my appreciation for Rev. Prof. B. Y. Quarshie (Akrofi-Christaller Institute of Theology, Mission and Culture) for reading through my proposal and offering insightful suggestions toward this current work and Dr. Hannah S. An for her encouragement at the initial stage of this work.

I am indebted to the staff of the Woodberry Institute for Muslim-Christian Relations for their cooperation, kindheartedness, and continuous prayers. They are wonderful. Thank you to my colleague, missionary Ivaneide Xavier de Sousa, who greatly encouraged me, peer-reviewed my work, and provided helpful corrections. I thank my friends, pastors J. W. Park and Yon Hyok Lim, for their bond of fellowship and support. In addition, I am grateful to Pastor Theophilus Agbemenu for his continuous encouragement.

Sister Emily Tregelles, an indefatigable, cooperative, and highly considerate editor, brilliantly edited the entire work. I am grateful to her for her sacrifice and time invested in this work. I sincerely thank Rev. Prof. J. Kwabena Asamoah-Gyadu, Rev. Dr. Robert Owusu, Apostle Dr. Lord Elorm Donkor, Apostle Dr. Samuel Ofori, and Apostle Dr. Emmanuel Anim for their encouragement and for offering relevant suggestions at the initial stage of this work. I am grateful to Professor John Azumah for taking personal interest in this work, giving informal tutorial sessions, and providing sources relevant to my context, despite his busy schedule. Apostle Nii Kotei Djani deserves special commendation for being a source of blessing to me. I would also like to express my profound gratitude to Apostle Eric Nyamekye (current chairman of the COP), Apostle Professor Opoku Onyinah (former chairman), Apostle Alexander Nana Yaw Kumi-Larbi (general secretary), Apostle Emmanuel Agymang Bekoe (IMD), and the entire executive council for their permission and support of this work.

Over the years, many people have genuinely expressed concern in the turning points of my life, especially Apostle Emmanuel Gyesi-Addo to whom I am particularly grateful for his role in my academic pursuit at various times. I cannot forget my elder sister Warrant Officer Grade 1 (WO1) Rtd. Elizabeth Nuekpe and the entire family for their continuous words of encouragement.

To my dear wife, Juanita Recamier Toffa-Nuekpe who nudged me to pursue this study, sacrificed her comfort, and stood firm with me while providing encouragement, prayers, suggestions, love, and peace of mind that enabled me to finish this work: Bravo! To my sons Jacques Morris and Jean Claude, may the Lord bless you for your moral support.

Introduction

Statement of the Research Problem

During the early spread of Islam in Africa, Islam was geographically confined to north Africa. Samuel Zwemer has noted that Islam was about to die as a religion because it contained "the germs of death."[1] However, instead of its predicted death, Islam has experienced a resurgence and rapid growth that has made its presence felt around the world and in Ghana. This spread of Islam in Africa and especially in Ghana is an undeniable reality. Although John Spencer Trimingham once described Ghana as a "resistant belt" to Muslims' influence in Africa,[2] it did not remain that way. Ghana's resistant belt has gradually collapsed, as evidenced by the proliferation of mosques in the capital city, Accra. John Azumah has noted that there is hardly any village in Ghana today where one cannot find Muslims, whether as a minority or majority.[3]

The collapse of this resistant belt has missiological significance for Christians living in Ghana. One major motivating factor that led Christian missionaries to west Africa in the early fifteenth century was their desire to stop the spread of Islam in Africa.[4] The Edinburgh Missionary Conference later emphasized this same objective of halting the spread of Islam when it stated that the "whole strategy of Christian mission in Africa should be

---

1. Zwemer, *Influence of Animism*, 18, quoted in Twumasi, "Understanding Folk Islam," 49.
2. Trimingham, *Islam in West Africa*, 19.
3. Azumah, "Controversy and Restraint," 23–26.
4. Onwubiko, *History of West Africa*, cited in Dovlo and Asante, "Reinterpreting the Straight Path," 214.

viewed in relation to Islam."⁵ Unless an appropriate awareness is developed among Ghanaians, the country that was once thought to be a Christian nation may become a Muslim one.

This awareness is especially needed among Pentecostals. The Ghana Pentecostal and Charismatic Council (GPCC) is the largest religious umbrella body in Ghana that spearheads the affairs of Pentecostal and charismatic denominations, and the Church of Pentecost is a leading member of this council in terms of influence and membership strength. Despite their size and influence, Rahman Yakubu has noted that the GPCC has "no policies or training for member churches on the issue relating to Islam and Christian-Muslim relationships."⁶ Member churches do not have a good understanding of Islam, and this is often seen in their confrontational and polemical approach to the Christian-Muslim relationship, which is characterized by bitter clashes between GPCC members and Muslims.⁷

In particular, a greater awareness of folk Islam is needed. Folk Islam is a variety of the faith that has resulted from Islam mixing with superstitions and traditional African religious practices, especially in sub-Saharan Africa. The lived experience and religious practice of folk Muslims, those who practice folk Islam, deviates from orthodox Islam on account of folk customs and beliefs from mysticism and animism.⁸

Because mission leaders of the Global South confidently rely on the supernatural workings of the resurrected Christ through power encounters, they may be especially suited to engage folk Muslims.⁹ Those from the Global South are generally less developed than the Global North, so they are more likely to appeal to supernatural encounters. Folk Muslims are more interested in God's interventions in their present reality than some form of dogmatic discussion about God. Thus, mission leaders in the Global South who rely on the sustaining power of the Holy Spirit are able to demonstrate God's work

---

5. Onwubiko, 214.
6. Yakubu, "Ghana," 307.
7. Yakubu, 307.
8. Hiebert, *Transforming Worldviews*, 46.
9. Livingstone, "Laborer from Global South," 86.

among folk Muslims. However, without appropriate training or methods of engagement, Pentecostals' mission to Muslims[10] will lack effectiveness.

Many Christians living in the Muslim majority world would not dare witness to their fellow Muslim citizens even if they were offered very good salaries to do so.[11] They suffer humiliation and physical attacks and are considered second class citizens, so regardless of countless seminars and training by Western missionaries to engage local people in the Middle East, Pakistan, India, Bangladesh, Malaysia, and Indonesia, they produce little result.[12] The Global South, therefore, has become a trusted disciple-maker for Muslims. Churches in Latin America, Africa, and Asia are looked upon by the world to engage Muslims with the gospel because of the growth of Christianity in these areas.[13] It is expected that by 2025, four out of five missionaries will come from the Global South, so the work of the harvest will be upon their shoulders.[14] Therefore, research from an African perspective is needed to raise awareness and reduce misunderstandings among Christian-Muslim relationships in Ghana and to develop a mission model for Pentecostal evangelism to folk Muslims.

As many people are striving to win Muslims to Christ, "we are not at the beginning of the end, but only the end of the beginning"; thus, more effort and fruitful practices are needed to share the gospel.[15] Due to the growth of Christianity in the Global South, including Ghana, there are both high hopes and some skepticism that the great increase in numbers will translate to a great increase in pioneer church planters among Muslims, thereby reducing the growth of Islam.

---

10. The phrase "Pentecostals' mission to Muslims" is used to mean the sharing of the gospel with Muslims by people of a Pentecostal background, whose identity is rooted in the events of Pentecost (Acts 2) and the Azusa Street revival of the early twentieth century, which emphasized the supernatural manifestations of the Holy Spirit through the gifts of the Holy Spirit. More specifically, the participation in the mission of God to folk Muslims by Pentecostals in the Southern Hemisphere is intended. Onyinah, "Movement of the Spirit," 273–86.

11. Livingstone, "Laborer from Global South," 42.

12. Livingstone, 42.

13. Livingstone, 41.

14. Livingstone, 43.

15. Livingstone, 39.

Background of the Study
The Growth of Islam and Its Implications for Pentecostals

Many people think the majority of Muslims reside in the Arab world. However, Arabs make up only 20 percent of the Islam population in the world.[16] Demographic studies show that Islam is the majority religion of fifty countries, especially in Southeast Asia. This implies that the presence of Islam is well represented in non-Arab nations, which is evidenced by the cultural diversity that is found in mosques all over the world. Islam has been ranked as one of the fastest-growing world religions,[17] and this trend may be linked to the decrease of Christianity in the Western world. There is enough visible evidence of Muslims' increasing presence in the Western world to bolster Muslims' motivation for Islam to assume a global dominance. An evaluation of the growth of world religions by country from 1900 to 2050 projects that Islam will grow from 0.2 billion to 2.5 billion people. Within this period, the world population will have grown almost six-fold while Muslims will have increased more than twelve-fold. Islam has considerably outgrown Christianity, considering that Christians in the West no longer have large families and the birthrate is low compared to Muslim families who have many children. The conversion into Islam through marriage, persuasion, and conviction accounts for no more than 10 percent of its growth while almost 90 percent of its growth is through birth rate.[18] The growth trend of Islam over the years has proven that the non-Muslim world has undergone historical transformations that have resulted in a tremendous crisis for Christianity.

Likewise, the influence of Islam is found in almost every sector of Ghana. For a few years now, Muslims have embarked on an aggressive, secular agenda to install Islamic education systems, and the government of Ghana, for political reasons, has gradually established Islamic education units that superintend English and Arabic government-funded schools. Since Ghana's independence, the international Muslim community has taken a keen interest in Ghana and strategically supported the Islamic agenda there through the provision of government loans and various aids for Muslim NGOs. They have also supported Ghana's agricultural and health sectors, among others. The Parliament

---

16. Johnstone, "Look at the Fields," 6.
17. Lipka and Hackett, "Why Muslims Are."
18. Johnstone, "Look at the Fields," 40.

of Ghana, for the first time since 1996, has granted two statutory holidays for Muslims, Eid-al-Fitr and Eid-al-Adha, a visible sign that Islam is gaining influence in Ghana. As of 2002, the Coalition of Muslim Associations (CMA) marked the growth of Islam in Ghana at 45 percent of the population of 21 million people.[19] Though the Ghana Statistical Service's census in 2000 contradicted the CMA's figure, the dispersion of Muslims across the country and their presence and influence in public spheres, especially in the northern region of Ghana, supports the CMA's claim.[20] Since the year 2000, Ghana has elected two Muslim vice presidents under the auspices of the National Patriotic Party. The influence of Islam in Ghana can no longer be underestimated, as evidenced by the visible presence of Muslims in politics and other ministries in the country. Even though it is expected of every Ghanaian to contribute to nation building and be politically conscious and active, Christians must be conscious about the effects of Muslims' presence. Mohammad Saani Ibrahim has stated that a reason that led to the ascendancy of Islam (Wahhabism) in northern Ghana was the election and influence of Muslims in the electoral politics in Ghana. In the 2008 parliamentary elections, Muslims won twenty-one parliamentary seats in the north and their political dominance eventually gave them "leverage in the power of disseminating their doctrinal beliefs and acceptance by the people."[21]

In the middle of the 1980s, there was a sudden emergence of Christian mission to Muslims in Ghana, which was spearheaded by specific Christian missions like "Xristomus Publications, the Converted Muslim Christian Ministries (CMCM), and the Markaz Al Bishara."[22] Despite the efforts of these groups in reaching out to Muslims, Islam continues to grow in Ghana. In 2010, according to the Pew Research Center's religious demography, 74.9 percent of the Ghanaian population was Christian, and Muslims constituted only 15.8 percent of the population. As of 2020, the Christian population dropped to 73.6 percent while the Muslim population increased to 17.5 percent. By 2050, it is estimated that the Muslim population will dramatically increase to 22.3 percent (11,030,000 people) while Christians will drop to

---

19. Dovlo and Asante, "Reinterpreting the Straight Path," 216.
20. Dovlo and Asante, 216.
21. Ibrahim, "Decline of Sufism," 2.
22. Dovlo and Asante, "Reinterpreting the Straight Path," 214.

67.8 percent (34,490,000 people).[23] While Samuel Huntington predicted that the population of Muslims would outnumber the Christian population by the early twenty-first century, Philip Jenkins asserts that Christianity will not likely succumb to the rising number of Muslims due to the rising number of evangelical Christians, especially in the Southern Hemisphere.[24] Patrick Johnstone also asserts that as some Muslims are converting into evangelical Christianity, one day it will be a wonder how many of Jesus's disciples will rise from Muslim graves.[25]

The early missionaries in Ghana first targeted the traditionalists, or the adherents of the indigenous religions, with the aim of preventing their conversion into Islam. By doing so, they tried to stunt the spread of Islam in Ghana. However, they made no deliberate efforts to engage Muslims with the gospel. Muslims and Christians coexisted in Ghana as rivals for the souls of "unconverted pagans." A few Muslims experienced some form of Christian influence in Christian mission schools, but there is no evidence that these mission schools successfully discipled Muslims in the Christian faith.[26] For this reason, despite the biblical mandate and the historic aspiration of missionaries in Ghana to engage Muslims with the gospel, adherents of Islam have been neglected more than any other population in Ghana.[27]

The Rise of African Pentecostalism

Despite the efforts of modern missionary movements, there were globally only three million followers of Jesus from Protestant churches by 1887.[28] Though the gospel message continued to be preached, after the Edinburgh Missionary Conference, from 1910 to 1960, the seed fell on hard ground characterized by modern, liberal theology that rendered it unproductive. After the 1960s, there was an increase in conversions resulting from the end of Western colonial imperialism.[29] Massive growth of Christianity occurred in the Southern Hemisphere, especially in Africa, Asia, and Latin America.

---

23. Pew Research Center, "Future of World Religions."
24. Johnstone, "Look at the Fields," 31.
25. Johnstone, 40.
26. Dovlo and Asante, "Reinterpreting the Straight Path," 215.
27. Dovlo and Asante, 214.
28. Broomhall, "Evangelization of the World," 33.
29. Johnstone, "Look at the Fields," 33.

The center of gravity of Christianity is now in the Southern Hemisphere, and this growth is specifically championed by the Pentecostal movement. According to Allan Heaton Anderson, Pentecostalism is the fastest-growing religious movement in the world today,[30] and it is spearheading global Christian outreach in the twenty-first century. Dana L. Roberts points out that the most populous Christian areas of the world by the mid-twenty-first century are projected to be in the Southern Hemisphere, in Africa and South America.[31] The massive growth of Christianity and its transformation in Africa is due to the influence of Pentecostalism, according to Kwabena Asamoah-Gyadu.[32] The increase of the Christian population in the Southern Hemisphere does not, however, translate into the reduction of the Muslim population as one may expect.

The Growth of the Church of Pentecost as Local African Pentecostalism

The Church of Pentecost (COP), which is the local version of African Pentecostalism, has emerged as the largest Protestant church in Ghana with a strong mission orientation.[33] Ghanaian Pentecostalism has tremendously impacted the growth of Christianity in Ghana. Like many Pentecostal denominations, one main factor that contributes to the COP's growth story is the pneumatic phenomena – the emphasis on the role of the Holy Spirit in mission, signs and wonders, and power encounters in evangelism. Its success story is based on "conversional" growth through soul-winning and evangelism.[34] This research assumes there is a lack of adequate awareness and effective practices in evangelism to Muslims that accounts for Pentecostals' failure to engage Muslims.

Azumah rightly asserts that there is a general lack of awareness and interest among Christians concerning issues involving Muslims. Many Ghanaian Christians and Christian leaders do not see the need for Islamic studies. The impression Ghanaian Christians have of Muslims is that of "a dirty, illiterate

---

30. Anderson, *Ends of the Earth*, 1.
31. Robert, *Christian Mission*, 9.
32. Asamoah-Gyadu, "Pentecostalism and Missiological Significance," 30.
33. Ghana Evangelical Committee, "Survey of Churches," quoted in Markin, "Spirit and Mission," 21.
34. Ghana Evangelical Committee, 9.

watchman from the north or an uncouth bunch of strangers living in the dirtiest and filthiest part of the city" who are objects of evangelism or conversion. Their presence in Ghana poses no challenge at all to "confront them with Jesus."[35] Since Pentecostals have contributed significantly to Christian growth in Ghana, they could be empowered to engage Muslims with the gospel in a more effective way if given an improved understanding of Islam and the use of appropriate methods.

Folk Muslims in Ghana

Zwemer points out that "Islam in its contacts with animism has not been the victor but rather the vanquished."[36] More than 70 percent of Muslims are influenced by folk Islam, and its practices provide opportunities for Christian-Muslim engagement. Many think of Muslims as homogenous, and deeply etched in the mind of the ordinary person is a monolithic image of Islam. However, what happens in the private life of Muslims goes beyond dead orthodoxy. All over the world, Muslims are in search of a practical Islam that meets their everyday needs and is not mere cognitive data in the form of guidelines and practices, which leave vacuums in the souls of adherents.[37]

The majority of African Muslims believe much more in folk Islam than in orthodox Islam,[38] because folk Islam readily provides solutions to the unanswered questions of African Muslims. As a result of folk Islam's potential to attract country people and the illiterate, missiologists perceive it as popular Islam in the sense that "it seeks to attend to the devotee's heart rather than to the devotee's head."[39] Muslims in Ghana are daily confronted with real issues like the fear of evil spirits and witches. Bill Musk sums up the practices of folk Islam as follows:

> Popular Islam has added a whole life-way of animistic beliefs and practices. The use of the rosary for divining and healing, the use of amulets and talismans, the use of hair-cuttings and nail-trimmings, the belief and practice of saint-worship, the use

---

35. Azumah, "Controversy and Restraint," 23–26.
36. Zwemer, *Influence of Animism*, quoted in Twumasi, "Understanding Folk Islam," 49.
37. Parshall, *Bridges to Islam*, 3.
38. Twumasi, "Understanding Folk Islam," 51.
39. Twumasi, 50.

of charms, knots, magic, sorcery, the exorcism of demons, the practice of tree and stone worship, cursing and blessing these and many other animistic practices belie the gap between the theological religion and the actual religion.[40]

Azumah writes that Islam is not a *"homo Islamicus"* and cannot be considered a monolithic entity that has a unified system of belief.[41] Islam is domesticated in Ghana according to various cultural contexts and people groups. For instance, Islam in northern Ghana is different from Islam in the Volta, Ashanti, or central regions (home of the Fante people). Irrespective of the form of Islam, their expressions are often swallowed up by the specific African heritage of the milieu. For example, Sufi Islam is viewed as "African Islam" because many elements of ATRs have found their way into it.[42] Even though there has been an increase in influence of the Wahhabi form of Islam in some parts of northern Ghana, especially in Tamale due to sociopolitical influence, Sufism remains the predominant form of Islam in Ghana.[43] Its expression is almost identical with folk Islamic practices.

Sufism is commonly called "Muslim mysticism,"[44] which is the knowledge of mysteries or "a communion with the divine through intuition and contemplation." The Qur'an differentiates "the world of Testimony," which is the visible or perceptible world, from the "the world of Mystery," which is not discoverable by natural sight. Sufism aims at piercing through the invisible world to discover the spiritual realities that cannot be obtained through simple faith. It refers to the state where humanity gives way to divinity and all human traces vanish.[45] The name Sufism stems from the Arabic verb *sufiya*, which means "it was purified." David W. Shenk defines Sufis as the mystics of Islam because their quest is to experience God.

The root of Sufi spirituality goes deep into the early history of Islam. Sufism is a syncretic movement that first arose in Baghdad two centuries after the

---

40. Parshall, *Bridges to Islam*, 2.
41. Azumah, "Fault Lines in African," 126.
42. Westerlund and Rosander, "African Islam and Islam," cited in Ibrahim, "Decline of Sufism," 23.
43. Ibrahim, 6.
44. Geoffrey, *Introduction to Sufism*, 2.
45. Geoffrey, 2.

Prophet Muhammad moved (*hijra*) from Mecca to Madina.[46] Al Hallaj, a Sufi saint in the early stage of the Sufi movement, was crucified after being accused of claiming the possibility of assuming divine presence. Besides him was a Sufi saint in Somalia, Shaikh Uways, who was martyred together with twenty-six of his disciples at Biyolay in 1909.[47] The dividing wall between Sufi and orthodox Islam is traceable to a qur'anic paradox that denies fellowship between God and humankind, *tanzih* (Qu'ran 112), and to a doctrine on friendship with God, *awilya* (Qur'an 5:53–54; 10:63).[48]

Sufism is a response to Muslims' ardent desire to experience God, which can be likened to Pentecostalism and Ghanaian Christians' yearning to experience God personally. In Sufism, Muslims believe that because they are imperfect beings, they cannot receive the blessing (*baraka*) of God without an intermediary or intercessor. The intercessor is expected to be a deceased person who led a holy life while on earth and qualifies to be a local saint.[49] The image of an intercessor in Sufism shares some nuances with the traditional African belief in ancestors, and so it has missiological significance. However, in the Qur'an, there can be no intercessor unless he is appointed by God. "None shall have the power of intercession, but such a one as has received permission from God most gracious" (Qur'an 19:87). While some Muslims struggle with the issue of an intercessor, some believe on the basis of the *ḥadīth* that Muhammad will act like an intercessor in Allah's court in the final judgment.

Islam posits that God is closer to Muslims than the jugular vein (Qur'an 50:16); however, that closeness does not lead to the knowledge of God. God reveals his qualities to Muslims but not his essence. Especially because God cannot meet Muslims, he may send down his will out of his great compassion, but personal relationship with people is out of the question. Thus, God cannot be known personally. Sufis desire to experience God personally, but the only way to do so is by reciting God's names and qualities to remember

---

46. Shenk, "Islamic Mysticism," 252.
47. Shenk, 252.
48. Shenk, 252.
49. Shenk, 255.

God (*dhikr*) and by recounting the ninety-nine names using the *tasbih* (the Muslim rosary of ninety-nine beads).[50]

The gospel, referred to as the Injil by Muslims, points to Jesus the Messiah as the one true intercessor, indestructible and eternal (Heb 7:23–28)[51] and says, "The Lord has sworn and will not change his mind: you [the Messiah] are a priest forever" (Heb 7:21). Additionally, Jesus himself promised that "The Father will give you whatever you ask him in my name" (John 15:16 NRSV). The intercessory ministry of Jesus responds to the quest of Sufi Muslims for an intercessor that permeates African Muslims' spirituality. Sufism, therefore, has bridges by which Pentecostal Christians can engage Muslims at their own level of understanding.

A majority of Muslims practice mysticism and see folk Muslim leaders as mediators between humans and God who have certain healing powers, so the mystic practice of Sufism sets the stage for the explanation of a divine healer and the restoring, sustaining power of the Holy Spirit. Many are fed up with their attempt to gain salvation through an interminable system of laws and rituals. Muslims with a mystical orientation lack assurance of salvation that Jesus alone provides (1 John 5:13). There is a spiritual vacuum that needs to be filled with a loving personal relationship with God through the Messiah, Jesus. This research, therefore, posits that folk Islam contains elements that serve as bridges to engage Muslims and that, with reliance on the Holy Spirit, Christians can share the gospel to meet Muslims' quest for a personal relationship with God.

Christians' Engagement with Muslims in Ghana

In 1984, a leader from a member of the Christian Council of Ghana (CCG), a mainline church, engaged Ghanaian Muslims in aggressive and confrontational public debates that resulted in his untimely death.[52] Later on 30 November 1996, eight people were injured in Kumasi, Ghana's second largest city, during a confrontation between Muslim youths and Christians. A polemical approach to Christian-Muslim engagement was the cause of the confrontation. Muslim youths destroyed the public address system used

---

50. Shenk, 259.
51. Shenk, 255.
52. Yakubu, "Ghana," 311.

by a group of Christian evangelists for street and public square preaching. Windows and security lighting systems at Presbyterian and Methodist churches in Kumasi were vandalized by the Muslim youths during the encounter while the Christian youths also smashed traditional stalls and sheds belonging to the Muslims.[53]

Since then, the CCG engages Muslims through a relational approach as part of their involvement with the Program for Christian-Muslim Relationships in Africa (PROCMURA). PROCMURA was founded in 1959 as the Islam in Africa Project with the aim of helping the church in Africa to understand its mission to Muslims and to interpret and share the gospel in the midst of Islam.[54] As Yakubu has emphasized, there is a high level of ignorance regarding Islam among Christians and a "reality of the potential for interreligious conflicts in Africa."[55] Thus, the essence of PROCMURA is to equip its coordinators to educate member churches for constructive engagement among Muslims. It produces literature publications to promote education about Islam along with quarterly newsletters to member churches. The CCG also runs seminars and workshops for churches about Christian witness and interfaith relationships, and it used to publish an annual newsletter for female leaders known as "Breakthrough" on issues involving Islam. However, it is no longer being published.[56]

The program's approach promotes a holistic manner of engaging Muslims rather than the conversion-focused approach of Ghanaian Pentecostals. PROCMURA works toward peace, tolerance, and mutual understanding conducive for Christian-Muslim engagement. Unfortunately, Pentecostal denominations do not form part of this council, predominantly due to doctrinal differences with the mainline churches, so they are not able to benefit from PROCMURA projects.

The Approach of the Roman Catholic Church

The Ghana Catholic Bishops' Conference, also referred to as the Bishops Conference (BC), forms part of the CCG and is an integral member of

---

53. Ephson, "Muslim-Christian Clashes," 102.
54. Yakubu, "Ghana," 308.
55. Yakubu, 309.
56. Yakubu, 309.

PROCMURA. The BC includes the Association of Episcopal Conferences of Anglophone West Africa-Inter-Religious Dialogue Commission (AECAWA-IRDC), which is in charge of the interreligious affairs of the BC. The commission aims to foster dialogue between Catholics and other religions and was formed in response to Pope John Paul II's address on 3 March 1984 that stressed the relevance of interreligious dialogue. His address has motivated Catholics to engage with people of other faiths, including Muslims, over the years. Through AECAWA-IRDC, Catholics in Ghana have engaged Muslims through joint study sessions and research into Islam during an annual event of two to three days that gathers Muslims, Christians, and ATR practitioners. During the event, they discuss issues of common interest. The Catholic church's approach is not unique to Ghana but is related to the Vatican's policy on engagement with people of other faiths.[57]

The approaches of the two non-Pentecostal councils, the CCG and the BC, demonstrate viable methods of relating to Muslims, creating awareness of the presence and influence of Muslims in Ghana, and dealing with the possible challenges they pose to Christianity. Their approaches have contributed to the gradual change of the Ghanaian Christian mentality toward Muslims from a nonentity to a force to reckon with and from violence to coexistence.[58] Though one cannot surely say the CCG's actions have resulted in the conversion of Ghanaian Muslims into Christianity, member churches can at least testify that their actions have led to peaceful relationships with Muslims. Although the CCG may have succeeded in educating their own members about Muslims, they seem to fail to speak to Muslims about Christ. The CCG adopts a "silent presence" to represent Christ to Muslims and the unbelieving world without sharing the gospel directly with Muslims.

It is rather unfortunate that the Pentecostal churches in Ghana are not part of these projects and still lack the requisite understanding to engage Muslims. Moreover, I have not yet come across any research done by a Ghanaian Pentecostal scholar on creating awareness for Christian-Muslim engagement with the gospel. As already demonstrated, Pentecostals are leading soul-winners in Ghana and in Africa in the twenty-first century. Their understanding of mission to Muslims is a requisite to reduce Islamic influence

---

57. Yakubu, 312.
58. Yakubu, 311–13.

in Ghana, which was once considered the resistant belt to Muslims' influence in Africa.[59]

Yakubu notes that, "to have good news but not know how to deliver that good news could make it bad news."[60] Pentecostals, like other Christ-centered Christian bodies, know the good news of Jesus and can share their message with the empowerment of the Holy Spirit. However, their lack of awareness about Islam can render their good message a bad one in the course of sharing the message with Muslims. Pentecostals, on the basis of Acts 1:8, boast of having the empowerment of the Spirit to share the good news to all nations from "Jerusalem, and in all Judea and Samaria, and to the ends of the earth" (NIV). However, Pentecostals must understand that Muslims are part of this universal mandate they have received and must work at reconciling Muslims to God through a better understanding of the Islamic faith. By understanding Islam, Ghanaian Pentecostals can engage Muslims responsibly without inviting avoidable conflicts.

Statement of Purpose

Most Christians have an "allergic reaction" to Muslims as evidenced by history. With the vast majority of Evangelicals (Pentecostals) living in Africa, African Christians need to adopt workable strategies to win and disciple Muslims. Protestant missional engagement was the result of William Carey's challenge to Protestant churches.[61] Pentecostals in Ghana need a similar challenge to become aware of the influence of Islam in Ghana and in neighboring countries like Nigeria and Côte d'Ivoire. Christians must not wait until extreme Islam takes over with suicide bombers before they rise up to evangelize Muslims. If the battle must be won and the next generation saved from the dangers of Boko Haram, ISIS, and civil wars (religiopolitical wars) that others have already faced, then mission to Muslims must be taken seriously now. Additionally, if Christians have love towards individual Muslims who are themselves victims of the dangers of extreme Islam, then the time to engage in a mission to Islam is now. In the light of the above, this research aims to

---

59. Trimingham, *Islam in West Africa*, 19.
60. Yakubu, "Ghana," 310.
61. Johnstone, "Look at the Fields," 33.

create an awareness of Muslims' influence in Ghana and develop an effective method to engage Muslims with the gospel.

Jesus told the disciples, "Every branch that bears fruit he prunes to make it bear more fruit" (John 15:1–2 NRSV). Pentecostalism and the COP, which represents the local expression of Pentecostalism in Ghana, are one branch of the vine that is producing fruit in their desire to reach out to the world. To bear more fruit, the COP must be "pruned" through the understanding of Islam and the development of effective mission practices to engage Muslims with the gospel. This work, therefore, aims:

- To raise awareness and reduce misunderstandings caused by a gap of ignorance among Christian-Muslim relations in Ghana.
- To develop a mission approach for Pentecostals to engage folk Muslims with the gospel.

Problem

- The COP is the fastest-growing Pentecostal denomination in Ghana with over one hundred branches but has no specific mission approach for evangelism to Muslims.
- The COP mission activities are centered on grassroots engagement but have no training manual for evangelism to Muslims.
- Pentecostals do not have enough understanding of Muslims in the context of folk Islam to engage them through needs-based ministry.

Assumptions

- Pentecostals are spearheading the growth of Christianity in the Southern Hemisphere; therefore, their understanding of and mission to Muslims will stunt Islamic influence in Africa.
- Pentecostals are unable to effectively engage Muslims with the gospel for a lack of appropriate models of evangelism to Muslims.
- Understanding folk Islam is a prerequisite to reaching Ghanaian Muslims with the gospel.

- Pentecostals and folk Islam share a similar spiritual heritage in Ghana; therefore, understanding the practices of folk Islam will result in effective sharing of the gospel with Ghanaian Muslims.

Methodology

I have used both descriptive and evaluative methods of textual analysis on a variety of literary sources, including books, archives, dissertations, and periodicals. In addition to my experience as a Pentecostal leader, I gleaned from the experiences of practitioners of Muslim evangelism, as echoed in "I planted, Apollos watered, but God gave the growth" (1 Cor 3:6).[62] The internet, the TTGU library, and the Woodberry Institute of Muslim-Christian Relations served as resources for my work.

Research is conducted not only to amass data but to discover answers to questions through the application of systematic procedures. It seeks answers by examining different social settings and people who inhabit these settings. In the context of this research, answers can be found by examining the social settings of Muslims who inhabit Ghana. In this sense, I have employed descriptive and analytic methodology with synchronous interconnections; this provided a means of accessing unquantifiable knowledge about Pentecostals and folk Muslims.[63] According to William Sebunje, descriptive research "describes phenomena, as they exist and [is] used to identify and obtain information on the characteristics of a particular issue."[64] This type of research answers "what" questions to ascertain and describe the issue's characteristics. Analytic research is a continuation of descriptive research that goes beyond describing characteristics to analyzing and explaining the issue at hand. An interdisciplinary approach to studies in the field of mission and Pentecostalism is essential,[65] so the current study in intercultural and Islamic studies has integrated knowledge from Pentecostal missiology, church history, cultural anthropology, and biblical theology.

---

62. Woodberry, *From Seed to Fruit*, 25. All biblical references are from the English Standard Version, unless otherwise noted.
63. Berg and Lune, *Qualitative Research Methods*, 62.
64. Sebunje, "Research Techniques."
65. Haustein, "Birmingham GloPent."

Analyzing the success and failure of practitioners of Muslim evangelism from diverse backgrounds led to the discovery of effective missiological practices. Historical data analysis was used to ascertain the historical development of Pentecostalism in Ghana, the presence and nature of Islam in Ghana, and the implication of these for Pentecostals today. David Bosch notes that the history of Christian mission is not merely carried out to satisfy curiosity but "with a view to getting a deeper insight into what mission for us is today. After all, every attempt at interpreting the past is indirectly an attempt at understanding the present and the future."[66] An investigation and analysis of how people have engaged folk Muslims in the past is carried out in the attempt to understand how folk Muslims must be engaged today and in the future.

Andrew F. Walls asserts that African Christians must develop an African approach to Muslims in African settings;[67] thus, Ghanaian Pentecostals need to develop a Ghanaian Pentecostal approach to Ghanaian folk Muslims. As a Ghanaian Pentecostal, and an active participant in the mission of the COP, especially in evangelism and church planting, I had the opportunity to carry out this research from an emic or insider's point of view. As the field of research relates to mission, my own observation and experience in practical evangelism, crusades, dawn broadcasting, rallies, radio, evangelism, and funeral and healing services further strengthened my understanding of the literary resource findings. As a member of a Pentecostal denomination, I already had some knowledge about the Pentecostal missiological practices within the chosen setting, Ghana, and this understanding made it easier to interact with the literature on the topic. As Sema Unluer indicates, insiders normally possess a great deal of knowledge that might usually take an outsider a long time to acquire or understand.[68]

I am, however, conscious of the effects of familiarity leading to bias and of unconscious assumptions based on previous knowledge. While cognizant of this potential to lose objectivity, I did not validate the findings based on insider experience but carefully relied on scholarly, interdisciplinary literature. I reviewed and referenced several non-Pentecostal scholars who have written on Pentecostal missiological practices to juxtapose this work against different

---

66. Bosch, *Transforming Mission*.
67. Walls, *Cross-Cultural Process*, 146.
68. Unluer, "Being an Insider Researcher," 2.

perspectives and remove any form of my personal bias. By weighing these perspectives equally, I carefully bracketed my own experience to acquire a fresh understanding of the topic. The Woodberry Institute for Muslim-Christian Relations (WIMCR), being fully an Islamic research center, provides a variety of resources helpful for understanding the research questions.

Limitations

I have no knowledge of Arabic and depend on English, French, and German translations. Additionally, the proposed methods of engagement may not be suitable for global Muslim evangelism because they are limited to the specific context of Pentecostals in the Southern Hemisphere, specifically Ghana. Moreover, the purpose of this work is not to research the entire history of Pentecostalism in Africa or Ghana; it is limited to a brief description of their growth using the COP as a specific, local version of Pentecostalism.

Thesis Statement

In Ghana, a common spiritual heritage of ATRs has created intersections between the practices of Pentecostals and folk Muslims that, when properly understood, can be used by Pentecostals as bridges to effectively share the gospel with folk Muslims.

Research Questions

Central Research Question

How can Ghanaian Pentecostals effectively share the gospel with folk Muslims in Ghana who share a common spiritual heritage with ATRs?

Subquestions

1. What is the perception of Pentecostals toward Islam in Ghana? What are the models of Muslim evangelism used by the COP as the fastest and biggest Pentecostal denomination in Ghana, and how can these models be reshaped to increase effective mission to Muslims?

What missiological strategies and/or structures were used to reach out to Muslims?

Which (existing) models of evangelism are best-suited for Christian engagement of Muslims in Ghana?
2. What are the general characteristics of folk Islam in Ghana?
3. What specific models should be used to engage folk Muslims in Ghana with the gospel?

Importance of the Research

Even though a few scholars have written on the COP mission, little research has been done so far on Christian evangelism to folk Muslims in Ghana or the COP's mission to folk Muslims. These findings shall provide new insight to further Pentecostals' understanding of folk Muslims and how to engage them with the gospel, especially for the COP and other denominations that strive to reach out to folk Muslims. The suggested ideas and recommendations from this research may serve as a guide for aspiring Christian leaders to effectively share the gospel in Ghana.

Definition of Terms

- Muslim: "Muslim" refers to someone who submits to the will of Allah and confesses and practices the Islamic faith. In this monograph, "Muslim" implies all who profess and practice the faith of Islam whether Sunni or Shi'a.
- African Pentecostalism: Lamin Sanneh states that "Christianity was delivered in the birth pangs of Pentecost and throughout its history it has not shed its birthmark."[69] That birthmark of the work and the manifestation of the Holy Spirit's gifts (pneumatological emphases) within the context of African cultures and spirituality is termed "African Pentecostalism." Pentecostalism (based on the pneumatological emphases derived from Acts 2) refers to the role of the Holy Spirit in mission as an expression of Christian faith within the religiocultural context of Africa.

---

69. Sanneh, *Pentecostal Mission*, vii.

- Mission (to Muslims): In this dissertation, "mission" implies participation with God in various activities and evangelistic methods for the redemption of Muslims within the context of Ghana and, more widely, Africa.

Structure of the Study

Chapter 1 is titled "The Historical Development of Christianity in Ghana and the Impact of Pentecostalism." It will present an overview of the current situation of Christianity in Ghana and shed light on the impact of Pentecostalism on Ghanaian Christianity. The chapter will also discuss the historical development of the COP's mission to Muslims, expressed as a local version of Pentecostalism.

Chapter 2 titled "The Development of Islam and the Nature of the Christian-Muslim Relationship in Ghana" will focus on the development of Islam in Ghana, highlighting the general history and orders of Islam. It will provide an overview of the emergence of Islam and its expansion in Ghana in the mid-twentieth century. It will also reveal the nature of the Christian-Muslim relationship in Ghana.

Chapter 3 titled "The Influence of Animism on the Beliefs and Practices of Ghanaian Folk Muslims" will describe the core beliefs and practices of Islam and how the worldview of folk Islam transforms these beliefs and practices in Ghana. The chapter details the everyday life of Ghanaian folk Muslims and identifies the practices from ATRs.

Chapter 4 is titled "Existing Methods of Sharing the Gospel with Folk Muslims." In addition to examining the existing methods and principles used to share the gospel with Muslims, it will provide a comparative theological study of Islam and Christianity. Based on the intersection between folk Islamic practices and Pentecostal practices, it will highlight bridges for sharing the gospel with folk Muslims.

Chapter 5 entitled "Pentecostals' Engagement with Folk Muslims in Ghana" will conclude the research by providing methods for Pentecostals' engagement of folk Muslims with the Holy Spirit through healing and deliverance, signs and wonders, and power encounters. Effective methods of sharing the gospel with folk Muslims within Ghana's context will be recommended in the hope that the recommendations will be applicable to other Pentecostals who wish to engage folk Muslims.

CHAPTER 1

The Historical Development of Christianity in Ghana and the Impact of Pentecostalism

Indigenous Religion in Ghana

Before Ghana obtained independence on 6 March 1957, the region was known as the Gold Coast because of the abundance of gold discovered there. Ghana forms part of the west African subregion and belonged to the British empire for more than one hundred years (1844–1957).[1] Before the arrival of missionaries in Africa, the people of the Gold Coast already had the concept of a supreme God, the creator of the universe, who local tribes such as the Ewes and the Akans referred to as *Mawu Ga* and *Onyankopon*, respectively. In the Ghanaian tradition, this supreme God was once closer to man, but due to the disobedience of a woman who continually hit him with a pestle in the process of pounding *fufu*, this God got angry and retreated to heaven. Fortunately, the supreme God did not abandon humans completely but resolved to engage in human affairs and exercise his power through lesser gods, *abosom* in Akan and *etro* in Ewe, which constituted his spirit sons and daughters in the form of local rivers, trees, mountains, rocks, forests, and other uncountable physical creatures. They, however, did not replace the identity of the supreme God with the lesser gods. The lesser gods could be discarded but not the supreme

---

1. Walker, "Pentecost Fire," 40.

God.² Thus, before the arrival of European missionaries, the people of the Gold Coast were "to [a] great extent rather monotheist than polytheist since they attributed the term for God [*Nyame* or *Mawu*] to only one supreme being"³ and held to the absolute uniqueness of a supreme God, which modern theologians define as "the incomprehensible term of human transcendence."⁴

The Ewe spiritual pyramid was headed by *Mawu*, a creator God to whom the minor deities, spirits, and ancestors were all subordinate mediators; the deities were generally viewed as the personifications of God's (*Mawu*'s) activities. There are references to *Mawu* as a female deity that forms one supreme being together with an inseparable male deity called *Lisa*: *Mawu-Lisa*, the unsurpassable supreme being. The intermediaries are referred to as *mawuviwo*, "children" or "servants" of *Mawu*. These various deities executed errands in a similar sense to the way angels go on assignments.⁵ In Akan, the deities were regarded as mediators between humans and God. The deities were invoked together with *Nyame*, the supreme God. In most of the festival prayers, the name for the lesser gods, *abosom*, was only mentioned after the name of the supreme being, *Nyame*. Henry St. John Tomlinson Evans has noted that "the evidence . . . makes it clear that there is a definite monotheistic background to the religion of the Akan and affords grounds for believing that this monotheism is one element, if not the predominant element, in their most primitive faith."⁶

Within the African concept of God, there was a tendency toward unity: humans tried to unite the different powers of the suprahuman world – the influences of which they experienced during the different events in their life – into a single whole. Humans' destiny may be determined by many gods, spirits, and magical things or events that take place, which resulted from many different suprahuman beings but were attributed to one "power": *Nyame*. God was simultaneously seen as unity and multiplicity: "What exists is a bundle of associations which attach themselves to a given point and are thereby made definite, although in actuality loose and kaleidoscopic."⁷

---

2. Larbi, *Pentecostalism*, chap.1.
3. Larbi, chap.1.
4. Larbi, chap.1.
5. Eggen, "*Mawu* Does Not Kill," 345.
6. Evans, "Akan Doctrine of God," quoted in Petterson, "Monotheism or Polytheism?" 49.
7. Petterson, "Monotheism or Polytheism?" 49.

The indigenous religions of the people of Africa, including Ghana, revolved around the notion of a supreme God, and Africans recognize these as deeply monotheistic, despite the variations from people to people and one place to another. Traditionally, African people named innumerable attributes about God, such as "Creator, Self-existent, Giver of children and rain, Father-Mother of people, holy, omnipotent, [and] eternal." Thus, the African name of God became the bedrock for the articulation of the biblical God within the African context.[8]

African religions and the concept of the supreme being cannot be analyzed by the exclusive Western categories of monotheism or polytheism. As these terms do not really reveal the religious experience of Africans, "it seems to be meaningless to ask the question whether African tribal religions are monotheistic or polytheistic."[9] Ryan Patrick has noted that the modern perspective of how Africans have traditionally viewed the transcendent betrays a tendency to impose Middle Eastern or Greco-Roman categories onto the African religious experience. He says, "to describe African conceptions of the transcendent in Semitic or Indo-European theological categories . . . implies that they impose on the forms of traditional African piety, without adequate interval equivalencies, alien patterns of thought."[10] The God whose name had been hallowed in indigenous Ghanaian languages in the pre-Christian tradition was found to be the God of the Bible, *Onyankopon*, the God and Father of our Lord Jesus Christ.[11] As John Mbiti has pointed out, the concept of the supreme being and the whole of African religious experience was preparation for the gospel, "*praeparatio evangelica*."[12] One can, therefore, speak of African monotheism, though it is different from Western monotheism.

The medium of worship to this supreme God was through the mediation of the lesser gods, to whom prayers were offered by various sacrifices and the pouring of libation on behalf of humankind. Sin was considered disobedience to the gods and abhorred because it attracted severe punishment from the supreme God through the lesser gods. Thus, the people of the Gold Coast

---

8. Mbiti, "Challenges," 147.
9. Petterson, "Monotheism or Polytheism?" 65.
10. Ryan, "'Arise, O God!'" 61.
11. Bediako, *Jesus and the Gospel*, 12.
12. Mbiti, "Future of Christianity," 36.

viewed the world as filled with a multiplicity of spirits capable of doing good or evil to humanity. They believed that premature death was the result of disobedience or bad conduct, whereas old age was a marker of good conduct.[13] They viewed their creator as the source of life and procreation as a divine blessing from the supreme God. Thus, a woman with many children was a testimony of divine blessing, while childlessness was a curse resulting from the activities of evil spirits.[14] Like other Africans, their world was classified into "two inter-penetrating and inseparable, yet distinguishable parts"[15] of the spiritual realm and the human realm.

Emmanuel Kingsley Larbi has observed that their general understanding of the spirit world falls within E. G. Parrinder's fourfold classification of west African religions, namely "the Supreme God, divinities or gods, ancestors, and charms or amulets."[16] The people believed that the spiritual forces could be manipulated for good or evil purposes through charms and amulets used in the physical realm. Thus, people who practiced juju (i.e. black magic) by using talismans and other mediums strove to change the course of life negatively or positively.[17] The activities of the forces of darkness were understood as directed to humankind to prevent them from fulfilling their destiny (*dzogbese* in Ewe and *nkrabea* in Akan). Therefore, the ultimate religious pursuit of the people of the Gold Coast was deliverance from evil, and this constituted their concept of salvation. Within this belief system, there was nothing like original sin from which one must be delivered. Rather, one had to be saved from the gods' punishment by appeasing them through ancestral purification and protective rites.

These cultural beliefs led the local people to yearn for any religious practice that would protect them from the forces of evil and give them the assurance of long abundant life, good health, wealth, or personal possessions, including many children and wives. Abundant life could only be obtained through the mediation of lesser gods and ancestors. The following example of a traditional

---

13. Walker, "Pentecost Fire," 41.
14. Assimeng, *Social Structure of Ghana*, cited in Walker, "Pentecost Fire," 41.
15. Larbi, *Pentecostalism*, chap. 1.
16. Larbi, chap. 1.
17. Walker, "Pentecost Fire," 41.

prayer, said by the head of the family during Christmas, reveals the people's concept of God and salvation:

> Almighty God, here is drink; Earth god, here is drink; Great ancestors, come and have a drink. . . . We are not calling you because of some evil tidings. The year has come again and you did not allow any evil to befall us. We are offering you drink, beseeching that the coming year will be prosperous. Don't allow any evil to come near our habitation. Bless us with rain, food, children, health and prosperity.[18]

Sutherland Rattray has made a similar observation about a prayer offered by an Ashanti king during an annual festival:

> The edges of the years have met; I pray for life. May the nation prosper. May the women bear children. May the hunters kill meat. We who dig for gold, let us get gold to dig, and grant that I get some for the upkeep of my kingship.[19]

The quest for salvation by the people of the Gold Coast was the search for concrete realities they could identify in everyday life. It involved rescue from immediate, physical dangers that suppressed peace, prosperity, and the fullness of life (*agbe* in Ewe and *nkaw* in Akan) for a community or individuals.[20] It was within this worldview that Christianity emerged in Ghana.

The Arrival of Christianity

Catholic Missions in Ghana

Christianity's beginning in Ghana is often associated with the arrival of Portuguese traders and explorers of the Gold Coast's coastal lands in January 1842. However, in 1471 a group of six hundred Portuguese led by Don Diogo d'Azambuja stepped on the shore of Elmina, Cape Coast in the central region of Ghana. On their arrival, they planted a huge wooden cross on the coast to signify the Christian gospel[21] and persuaded the chief of Elmina

---

18. Larbi, *Pentecostalism*, chap. 1.
19. Rattray, "Religion and Art," 138, quoted in Larbi, *Pentecostalism*, chap.1.
20. Larbi, *Pentecostalism*, chap. 1.
21. Mobley, "Ghanaian's Image of Missionary," cited in Walker, "Pentecost Fire," 43.

to give them a plot of land, where they built a fort and a chapel.[22] Larbi writes that the earliest Christian body to step foot on the shore of the Gold Coast was the Roman Catholic Franciscan friars who came not to evangelize Ghanaians, but to provide chaplaincy services to the Portuguese explorers.[23] These Roman Catholic Franciscan friars later introduced the indigenous people of the central region to the Catholic faith. The king of Efutu and his subordinates accepted the Christian faith on 2 January 1513, and in 1529, the king of Portugal instructed the chaplain of the fort to teach the children in Elmina "to read and write, sing and pray . . . and carry out all other duties connected with divine service."[24]

By 1637, four hundred inhabitants of Elmina had become Christians, even though the chaplain of the Elmina fort admitted they were Christians only by name. The people of Efutu and Komenda killed three of the Catholic fathers who were trying to Christianize the indigenes, which disrupted the early Portuguese missionaries' activity in the central region. Dutch Protestant missionaries took over from the Portuguese Catholic missionaries and they then established a school and an educational center for mixed children in 1641.[25] Disturbing rivalries among the Portuguese, English, and Dutch resulted in raids on the towns of Axim and Elmina from 1607 to 1642, and by 1650, there was no longer a trace of Catholicism in the area. Peter B. Clarke asserts that those conflicts notwithstanding, the early missionaries in Ghana did not concentrate on spreading the gospel message. They focused on trade and commerce, and for that reason, they centered their activities around communities close to the forts.[26] It was not until 1880 that the Catholic faith was revived through the work of Father Auguste Moreau and Father Eugene Murat who stepped in following Sir James Marshall's appeal. The two fathers mainly focused on the building of schools, health care centers, and chapels, which they used as mission tools to preach the gospel.[27]

---

22. Agbeti, *West African Church History*, cited in Walker, "Pentecost Fire," 43.
23. Larbi, *Pentecostalism*, chap. 2.
24. Asem, *Church of Pentecost*, 11.
25. Asem, 12.
26. Clarke, "West Africa and Christianity," cited in Walker, "Pentecost Fire," 44.
27. Agbeti, *West African Church History*, cited in Walker, "Pentecost Fire," 43.

Protestant Missions in Ghana

To establish their missions in the Gold Coast, the Dutch missionaries sent Frederick Pedersen Svane, a Gan and native of Accra who had graduated from the University of Copenhagen and was married to a Danish woman. In 1735 together with his wife, he arrived at the fort in Accra, Christianborg, to serve as the first African Protestant missionary to his fellow Africans. Unfortunately, Pedersen had forgotten his native Ga language and was not effective as a missionary due to communication barriers.[28] Missionaries Christian Protten and Henry Huckuff followed Pedersen (1737–72) but lost their lives due to unfavorable weather conditions. The mission activities in the Gold Coast then halted until the nineteenth century when mission activities reemerged,[29] so there was not a substantial witness of Christianity during this period.[30]

The first evidence of permanent mission stations is of the arrival on 18 December 1828, of one Bremen missionary from the Evangelical Presbyterian Church and four Basel missionaries: three Germans, Karl F. Salbach, Gottlieb Holzwarth, and Johannes Henke, and one Swiss, Johannes Gottlieb Schmidt. They first settled in Christianborg and later moved to Akwapim in the mountains for more favorable climatic conditions.[31] The first Wesleyan Methodist missionary, Joseph Dunwell, came in 1835 and settled in Cape Coast. Thomas Birch Freeman, born to an African father and an English mother, followed him and established the Methodist church among the Ashanti people in 1838.[32] The Methodist Mission established the Kwadaso Women's Training Centre, Freeman College, and Trinity College.

More German Bremen missionaries arrived in 1847 and settled in British Togoland, known today as the Volta Region. Within the span of seventy-two years, the Northern German Missionary Society (i.e. the Bremen) opened forty mission stations in the region with 11,682 adherents, 8,100 school children, and 198 catechists.[33]

In 1850, Johannes Zimmerman of the Basel mission joined the missions work in the Gold Coast, and through his leadership, the Basel Mission grew

---

28. Walker, "Pentecost Fire," 44.
29. Clarke, "West Africa and Christianity," cited in Walker, "Pentecost Fire," 45.
30. Larbi, *Pentecostalism*, chap. 2.
31. Larbi, chap. 2.
32. Neill, "History of Christian Missions," cited in Walker, "Pentecost Fire," 46.
33. Walker, "Pentecost Fire," 47.

and spread to other parts of the country. Johann Gottlieb Christaller, another Basel missionary, translated the Bible into the local language, Twi, in 1871. His contribution spurred the growth of the Basel Mission as it facilitated vernacular worship.[34] The Basel Mission built schools, vocational training centers, and missionary residences in communities known as Salem. Often the residents within these Salem areas were expected to adhere to rigorous Christian principles that further helped the missionaries build strong local churches.[35]

The Roman Catholics reentered the Gold Coast in 1881 and settled in the central province of Elmina. They were followed by the African Methodist-Episcopal Zion Mission, an African American church established in Cape Coast by Rev. Frank Arthur Osam Pinanko who had received pastoral training from the United States of America.[36] The Anglican denomination originating from England was the last to arrive in Ghana in 1906.[37] Due to the First World War, the Bremen missionaries were deported in 1916, followed by the German Basel missionaries in 1917.[38]

The Impact of Western Missions

The churches that sent missionaries to Ghana were known as the mainline churches, and they strictly followed the conventional forms of their sending bodies.[39] They impacted Ghana through church planting, hospitals, education, and many other social services to the extent that Governor Guggisberg of the Gold Coast described the expulsion of the Bremen missionaries as "the greatest blow which education in Ghana has ever suffered."[40]

The missionaries contributed massively to the religious space of the Gold Coast and were very instrumental in training Ghanaians who eventually became freedom fighters for Ghana's independence. However, they had very little missionary success in terms of the spread of the gospel. Among the challenges the missionaries confronted was their inability to provide an

---

34. Walker, 45.
35. Falk, *Growth of the Church*, cited in Walker, "Pentecost Fire," 45.
36. Walker, "Pentecost Fire," 48.
37. Larbi, *Pentecostalism*, chap. 2.
38. Larbi, chap. 2.
39. Anim, "Mission, Migration, and World," 40.
40. Larbi, *Pentecostalism*, chap. 2.

alternative practice to Ghanaian converts' traditional medicine and divinities after they taught them to abandon these practices. The people of the Gold Coast believed that not all sicknesses had natural causes and sought spiritual solutions, but they abandoned their gods for the "Westerners' worship" while continuing to suffer from sickness and demonic spirits. Missionary activities only changed their behavior, without affecting their worldview. For instance, the *Tigare* divinity was despised by the missionaries, but many local people feared being destroyed by *Tigare*, and so they turned to its cult.[41]

The belief in supernatural powers, witchcraft, juju, and idols remained a reality for the people of the Gold Coast, but the missionaries saw these beliefs as superstitions and rejected them as illusions. This Western mindset, which was not by its "nature and purpose holistic, addressing the total needs of the total person, spiritual, physical and emotional,"[42] left the people of the Gold Coast to continue to search for solutions outside the church. Becoming a Christian was seen as a change of name – from an African name to a Western name – and the participation in Western religious rituals.

The philosophical frame of the Western missionaries opposed the ancestral ways of the people's lives. Western missionaries celebrated reason as the power by which people had to understand their world and improve their life. Because the missionaries engaged the people from a post-Enlightenment, rational background, the people considered Christianity to be the "white man's religion" that was only capable of providing material blessings. The total denial of the existence of spirit forces, witches, sorcerers, fetish magic, charms, and local deities greatly undermined the missionaries' work and led to the people's double allegiance, one to the missionaries' God and the other to the African gods. Walter J. Hollenweger describes the evangelistic efforts of the Western missionaries in Africa as a "truncated and distorted form of evangelism because the colonial takes his or her culturally-conditioned interpretation of the gospel to be the gospel for everybody else."[43] The quest for solutions outside mission churches led to the emergence of African revivalists in Ghana.

---

41. Larbi, chap. 2.
42. Larbi, chap. 2.
43. Hollenweger, "Evangelism," 107.

Origins of Global Pentecostalism

Before describing the historical development of the COP in Ghana, it is helpful to understand the spread of Pentecostalism worldwide and Pentecostal practices. The root of the Pentecostal movement can be traced to the Holiness movement,[44] "which was itself based on a particular interpretation of the teaching of the founder of Methodist John Wesley (1703–91) and that of Wesley's theologian John Fletcher."[45] According to Gary B. McGee, forty years before the occurrence of North America's experience of Spirit baptism, it had already occurred in India, implying that Pentecostalism began far before the event of the Azusa Street Revival, which is generally reported by scholars as the beginning of Pentecostalism.[46]

Other revivalists who thought along the lines of John Wesley from varied angles include Jonathan Edwards, Charles Finney, Dwight Moody, and Reuben Torrey. The Keswick Convention fine-tuned the position in 1875 during an annual meeting in the English Lake District. The Keswick Convention posited that the baptism of the Spirit was characterized by an enduement of power for service; thus, by the close of the nineteenth century, this position became prominent among the North American revivalists. A third position emerged, "the third blessing," which tied both the "second blessing of sanctification" and the "third blessing of the baptism with fire," which was also characterized by enduement with power.[47] Pentecostalism was birthed out of these preparations. However, both Wesley and Fletcher's positions were influenced by early German Pietism. Earlier in the seventeenth and eighteenth centuries, the Pietists (i.e. Pietistic Lutherans) laid emphasis on a personal experience of God, which they referred to as the "new birth" by the Holy Spirit. This new birth was considered better than head knowledge. Pietists

---

44. The Holiness movement was a religious movement that emerged in the nineteenth century among Protestant churches in the United States. It began when Nathan Bangs, Timothy Merritt, and Phoebe Palmer, a group of influential members of the Methodist Episcopal Church, started to promote the doctrine of Christian perfection through preaching and publications. The movement was characterized by John Wesley's doctrine of entire sanctification, which was considered to be wrought by the baptism of the Holy Spirit, or the "second blessing" – a post conversion experience attained by self-denial. See Samuel M. Powell, "Theological Significance," 126.

45. Onyinah, "Movement of the Spirit," 274.

46. McGee, "Pentecostal Phenomena and Revivals," 112.

47. Anderson, *Introduction to Pentecostalism*, 29, quoted in Onyinah, "Movement of the Spirit," 274.

drew inspiration from Catholic mysticism, which placed importance on emotions in the Christian experience and promoted a personal relationship with God. "The Reformation's doctrine of the priesthood of all believers and the working of the Spirit to bring about a changed, morally ascetic Christian life separated from the world"[48] was encouraged by Pietism. Through Pietism, Nicolaus Zinzendorf's (1700–60) Moravian movement was revived and his round-the-clock prayer meetings lasted for hundreds of years thereafter. This Moravian movement, in turn, had a profound impact on Wesley and the revival he led. Thus, Pentecostalism has drawn its strength from the spiritual experiences of various traditions, including "Catholicism, Protestantism, and Evangelicalism."[49]

Charles Fox Parham (1879–1929), a former Methodist minister and a preacher of the Holiness movement, taught that speaking in tongues was the conclusive evidence of the Holy Spirit's baptism. Originally from North America, he ignited the flame of Pentecostalism at the Bethel Bible School in Topeka on 31 December 1900, during a prayer meeting. It is reported that Agness Ozman received the Holy Spirit baptism with evidence of speaking in tongues after the laying on of hands.[50] A few years later, in 1904, the Welsh revival began; it emphasized "repentance of sin, sanctification, and the presence of God in people's lives"[51] and was the precursor to Pentecostalism in western Europe. However, the seeds of what would become the Pentecostal denomination grew from the 1906 Azusa Street Revival led by William Seymour, a Black Holiness preacher in Los Angeles.[52] Pentecostalism was not originally intended to be a denomination of its own but rather an interdenominational movement whose adherents were Christians from any background who had experienced the impact of the Holy Spirit. Unfortunately, the new experience of the Spirit led to the ejection of members from mainline churches, and this gave rise to denominational movements from 1909 onwards. The fire that was rekindled on Azusa Street soon spread to the rest of the world.[53]

---

48. Onyinah, 274.
49. Onyinah, 274.
50. Onyinah, 274.
51. Onyinah, 275.
52. Vinson, "Charismatic Renewal," 9.
53. Johnson, "Demographics," in Vinson, *Spirit-Empowered Christianity*, 57.

Thomas Ball Barratt (1862–1940), a pastor of the Methodist Episcopal Church in Oslo, Norway, attended the Azusa Street meeting and "caught the fire," which led him to conduct revival meetings in Norway that spread throughout northern Europe. Thus, many of the Pentecostal churches in northern Europe are attributed to Barratt. In Asia, although the Pentecostal phenomenon may have occurred long before the emergence of modern Pentecostalism, the Azusa Street Revival had a great impact on Korea, India, China, Indonesia, and the Philippines in the twentieth century.[54]

In Latin America, the first recorded Pentecostals were in Chile, where Pentecostalism originated from the revival associated with Willis Collins Hoover (1858–1938), a minister of the largest Methodist church at the time. In Africa, before the emergence of Pentecostalism, the manifestation of the Spirit had been prominent in the lives of some individuals referred to as "prophets" and churches that emanated from the mainline (i.e. historic) churches. Most of these "prophets" were former traditional priests and priestesses who turned to Christ. Outstanding among them were William Wade Harris of Liberia, Joseph Babalola of Nigeria, Simon Kimbagu of Congo, and Joseph Appiah of Ghana – whose prophetic ministry led to the establishment of the African Initiated Churches, also known in Ghana as the "Spiritual Churches." The name Spiritual Churches reveals the type of practices they engaged in – prophecies, healing, and casting out demons.[55]

Similarly, Pentecostal groups hold to the specific teaching that all Christians must pursue a form of postreligious experience by the baptism of the Holy Spirit, which produces evidence of speaking in tongues, exercising supernatural spiritual gifts, and casting out demons. Todd M. Johnson enumerated some of their practices as follows:

> Divine healing through prayer, to speak in tongues (glossolalia), or to interpret tongues, singing in tongues, singing in the Spirit, dancing in the Spirit, praying with upraised hands, dreams, visions; discernment of spirits, words of wisdom, words of knowledge, miracles, power encounters, exorcisms (casting out demons), resuscitations, deliverances; signs and wonders.[56]

---

54. Yung, "Pentecostalism and Asian Church," 38.
55. Onyinah, "Movement of the Spirit," 276.
56. Johnson, "Demographics," in Vinson, *Spirit-Empowered Christianity*, 57.

Asamoah-Gyadu defines Pentecostalism more broadly as:

> Christian groups which emphasize salvation in Christ as a transformative experience wrought by the Holy Spirit and in which pneumatic phenomena, including "speaking in tongues," prophesies, visions, healing, and miracles in general, perceived as standing in historic continuity with the experiences of the early church as found mainly in the Acts of the Apostles, are sought, accepted, valued, and consciously encouraged among members as signifying the presence of God and experiences of his Spirit.[57]

This implies that the Pentecostal movements operate under such a great diversity of practice and doctrines that it is increasingly difficult to clearly find a definite factor that may describe what Pentecostalism truly is.

Yan Suarsana notes that "neither theological nor phenomenological or historical approaches to define the subject have been spared from attacks of scholars viewing this immense religious phenomenon mostly from a post-structural or postcolonial perspective."[58] A look at the historical discourse that traces the birth of the phenomenon of Pentecostalism to radical branches of the Holiness movement at the onset of the twentieth century reveals that even at that time, there was no clear distinctive definition of Pentecostalism. Cecil Robeck observes that "Pentecostals had not resolved the problem of identity and did not agree as to what constituted a Pentecostal, and that this hindered Pentecostals from being truly ecumenical."[59] Thus, the term remains open-ended. James Goff defines Pentecostalism on the basis of the theology of supposed founder, Charles Parham (1873–1929), regarding the experience of glossolalia.[60] However, committed Pentecostal activists of the time, including "Willis C. Hoover (Chile), T. B. Barratt (Norway), the works of Minnie Abrams (who has recently been declared as founder of Indian Pentecostalism) and the activities of Stone Church in Chicago can show that Parham and Seymour's initial evidence doctrine was far from being acknowledged as the

---

57. Asamoah-Gyadu, *African Charismatics*, 12.
58. Suarsana, "What is Pentecostalism?" 1.
59. Robeck, "Pentecostal Theology," quoted in Anderson, "Diversity," 40.
60. Suarsana, "What is Pentecostalism?" 1–2.

core of Pentecostal theology."[61] Walter Hollenweger proposes a "black origin" of Pentecostalism, tracing its root to the worship practices of Afro-American churches.[62] Allan Anderson describes the origin of Pentecostalism as a "'multi core' origin of Pentecostalism that took place . . . in parallel awakenings all over the world at the turn of the nineteenth century."[63]

Further, numerous people in mainline denominations have experienced the baptism of the Holy Spirit and the spiritual gifts but do not classify themselves as Pentecostals. Thus, Pentecostalism could be described as the move of God through the Holy Spirit in various forms through the visible church – irrespective of denomination – to attain God's mission, "Missio Dei." Since the Spiritual Churches shared these characteristics with Pentecostalism, they laid the groundwork for the emergence of Pentecostalism in Ghana.

Pentecostalism in Ghana

The Precursor to Pentecostalism: Spiritual Churches

The African spiritual identity was crucial for the survival of Christianity in Ghana. Lamin Sanneh observes,

> The missionaries from the West, aware of the significance of the local springs of religious vitality, could no longer dispense with African agents and would themselves have to clothe their thinking in the indigenous cultures of their endeavours, if they were to bear any lasting fruit.[64]

African evangelists emerged in the twentieth century, and through their activities, Ghanaian independent churches were planted free of Western attachments. Among the well-known Ghanaian revivalists were William Wade Harris, John Swatson, and Sampson Oppong. The most prominent among the three was the Liberian preacher William Wade Harris (1860–1929) from the Grebo tribe. He impacted the Ghanaian religious landscape with his preaching, beginning from 1914 in the Nzema, a southwestern region of Ghana. While serving a prison sentence for desecrating the Liberian flag and

---

61. Suarsana, 2.
62. Suarsana, 5.
63. Suarsana, 5.
64. Sanneh, *West African Christianity*, 106.

protesting against the repressive Americo-Liberian government, he was said to have received an angelic visitation that commissioned him as a prophet of God. He immediately launched into missions after serving his term in prison. Even though he did not have much impact in Liberia, his ministry in Côte d'Ivoire and Ghana was marked with great success: Harris was said to have won and baptized more than one thousand people from Côte d'Ivoire and a thousand more in Ghana.[65] Harris's work was a success in Ghana due to his understanding of the African worldview and his adaptation to the Ghanaian culture and indigenous forms of worship, coupled with his in-depth knowledge of the gifts and work of the Holy Spirit.[66] He preached Jesus as the supreme God and that allegiance to him gives converts the divine protection needed against the onslaught of evil spirits. His attack on the tribal gods earned him a reputation as a prophet of God. He inspired awe and fear among the people as he destroyed fetishes and exercised a total mastery over the dark forces that the people of Ghana dreaded. His evangelistic approach to mission in Ghana was quite different from Western missionaries. G. O. M. Tasie notes that Harris contextualized the gospel message by wearing clothing that appealed to the primal worldview of his audience: the very colors of his gown had meaning to Ghanaian audiences. His approach "was indiscreet, imprudent, and undiplomatic. When he attacked traditional religion, he directed his message to the root of the matter."[67]

John Swatson was a disciple of Harris. Swatson was born in Apollonia (Nzema) in the western region of Ghana to a Ghanaian mother, a member of the royal family, and a European father who was attached to the royal court of Omanhene Amakyi I. Swatson, formerly a teacher-catechist in the Methodist Church. He met Harris in Côte d'Ivoire in 1914 and "begged him to teach him his powers of baptism." Harris later commissioned him as a bishop and apostle for the Côte d'Ivoire and Ghana. Through Swatson, the Anglican Church opened a mission station in the interior of Ghana and helped to translate the Anglican hymns and the Book of Common Prayer into the Nzema language.[68] Like Harris, Swatson healed the sick and drove

---

65. Markin, "Spirit and Mission," 62.
66. Larbi, *Pentecostalism*, chap. 4.
67. Tasie, "Christian Awakening," 296, quoted in Walker, "Pentecost Fire," 54.
68. Walker, "Pentecost Fire," 56.

out demons by placing the Bible on the head of the demon-possessed person until the spirit departed from them.

The third well-known revivalist was Sampson Oppong, who started preaching in the Gold Coast in 1917. Sampson had no formal education when he was converted to Christianity from his background as a fetish priest. He asserted that, during his conversion, the Holy Spirit instructed him to burn all his fetish items and to build a wooden cross and wrap a stone in a handkerchief, which later became his companions throughout his ministry. Even though he was not educated, he had a remarkable knowledge of the Bible, which he attributed to the work of the Holy Spirit. By 1923, his Methodist church could claim twenty thousand converts.[69]

The ministry of these three people in Ghana emerged "in reaction to a Christianity which denied or explained away the miracles and mighty works attested in the New Testament." They themselves did not found churches, but through their ministry, followers started congregations in Ghana that are now referred to as the Spiritual Churches.[70] The first of these churches was the Twelve Apostles Church founded in 1914 by Grace Tani, John Nackabah, and John Hackman, all converts of Harris. The church was like Aladura churches, which are identified by their "central beliefs about revelation from the Spirit through prophets and a practical salvation in which healing is prominent," and the Twelve Apostles Church's worship involves different activities considered to invoke the work of the Holy Spirit upon the worshipers.[71] Two essential tools were used by the Spiritual Churches: the Bible and a traditional African "gourd-rattle made from a calabash with a white neck netted with strings of white beads." The Bible was not primarily meant for reading; rather, adherents of Spiritual Churches placed it under their pillow or used it to ward off evil spirits. Likewise, the sound of the gourd was believed to invoke the presence of God and ward off evil spirits.[72] The Pentecostal movement in Ghana began after the Spiritual Churches were established.

---

69. Larbi, *Pentecostalism*, chap. 3.
70. Larbi, chap. 3.
71. Larbi, chap. 3.
72. Breidenbach, "Spatial Juxtapositions," 95.

The Emergence of Pentecostalism

As Larbi asserts, the emergence of Pentecostalism was in response to a search for answers to life's difficult situations that both ATRs and the Western forms of Christianity did not fully address.[73] Ghanaians came to a crossroads where they needed practical answers to health problems, economic issues, deliverance from evil, and ancestral powers. The origins of Pentecostalism in Ghana can be traced to the ministry of one Peter Anim who was born in Boso, in the Volta Region of Ghana, on 4 February 1890. Anim benefitted from an education through the Basel Mission and in 1917 began reading the *Sword of the Spirit*, a religious magazine published by Pastor A. Clark who founded Faith Tabernacle in Philadelphia, Pennsylvania, USA.[74]

In the process of reading the teachings and advice of the founder of the Faith Tabernacle in *Sword of the Spirit*, Anim received divine healing from a chronic stomach ailment and a guinea worm attack he was suffering from.[75] Impressed by the content of this magazine, Anim remarked, "Though I had intellectually believed the Bible before, I never had the truth presented in a more realistic way that posed faith as a voluntary trust instead of an intellectual attainment."[76] Anim, however, continued with the Basel Mission in a Presbyterian church until the death of his wife in 1920. Then, he finally left the Basel Mission and resolved to start his own church in 1922 under the umbrella of Faith Tabernacle.

In 1923, Anim was given a certificate of ordination by Pastor Clark with the mandate to baptize souls won, call new workers, and exercise pastoral ministry. Several divine healings occurred during Anim's ministry, and his own healing testimony drew several converts to the Lord in Asamankese, Ghana. Unfortunately, in 1926, the founder was dismissed from the USA based on charges of adultery, and thus in 1930, Anim and his members severed their relationship with Faith Tabernacle and sought affiliation with the Apostolic Faith Church in the UK.[77]

---

73. Larbi, *Pentecostalism*, chap. 3.
74. Wyllie, "Pioneers," 109.
75. Larbi, *Pentecostalism*, chap. 5.
76. Wyllie, "Pioneers," 110.
77. Wyllie, 112.

On 2 March 1937, the first resident missionaries from the Apostolic Faith Church, James McKeown and his wife Sophia, arrived in Ghana to assist Anim's group. McKeown contracted severe malaria and resorted to treating it with medicine, and Anim and his group interpreted this move as having no faith. The main doctrinal base of Anim's group was a "strong emphasis on prayer, strong belief in divine healing without recourse to any form of medicine, preventive or curative, the experience of glossolalia with evidence of speaking in tongues, and strong evangelistic ethos."[78] In contrast, McKeown's group believed they could depend on God for healing but also seek the assistance of preventive and curative medicine. This unresolved difference led to a sharp division between the groups. Anim and McKeown separated in 1939, and this division led to the formation of two churches: the Christ Apostolic Church headed by Anim and the UK Apostolic Church, which McKeown left later (1953) to form an indigenous church culminating in the Church of Pentecost (COP). These three Pentecostal bodies became significant loci of the Pentecostal movement in Ghana,[79] besides the Assemblies of God denomination that was registered in 1930.[80]

The First Phase of Pentecostalism

The four Pentecostal groups – the Apostolic Faith Church, the Christ Apostolic Church, the COP, and the Assemblies of God – constituted the first surge or wave of Pentecostalism in Ghana,[81] which drew from the Azusa Street Revival led by William Seymour. They were a group of Christians who explicitly belonged to Pentecostal denominations, a group of people characterized by the exercise of the supernatural, such as speaking in tongues and the quest for the miraculous through the working of the Holy Spirit.[82] In Ghana, these Pentecostal groups emerged as independent churches who came out from mainline denominations in search of the miraculous and who strictly observed holiness and perfection, a peculiarity inherited from the Holiness movement.

---

78. Larbi, *Pentecostalism*, chap. 5.
79. Wyllie, "Pioneers," 118.
80. Daswani, "(In-)Dividual Pentecostals," 259.
81. Johnson, "Demographics," in Vinson, *Spirit-Empowered Christianity*, 57.
82. Johnson, 57.

The main factor leading to the emergence and rapid spread of Pentecostalism was the quest of Ghanaians to see a superior power overthrow their gods and provide a solution to the numerous spiritual questions and anxieties of life. The mainline denominations founded by the Western missionaries provided education, and their type of Christianity was centered on the physical and the unseen realms of reality. But they could not resolve the Ghanaian's challenges with incurable sicknesses induced by evil spirits or the powers of African black magic. Thus, their form of Christianity was not appealing to Ghanaians, a people whose worldview revolved around power encounters between ancestral spirits and dark powers. Charles H. Kraft asserts that power-oriented people require proof of power, not solely reasoning or academic knowledge.[83] Ghanaian Pentecostalism was in response to the inner desire of Ghanaians to see the power of the Holy Spirit that is attested in the New Testament restored to ordinary Christians. The movement emphasized the cultural continuity of Ghanaian traditional religion, spiritual causalities, and deliverance from evil here and now.

The Second Phase: Neo-Pentecostalism

The charismatic movement emerged in 1907 but became popular in 1950, marking the second wave of the charismatic movement. Adherents were Christians from Anglican, Catholic, Orthodox, and Protestant backgrounds affiliated to nonclassical Pentecostal denominations but who had also experienced the baptism of the Spirit.[84] Instead of leaving their mainline churches to join Pentecostal denominations, this group of people formed a renewed group within their respective churches. They believed and demonstrated the *charismata pneumatic*, the gifts of the Spirit through signs and wonders, without necessarily ascribing to the belief that glossolalia is evidence of Spirit baptism. Because of their emphasis on *charisma* (gifts), they constituted a new form of Pentecostalism in Ghana, termed neo-Pentecostalism, or the Charismatic Renewal group.

After the Second World War, thousands of Christians came out from the neo-Pentecostal or charismatic movement and formed independent churches with much emphasis on the prosperity gospel and the manifestation of

---

83. Kraft, *Power Encounter*, 2.
84. Johnson, "Demographics," in Vinson, *Spirit-Empowered Christianity*, 59.

the gifts of the Holy Spirit. These churches were departures from evangelical Christianity, which does not recognize Holy Spirit baptism as separate from the conversion experience and does not regard speaking in tongues as evidence of baptism in the Holy Spirit. They considered themselves utterly separate from Pentecostals and charismatics, but at the same time, they engaged in some of the Pentecostal-charismatic practices of healing, signs and wonders, power encounters, and miracles.[85] Johnson asserts that they referred to themselves as denominationalists, restorationists, radical charismatics, neo-apostolics, or the "third wave" of the twentieth century.[86]

In Ghana, Nicholas Duncan-Williams of Action Faith Ministries International (AFMI) has been identified as the father of the charismatics. Duncan-Williams was born to a diplomat and a nurse who worked in the Wa and Bolgatanga in northern Ghana. Raised by his mother alone after his parents' separation, Nicholas led a wild life until 1976 when he got converted to the COP while recovering from an ailment in a hospital. During that same year, Duncan-Williams travelled to Nigeria and was mentored for two years at the Bible college founded by Benson Idahosa. He completed the course in 1978 and returned to Ghana, where he founded his own exuberant church in 1979. Thus, the AFMI would later become the motivating example for many other independent charismatic groups in Ghana.[87]

Paul Gifford has criticized the AFMI's theology for being based on the faith gospel of success, health, and wealth, which is evident from Duncan's first book *Destined to Make an Impact*.[88] However, Gifford's criticism was as an outsider who did not fully understand the cultural and socioeconomic context within which the AFMI church originated. The AFMI theologized within a context when many Ghanaians were socioeconomically oppressed and needed a "theology brewed in an African Pot"[89] – one that was not confined to some "professional Christians" but a theology meaningful to a specific audience, Ghanaian men and women who needed to identify their faith with the realities of the time. Duncan-Williams, therefore, believed that

---

85. Johnson, 59.
86. Johnson, 60.
87. Gifford, "Ghana's Charismatic Churches," 242.
88. Gifford, 242.
89. Orobator, *Theology Brewed*, 8.

God never planned sickness, fear, inferiority, defeat, or failure for anyone, based on Genesis 1:29–30.[90] He interpreted the entire Bible as a tree of life that produces riches, honor, promotion, and joy, heavily drawing inspiration from all prosperity preachers of the time: "Robert Schuller, Oral Roberts, Casey Treat, John Avancini, Kennneth Hagin, T. L. Osborn, Paul Yonggi Cho, and Benson Idahosa."[91] Thus, the prosperity gospel became the pillar of all charismatic movements in Ghana through the teachings and ministry of Duncan-Williams, a beacon for Ghanaian charismatics.

Duncan-Williams was followed by Mensa Otabil of the International Central Gospel Church (ICGC). Otabil, a member of the Anglican Church in Ghana, broke out from the Anglican Church and started the ICGC in February 1984. The church was distinguished by its evangelistic outreach, and in April 1987, it increased from seven hundred to fifteen hundred people within one week. However, like Duncan-Williams, Otabil mainly built his preaching on the biblical texts commonly used in the prosperity gospel.[92] Otabil's messages preached success: "Every problem is temporary, every problem can be solved . . . God did not create you with failure in mind, but with success." Similarly, Duncan-Williams taught that "success [is] achieved inexorably by the operation of immutable laws of sowing and reaping."[93]

The Impact of Pentecostalism on Ghanaian Christianity

Since the turn of the twenty-first century, Pentecostalism has grown both globally and in Ghana. Patrick Johnstone has stated that the Pentecostal-charismatic movement is now more visible in church life and is increasing: he predicts that Pentecostal-charismatic adherents will constitute an estimated 11 percent of the world population by 2050, which is a 5 percent increase from the 6 percent reported in 2000.[94] In Ghana, the Population and Housing Census conducted in 2000 indicated that 61.1 percent of the

---

90. Gifford, "Ghana's Charismatic Churches," 243.
91. Gifford, 242.
92. Gifford, 242.
93. Gifford, 246.
94. Johnstone, *Future of Global Church*, 125.

population identified as Christians, and Pentecostal-charismatics constituted 24.1 percent of that number. In 2010, the number had rapidly increased: among the 71.2 percent of the population who identified as Christians, 28.3 percent of Christians identified as Pentecostal-charismatics. The rest of the Christian population was comprised of 13.1 percent Catholics, 18.4 percent Protestants, and 11.4 percent who identified as "other."[95] The fast growth can be ascribed to the nature of the Pentecostal gospel. Francis Benya suggests that the emergence of Pentecostalism coincided with the socioeconomic challenges suffered by sub-Saharan Africa in the 1980s; the economic hardship provided a conducive context for the prosperity gospel.[96]

A common practice of the Pentecostal-charismatics is their emphasis on wealth and health as an indicator for being born again, along with blessing, restoration, supernatural empowerment, and material possessions.[97] In this way, they have succeeded in making Ghanaian Christianity materialistic. The gospel has become a commodity that is being marketed in Ghana. Ghanaian churches have become marketplaces where the gospel is packaged to appeal to the people and not to bring spiritual transformation that is evidenced in godly character and upright social values. The nature of Christianity in Ghana, unfortunately, has turned out to be nominal. The lifestyle of the people in all aspects of life does not reveal the nature of Christ. Religious charlatans pervade Ghanaian churches more than genuine ministers of the gospel who desire to prepare people for heaven.

Exorbitant fees for religious counseling and various forms of harmful practices, like the sale of anointing oil, car stickers, handkerchiefs, water, wrist bands, porridge, and other services, are common. Paul Hiebert has noted that these practices do not lead to a genuine conversion of people. The people just change their symbols or fetish; they may give Christian names to their pagan gods and spirits or change their own traditional names to Christian names, but they are not truly converted.[98] The practice is simply a reinterpretation of Christianity as a new charm or magical power that helps the individual gain more influence.

---

95. Benyah, "Commodification of Gospel," 116.
96. Benyah, 116.
97. Benyah, 135.
98. Hiebert, *Transforming Worldviews*, 11.

The use of mass media to advertise Pentecostal-charismatic services is quickly spreading the faith and turning Ghanaian Christianity into the religion of the charlatans. There is a striving for power encounters without an element of truth encounters or "commitment encounters."[99] Churches promise to help assuage socioeconomic difficulties and offer material blessings, which attracts the ordinary Ghanaian and is causing the youth to chase after easy money and a comfortable life. For most Ghanaian youth, Christianity has become an avenue for making money and improving social status. The promise of the Pentecostal-charismatic churches to provide answers to life-debilitating situations, such as demonic oppression, alcoholism, poverty, depression, a lack of spiritual direction, and drug dependence, is a form of bait used by the Pentecostal-charismatics in Ghana.

Pentecostalism in Ghana is progressing along the same lines as what Anderson observed in South Africa: religious syncretism. Even though Christians claim they speak in tongues, heal the sick, and prophesy, they engage in strange, unbiblical rituals that can best be described as the practices of ATRs.[100] Ghanaian Pentecostalism has also led to ecumenical divisions. Anderson has rightly observed that most Pentecostals hold to the assumption that they are right and all other denominations are wrong and that real Christians are those who believe and practice the Pentecostal faith.[101] Such religious ideology is gradually leading many Pentecostals in Ghana to sectarianism and the erecting of religious barriers that are seemingly difficult to erase.[102]

Nevertheless, Pentecostal-charismatics have contributed massively to the social development of Ghana. Currently, all the major Pentecostal-charismatic movements in Ghana own institutions of higher education or universities, hospitals, and centers for youth retreats. Among them are Central University College (founded by Mensa Otabil), Pentecost University College, Seminary of the Church of Pentecost, Dominion University (founded by Duncan-Williams of AFMI), and Perez University (founded by Rev. Charles Agyinasare of Perez Chapel). These institutions do admit people of other

---

99. Kraft, *Power Encounter*, 18.
100. Anderson, "Diversity," 42.
101. Anderson, 42.
102. Anderson, 42.

faiths and can become a great opportunity to reach out to Muslims. Moreover, Pentecostal-charismatics in Ghana are championing various forms of missions inside and outside Ghana that are contributing to the massive growth of Ghanaian Christianity.

Due to the aggressive evangelistic efforts of the Pentecostal-charismatic churches through media, many historic mainline churches are forced to reconsider their theology, practices, and the general ethos inherited from Western colonialism in an attempt to retain membership lost to the Pentecostal-charismatic movement. Pentecostal-charismatic music and videos are not only played in religious circles but have also influenced Ghanaian politics and culture, and their well-advertised gospel messages on healing, deliverance, and success have almost become a guide to both Christians and non-Christians.[103]

Summary

Before the arrival of Western missionaries and the introduction of Christianity, the people of the Gold Coast (that is, Ghana) held a worldview that emphasized the concept of a supreme God and salvation from harm or the punishment lesser gods could deliver. In light of that, the evangelistic activities of the early Western missionaries could not effectively meet the spiritual needs of the people of Ghana, even though they succeeded in providing them with socioeconomic development. Thus, the quest for spiritual solutions congruent with the African spirituality and worldview led to the emergence of African revival movements, which gradually culminated in the formation of African independent churches that gave birth to Ghanaian Pentecostal and neo-Pentecostal movements. The ministries of William Wade Harris, John Swatson, and Sampson Oppong ushered in the Pentecostal and neo-Pentecostal movements, which largely led to a nominal Christian practice based on prosperity gospel teachings. The COP, whose adherents account for nearly 14 percent of the total Christian population, has emerged as the local version of Pentecostalism and as a leading denomination in Ghana.

---

103. Gifford, *Ghana's New Christianity*, 35.

CHAPTER 2

The Development of Islam and the Nature of the Christian–Muslim Relationship in Ghana

Islam in West Africa

The people of west Africa first encountered Islam in the eighth century. By the end of twentieth century, a combination of forces led to the spread of Islam throughout Sudan, Savannah, and west Africa, where migrant traders and Muslim missionary teachers had formed Muslim communities. In Sudan and east Africa, local rulers were converted to Islam and helped form Muslim states, whereas in other places, the Muslim ulama[1] and holy men waged jihad[2] to form new states. Unfortunately, by the end of the nineteenth century, European invaders had defeated and dislocated the existing states in west Africa and imposed a new Western imperial regime to which Muslims were economically and politically subjected.[3]

---

1. *Ulamā* is the plural form of the Arabic word *ālim*, which literally means "man of knowledge." The root word *ilim* means knowledge and is often the opposite of *jahl* which implies ignorance. This kind of knowledge is related to the revelation God gave to Prophet Muhammad, or the knowledge of God. One is an *ālim* on account of particular religious knowledge of the Qur'an, the *ḥadīth*, and *fiqh* or religious law. *Ulamā* are therefore the professional religious scholars of Islam. Esposito, *Oxford Encyclopedia*, s.v. "Ulama."

2. Originally, *jīhad* carried the meaning of the believer's internal struggle to live out their faith, but this later carried different meanings, including fighting in defense of Islam.

3. Lapidus, *History of Islamic Societies*, 732.

The new states in west Africa were ruled by Western military elites, so the administrative structures, territorial boundaries, and general ideological concepts did not reflect the values, identities, and interests of the west African people. Most of the new rulers, like Dr. Kwame Nkrumah of Ghana, Felix Houphouet-Boigny of Côte d'Ivoire, and a few military elites and chiefs used as intermediaries of the French and British imperialists, were not Muslims and were interested only in political and economic modernization; thus, they accepted Islam as a "personal religion" on par with Christianity.[4] The colonial administration indirectly promoted Islam by promoting circular, nonreligious elites who maintained peace and order, stimulated trade, and opened markets for trade that lured Africans to migrate to growing cities. The colonial administration broke down the traditional structures of African society and introduced new ideas of education and society that promoted Islam as a form of authority and expression of cohesion among displaced peoples. These French and British colonial powers considered Muslims to be more educated and culturally advanced than non-Muslim Africans, so they appointed Muslim chiefs and clerks as administrators of non-Muslim areas. They allowed Muslim religious teachers and missionaries to rally communities, and in some cases, the colonial rulers helped establish courts of Islamic law in non-Muslim areas. This strategy led to the conversion of many people from ATRs into Islam. From the years 1900 to 1960, Muslim communities doubled in west Africa.[5] A significant number of people converted to Islam among pagan people during the colonial and independence eras.

History of Islam in Ghana

Islam preceded Christianity in Ghana.[6] From its outset, Islam was considered the religion of a small group of migrants who originated from north Africa and moved to Ghana through the northern and southern parts of the nation in the fourteenth century.[7] Their presence and movement in Ghana was in a scattered manner and has been described by Johnson A. Mbillah as a

---

4. Lapidus, 736.
5. Lapidus, 736.
6. Azumah, "Muslim-Christian Relations," 1–5.
7. Dovlo and Asante, "Reinterpreting the Straight Path," 215.

dispersion of Muslims rather than the spread of Muslims.[8] The influx of Islam as a religion came to Ghana through Muslim traders and campaigns conducted in the nineteenth century by a group of slave raiders in the northern part of Ghana. However, the campaigns, rather than converting the locals to Islam, made the locals averse to Islam.[9] The traders often moved with Muslim clerics, referred to in Ghana as *mallam, alfa,* or *Kramo* (Muslim). Because they could write skillfully, tell fortunes, and prepare amulets or protective charms, they attracted the indigenous people and especially the chiefs, who relied on these clerics for magical and spiritual powers.[10]

The first identified group of Muslim traders to have arrived in the northern territories of the Gold Coast between the fourteenth to fifteenth centuries were Dyula Muslims.[11] They were made up of the Wangara, Yase, and Hausa people of Malian or Mande descent who travelled to the Gold Coast for the purpose of business and commerce.[12] They settled among the Gonja, Wa, Banda, Mamprussi, and Dagomba in the North, and due to their economic and political exploits, they moved to the southern part of Ghana when invited to trade in gold by the chiefs of southern states, such as Bono and Asante.[13] The rulers were specifically interested in the talents and gifts of Muslim *sharifs* who claimed to be descendants of the Prophet Muhammad's family; they said they were endowed with *baraka*[14] and had the ability to confer on other people blessing and spiritual power that healed and ensured success.[15]

Dyula Muslims practiced Islamic mysticism, Sufism, and introduced the people of the northern Gold Coast to Sufi traditions. The followers of this branch of Islam in the Gold Coast were ordinary, practicing Muslims who

---

8. Mbillah, "PCG," 27, cited in Dovlo and Asante, 215.

9. Azumah, "Muslim-Christian Relations," 1–5.

10. Mbillah, "PCG," cited in Dovlo and Asante, "Reinterpreting the Straight Path," 215.

11. Sanneh, *Crown and Turban*, 12.

12. Hiskett, *Development of Islam*, 45.

13. Sarbah, "Critical Study," 32.

14. *Baraka* is derived from the Arabic root word b/r/k, which in plural is *barakāt*, and fundamentally means "blessing," "beneficent force," or "supernatural power" that God confers on humankind. The concept carries different implicit and explicit meanings according to the historical and cultural context but is usually linked to Islamic mysticism and spirituality. Pious individuals like Prophet Muhammad and those from his house are deemed to possess this type of blessing and can transfer material benefits and spiritual rewards. Esposito, *Oxford Encyclopedia*, s.v. "Barakah."

15. Clarke, *West Africa and Islam*, 106–7.

neither had accurate knowledge of the philosophical, theological, and doctrinal aspects of Islam nor saw doctrine as essential in the practice of faith. The Dyula Muslim traders who brought Islam to the Gold Coast were not experts in Islamic laws but African people with humble dispositions who identified with their fellow Africans' local, traditional, and cultural context.[16] The Dyula Muslims neatly fitted into the traditional cultural context of the people of the Gold Coast and easily assimilated into everyday life. They did not adopt a methodological approach toward the indigenous cultures but intermingled with them in a way that made it possible to contribute to the development of the community.

Dyula Muslims also played an immense role in the royal court.[17] For instance, at the Gonja royal court, their support included administration and military warfare. Due to their literary skill, they assisted as scribes, preserving the names of past chiefs and imams and the history of the kingdom.[18] Their work greatly helped to consolidate the position of the chiefs.[19] Gradually, these Muslims became part of the royal families and held great influence. In Kumasi, the capital of the Ashanti kingdom, they played the role of advisors to the king on matters pertaining to the gold trade, kola, salt, and slaves. Due to their skills in trade, they controlled the cattle industry and "wielded a considerable economic and political power."[20] They helped the administration of northern states, such as Gonja, Dagomba, Wala, Banda, and Mamprussi,[21] as civil servants, physicians, and astrologers.[22]

Due to their adaptability to ATRs, they succeeded in dispersing Islam in Ghana, especially in the North. The Dyula Muslims did not require the people of the Gold Coast to break from their past traditions; they introduced them to Sufi Islam, which is based on nonviolence, a noncompulsive form of ritual prayer, "the Ramandan fast, simple death and marriage ceremonies, and the laicization of religious functions." Where the Islamic faith confronted elements of ATRs, the traditional practices prevailed because the Dyula Muslims

---

16. Sarbah, "Critical Study," 33.
17. Sanneh, *Crown and Turban*, 12.
18. Levtzion, *Muslims and Chiefs*, 51.
19. Sarbah, "Critical Study," 33.
20. Sarbah, 33.
21. Sarbah, 34.
22. Clarke, *West Africa and Islam*, 106–7.

themselves were spiritual Africans.²³ Thus, like the ancient Assyrians, "they feared the LORD but also served their own gods, after the manner of the nations from among whom they had been carried away" (2 Kgs 17:33).

The Characteristics and Spread of Islam in Ghana

After the seed of Islam was sown in northern Ghana, its tenets and practices were assimilated into the country in a gradual manner. Trimingham remarks that there were three stages of assimilation that Islam underwent in west Africa. The first stage, the preparation stage, involved visibly expressing the Islamic way of life through wearing amulets and ornaments while dressing traditionally to suit the way of life of the indigenous people. This stage helped break down traditions that could impede the reception of Islam, and it subtly introduced elements of the Islamic faith to which the indigenous people were indifferent.²⁴ The second stage was the conversion stage, when kings and the royal families gradually broke with the traditional religion without completely adopting the Islamic faith. As this happened, the major elements of the Islamic practices coexisted alongside traditional religion and culture, which began to weaken.²⁵ However, even though Islam attempted to weaken the Ghanaian culture and tradition, the faith was swallowed by the Ghanaian way of life. As indicated by Zwemer, "Islam in its contacts with animism has not been the victor but rather the vanquished,"²⁶ and ATRs became fertile ground for Islam to spread and take root among the people, especially in the North. The third stage involved a gradual reinterpretation of the old culture through Islam so that the indigenous community would fully adopt Islamic culture. This stage emphasized the strong belief in the Islamic faith and practices as an effective vehicle to change conduct and social customs. The individual adherents at this stage gained a strong feeling of belonging to the worldwide Islamic community, *ummah*, which produced a natural disintegration and reintegration of the adherents.²⁷

---

23. Sarbah, "Critical Study," 34.
24. Trimingham, "Influence of Islam," cited in Sarbah, "Critical Study," 34.
25. Sarbah, 35.
26. Zwemer, *Influence of Animism*, quoted in Twumasi, "Understanding Folk Islam," 49.
27. Sarbah, "Critical Study," 35.

These stages of the integration of Islam in northern Ghana explain the development of three distinct social classes of Muslims that exist in northern Ghana: the *gbanga*, the *nyamase*, and the *karamos*. The *gbanga* is mainly made up of the rulers and royal family members who were associated with the Dyula Muslims. This class, though they accepted Islam, practiced adulterated Islam. The *nyamase* is made up of commoners who were not impacted by Islam and continued in their traditional religion. The third class, *karamos*,[28] is comprised of local Muslim communities of different ethnic origins. These social distinctions existed for many years in the North, especially in Gonjaland where the entire area eventually adopted Islam.[29]

While the Dyula Muslims succeeded in impacting the northern people with Islam by simply accommodating northern culture and traditions, this strategy did not work in the southern states, such as Asante and Bono. The process of assimilation did not work in these areas because Islamic practices angered the Asante people.[30] The Dyula Muslims in the south tried to change traditional Asante and Bono rituals that they deemed un-Islamic by substituting them with Islamic prayers. In that way, the Asante people would grow accustomed to using Muslim amulets and become dependent on them for healing, divination, and protective charms. Islam had such an influence in the southern states during the reign of *Asantehene* (King of all Asante) Osei Kwame (1777–1801) because he had believed in the Islamic faith. However, he was removed from power ("destooled") because the Asante realized that their customs and traditions were being replaced with Islamic practices. Thus, his successor Asantehene Osei Bonsu (1801–24) became an enemy to Islam and eventually executed several Muslims in an attempt to win back his people's hearts. The Asante feared the growing Islamic influence in the North, and the dominance of the Asante in the south was threatened by Muslims. For this reason, the Asante and the Bono remained unreceptive to Islam.[31] However, Muslim traders who dwelled in the southern states soon integrated into society without needing to abandon their faith. Through them, Islam resurged in the southern part of Ghana.

---

28. Levtzion, *Muslims and Chiefs*, 55.
29. Sarbah, "Critical Study," 35.
30. Clarke, *West Africa and Islam*, 107.
31. Sarbah, "Critical Study," 36.

The other group of Muslims in Ghana were freed Muslim slaves who returned to settle in the Gold Coast after the abolition of the slave trade. In 1836, the American colonization society dispatched a group of slaves – the "Tabons," believed to have come from Brazil – to settle on the west African coast in Freetown, Monrovia, Lagos, and Accra.[32] The first batch of Tabons returned from Brazil and settled in Accra at Fort James and Ussher Fort and in the town of Keta in the Volta Region. In July 1872, three hundred Hausa Muslims were brought to Ghana who settled in the *zongos*[33] (designated as the Muslim quarters). A group of immigrant Muslims originating from Wangara, Kotokoli, and Nigeria (the Hausa, Yoruba, and Fulani) arrived in Ghana in search of work in plantations and mines.[34] Some of them moved to the commercial and mining areas like Tarkwa, Prestea, and Takoradi. Unlike the Dyula Muslims in the northern part of Ghana who got involved in the political, social, and religious affairs of the chiefs and people, immigrant Muslims in the south were disengaged from the chiefs and the local people. As a result, they could not influence indigenous Ghanaians with their religious practice. The nonengagement of the Muslim immigrants, mainly the Hausa and the Dyula in the southern coastal towns, could be explained by the fact that the people in the coastal areas were not impressed by their lifestyle and despised them because of their lack of formal English education.[35]

Islam in Ghana encountered ATRs and the Ghanaian culture. The encounter between the two religions and cultures produced a new brand of Islam in Ghana. Irrespective of the form of Islam adopted by adherents of the Islamic faith in Ghana, the Islamic faith became a chameleon that took up the colors of the various traditional and cultural milieu it was in. This type of Islam is generally described by scholars with derogatory language, such

---

32. Samwini, "Muslim Resurgence," 32.

33. *Zongo* is a word that originates from the Sahel region of north Africa. It means "caravan" and was originally the stopover place for trans-Saharan traders. They were places in the south where traders offloaded their camels and took rest. Zongos were usually on the outskirts of towns and settlements where the trans-Saharan Muslim traders bartered cattle and cloth for salt and Asante gold. These settlements in the twentieth century became "out-of-sight, out-of- mind" locations for British colonial overseers to accommodate the northern economic migrants they exploited as a source of cheap labor. In modern Ghana, these areas are overcrowded with dilapidated buildings, generally with northern settlers in poor living conditions. Samwini, "Muslim Resurgence," 37.

34. Samwini, 31.

35. Sarbah, "Critical Study," 37.

as "spiritual dualism," "syncretism," "new Islamic religion," "infidelity," "half Islamization," and "mixed" religion, and the religious life of the converted chiefs who practiced Ghanaian Islam has been described as folk in nature.[36]

Even though Islam in Ghana has taken different forms from one geographical area to another, it shares some common features with Islam as practiced in the other parts of west Africa. These common features include the "recognition of common Islamic law, the qur'anic school as an essential feature of village life, the five pillars as evidence of being a Muslim, observance of the common taboo[s] and common calendar rites."[37] Ghanaian Muslims commonly include Islamic elements in naming ceremonies, rites of circumcision, marriage, and death, and they maintain faith in Islamic clerics to invoke supernatural powers through ritual words and activity.[38]

The Emergence and Expansion of Islam Since the Mid-Twentieth Century

Islamic Reformist Movements in Ghana

With the religious syncretism, some Islamic revivalist movements emerged in Ghana that aimed to portray Ghanaian Islam with its traditional cultural elements as syncretic, corrupt, and compromising of the Islamic faith.[39] The revivalist movements operated under the belief that the practice of blending indigenous traditions with Islamic traditions and anyone who did so was deviating from orthodox Islam. Their goal, therefore, was to produce a shift in attitudes among Ghanaian Muslims through the power of teaching, preaching, education, and training regarding the right application of Islamic laws. For instance, the revivalists sought to correct praying to ancestors or saints, wearing charms to ward off evil spirits, and the belief that saints could grant blessings and perform miracles, which were practices that were abhorrent to orthodox Muslims. The revivalists advocated a return to one God, *tawḥīd*, which is a concept in Islam that teaches Allah alone is worthy of worship and prayer. Allah alone must be recognized as "the creator, sustainer of all life,

---

36. Sarbah, 39.
37. Sarbah, 39.
38. Sarbah, 39.
39. Sanneh, *Crown and Turban*, 23.

and the ultimate sovereign lawgiver." *Tawḥīd* includes a return to the Qur'an alone as the revealed word of God to Prophet Muhammad and the *ḥadīth*[40] as the right pattern for religious and moral guidance.[41]

Muslims of Fulani, Hausa, and Tuareg descent were among the Muslim scholars who initiated this type of puritan Islam in Ghana. These scholars had opportunity to study Islam abroad and had contact with north African and Middle Eastern traditions. However, despite their efforts, they were unable to eradicate the elements of ATRs from Ghanaian Islam. The Muslim community in Ghana continued to desire a version of Islam that was congruent with their spiritual aspirations and which met the spiritual and cultural needs of the people. Thus, the work of the puritan Muslims in Ghana led to the evolution of two main groups of Muslims: the *yarnas*[42] who practiced the ancient Islam of the Dyula, and the Sunnis, who practiced the very literal Islam of the Hausa immigrants. The *yarnas* were accommodative to the Ghanaian cultural norms, and the Sunnis were conservative and uncompromising.[43]

The majority of Muslims in Ghana are part of the mainstream Islam, a category of Muslims with unique ethnic and doctrinal diversity. The adherents of mainstream Islam are unique in Ghana in the sense that they identify first and foremost as Ghanaian before becoming Muslims; thus, they respect and adjust to the local culture and tradition. Until 1921, Muslims in Ghana were organized along ethnic lines and not on the basis of the religion's orthodox or heterodox labels.[44] Ethnic Islamic affiliations received special identification tags (special nicknames) that superficially identified the origin of the various Muslim groups, but in reality, they marked the distinction between pure and mixed Muslims. Converts from the southern ethnic groups who were not considered pure Muslims had tags like Fante Kramo or Asante Kramo.[45] Those from the north were considered pure Muslims, so they had no identification tags, unlike the southerners. There is no identification like

---

40. The *ḥadīth* is the account of the sayings and deeds of Prophet Muhammad.
41. Sarbah, "Critical Study," 40.
42. The *yarnas* engage in divination by sand and stars and believe spirits inhabit wells, streams, rivers, and mountains, which make the group almost identical with ATRs.
43. Sarbah, "Critical Study," 41.
44. Samwini, "Muslim Resurgence," 16.
45. *Kramo* is a nickname or a kind of ethnic affiliation tag given to Muslims seen as mixed Muslims from the southern and coastal areas of Ghana. The name marks a distinction between Muslims from the northern part of Ghana and those from the south.

Hausa Kramo or Kotokoli Kramo. However, the Fante, Asante, Ga, Ewe, and northern Muslims each have their ethnic and doctrinal differences. Ethnicity also gave rise to an increase in the number of mosques in the country in the sense that each ethnicity desired their own mosque.[46]

Until August 1997 when the *Alh al-Sunnah wa 'I-Jama'a*[47] was inaugurated, mainstream Muslims in Ghana were the sole custodians of Sunni Islam, which largely practiced Sufi mysticism.[48] The mainstream Sunni Muslims followed the Maliki[49] *madhhab* (legal thought) with an inclination toward "Quadiriyya[50] and Suwarian/Tijaniyya tariqa,"[51] which is the Sufi brotherhood.[52] They belong to the Dyula tradition's flexible doctrinal position that tolerates the viewpoints of other faiths and cultures. While maintaining some level of distinctiveness, they generally embrace the viewpoints of pluralistic society and respectfully work among non-Muslims without losing their Muslim identity. As followers of the Suwari school of thought, they subscribe to a pluralistic ideology that accommodates, respects, and tolerates other worldviews and is able to serve the community and its leader, irrespective of whether the leader is Muslim or not. The Suwarians/Tijaniyya *shuyukh* have demonstrated a level

---

46. Samwini, "Muslim Resurgence," 102.

47. *Alh al-Sunnah wa 'I-Jama'a* means the people of the Sunnah and the community. This group emerged from Ghanaian scholars' contact with the Arab/Muslim world. Among the early leaders were Alhaji Afa Ejura and Umar Ibrahim Iman (a Ghanaian from Benin and the first Ghanaian to graduate from the Islamic University of Madinah). They are a legalistic group that emerged from Sunni Islam in Ghana and fought against all forms of innovations from other Islamic groups, especially the Tariqa Tijaniyya. They contend that their religious practices are based solely on the *ḥadīth* and do not undertake any religious activity that is not in compliance with the Qur'an and Sunnah. They are militant and accuse the Tariqa Tijaniyya of being "mixed," "syncretic," and "Seers of God" because of their inclination toward magic and divination. Samwini, 223–24.

48. Samwini, 106.

49. The Maliki Order was founded by Malik Ibn Anas and is a special school of thought from Sunni Islam. It lays emphasis on the Madina Sunnah (the customary practice of Muhammad) as the true practice and customs, the *ḥadīth* that reflected the actual prophetic practices of Muhammad during the Madina period.

50. The Qādiriyya Order originated from Baghdad. It was founded by Shaykh 'Abd al-Qādir al-Jaylānī during the twelfth century. Although their doctrines have varied over the years, they interpret the Qur'an and the *ḥadīth* mystically. Hiskett, *Development of Islam*, 244–46.

51. Suwari is a school of thought founded by Alhaji Salim Suwari and has been adopted by many west African Muslims, including those in Ghana. It is reported to have a long history in Ghana.

52. The word *tariqa* is used to denote an order of Islam, that is, the Tariqa Tijaniyya is the Tijaniyya Order.

of tolerance to Ghanaian customs and traditions to the point of adopting some of them into Islamic practices. By doing so, Islam has been brought closer to Ghanaians. The Tariqa Tijaniyya has assumed exclusive claims of spiritual and sociopolitical authority in Ghana.[53]

Emergence of Ghana's Islamic Groups

The overwhelming majority of Muslims in Ghana are Sunni Muslims. However, Sunni Islam is not monolithic; it consists of many theological and legal schools of thought shaped by history and the prevailing local and cultural circumstances. The four schools of thought that exist among the Sunni sect were founded by "Abu Hanifah (d. 767), Malik Ibn Anas (d. 797), al-Shafi'I (d. 820), and Ibn Hanbal (d. 855)."[54] Ghanaian Sunni Muslims subscribe to the Maliki legal tradition and only a minority adopt the Shafi'i school of thought.

Sunnis recognize the first three caliphs after Muhammad, Abu Bakr, Umar, and Uthman, as the rightful leaders of the Islamic community. Sunni Islam is generally based on the Sunnah, which is preserved in the *ḥadīth*. Both the Qur'an and tradition form the basis of Sunni religious law. However, they also value the *ijma*, which is the religious consensus of Muslim scholars. This value for the *ijma* reflects Sunni Muslims' emphasis on community and collective wisdom that is guided by the Qur'an and the Sunnah. The Sunni Muslims in Ghana, on the basis of this community life, refer to themselves as *ahl al-sunnah wa al-jama'ah*, "the people of the sunnah and the community."[55]

Four major developments of Islam in Ghana between the years 1900 to 1950 characterized the beginning and subsequent resurgence of Islam in Ghana. These developments also shaped the Muslim-Christian relationship and Muslims' relationship with fellow Muslims. During this period, the Tariqa Tijaniyya grew in Ghana and the Ahmadiyya Muslims Mission was established. Ghanaian Muslims formed the Muslims Association party in an attempt to unify the ummah. By the mid-nineteenth century, specifically in the 1950s, Ghanaian Muslims were clearly divided on doctrinal and ethnic fronts. Doctrinally, they were divided between the Ahmadiyya and the Sunnis/Tijaniyya, and ethnically, the southern Ghanaians established their

---

53. Sarbah, "Critical Study," 41.
54. Esposito, *Oxford Encyclopedia*, 257.
55. Esposito, 256.

own missions. This brought a shift in Ghana; Muslims were formerly tolerant, but by the year 2000, Islam was made up of intolerant groups. These groups experienced an identity crisis, as the "more authentic" or "orthodox" groups confronted the "heterodox" or "non-Islamic" inclinations of other groups.[56]

In 1971, the Islamic Reformation and Research Centre, which is a Muslim missionary organization, opened in the city of Accra. The activities of the organization are called the Wahhabi missionary order. The organization is reportedly financed by the *Dar al-Ifta* (a state advisory institution on Islamic matters) of Saudi Arabia, which has sponsored numerous Ghanaian Muslim students to universities in the Arab world since then.[57] These students then return to Ghana to engage in missionary activities. Besides these groups of Islamic organizations, it is worth mentioning that in 1990 the leader of the Nation of Islam, Louis Farrakhan, was invited to Ghana by the then Provisional National Defense Council (PNDC, which was Ghana's military junta), and in October 1996 the PNDC held a national convention in Ghana that was fully telecasted by the national television, radio, and print media. Despite this, the Nation of Islam did not gain many followers in Ghana.[58]

The Sufi Order: Tariqa Tijaniyya

The main Sufi order (*tariqa*) in Ghana is the Tariqa Tijaniyya.[59] The Tijaniyya, founded in the eighteenth century in north Africa, traces its origins to 'Abul-Abbas Ahmad b. Muhammad b. al-Mukhtar b. Salim al-Tijani (1737–1815).[60] The order entered Ghana through British colonialists who brought with them a number of police and soldiers who were adherents. Additionally, the Ghanaian Muslims who went on *hajj* (pilgrimage) returned home with strong Tijaniyya ties and propagated the tariqa among their families. Among those who popularized the Tijaniyya in Ghana, especially in the 1920s, were Imam Muhammad Abbas, who became the Imam of Accra and the *muqaddam* (the head official) of the tariqa, Shaikh Muhammad Tayla, and Mallam Alhassan Atta. Alhaj 'Umar of Kete-Krachi was the head of the Tijaniyya of

---

56. Samwini, "Muslim Resurgence," 78.
57. Azumah, "Muslim-Christian Relations," 1–5.
58. Azumah, 1–5.
59. Azumah, 1–5.
60. Ryan, "'Arise, O God!'" 208.

the Gold Coast from 1913 to 1934. By 1950, many parts of Ghana including Accra, Banda, Kumasi, Tamale, Wa, and Yendi became the strongholds of the Tijaniyya. The work of visiting *shuyukh* and *mallamai* contributed to the spread of the Tijaniyya in Ghana. One such visiting Shaikh was Hadi Idaw 'Ali who paid a visit to Wenchi: his words are still followed in that part of Ghana. It has been said that the most influential shaikh[61] among the visitors was Shaikh Alhaj Ibrahim Niasse of Kaolack. He paid a visit to Ghana as an official guest of the first president of Ghana Dr. Kwame Nkrumah (1957–66), who was reported to have sent presents to the shaikh in exchange for *baraka*.[62]

The young proficient Muslim scholar, Shaikh Niasse, was a strong Tijani leader. He visited Ghana to assist in reuniting Ghanaian Muslims; however, his teachings generated doctrinal controversies that led to the development of another phase of Islam in Ghana. His major spiritual and intellectual contribution to the tariqa denigrated the Muslim community when some of his followers in Ghana claimed they had seen Allah and began an "antinomian movement hitherto unknown to Ghanaian Muslims."[63] Shaikh Yussif Afajura, a political activist of Kwame Nkrumah's Convention People's Party, stood against the teachings of Niasse and the Tijaniyya, leading to the Ahl-al-Sunnah reform movement in Ghana, which struggled against Sufism.[64]

The Tijani venerate the Prophet Muhammad and Shaikh Ahmad al-Tijani. Unlike other Muslims, the Tijani exalt Muhammad beyond a mere mortal messenger of God and consider him to be a mediator between the transcendent God and the mortal world.[65] They recite the *salat alfatih* daily, one hundred times in the morning and evening, and reciting this prayer is regarded by some as more meritorious than all *du'a* invocations, prayers of remembrance (*dhikr*), and the glorification to God (*tasbih*).[66] Besides *salat alfatih*, they also pray the *Fawharat al-Kamal* (Jewel of Perfection) which they

---

61. Shaikh, also written as shaykh or sheikh, is an Arabic title since pre-Islamic times given to distinguished men who possess some level of scriptural learning, such as the heads of Islamic religious orders. The honorific term connotes "leader, patriarch, notable, elder, chief, or counselor." Quranic scholars, those who preach and lead prayers in mosques, and jurists use the title shaikh. Esposito, *Oxford Encyclopedia*, s.v. "Shaykh."

62. Samwini, "Muslim Resurgence," 85.

63. Kobo, "Promoting Good," 190.

64. Kobo, 191.

65. Ryan, "Mystical Theology," 210.

66. Ryan, 210.

claim was revealed in 1782 by Muhammad himself to Ahmad al-Tijani while he was awake during the day.⁶⁷ This prayer is recited twelve times daily by all Tijani as part of their *wazifah* (devotion). The *Fawharat al-Kamal* prayer contains three blessings for Muhammad, which describe him "as a water source (*'ayn*), the spring from which a river flows,"⁶⁸ as light, and as a jewel. It also claims that he is the source of divine mercy and truth, like lightning in a storm that brings rain. For the Tijani to see Muhammad is to see God emanate, reminiscent of Christians' perception of Jesus (John 14:9: "Whoever has seen me has seen the Father.")

Ahmad al-Tijani regarded himself highly, proclaiming himself to be the "seal of Muhammad-like sainthood" (*Khatm al-wilayah al-muhammadiyya*) and the "supreme axis" (*qutb al-qatb*), which Ryan J. Patrick describes as "the source of saintliness of all those close to God before and after his day."⁶⁹ Knut Vikor writes, "He [Ahmad al-Tijani] was in fact the 'seal of *wilaya*,' in the same way that the Prophet Muhammad was the seal of prophethood; for this reason, his Way was the ultimate one, and no other Way was acceptable."⁷⁰ An affiliation with the Tijaniyya implies abandoning all other *wird* (liturgy) and adopting the tariqa as one's sole religious identity.

Patrick Ryan notes that the Ghanaian Tijani he knew in the 1970s and 1980s "revered relics of the late Shaykh Ibrahim's turban and had drunk water left over after he had finished his ritual ablutions during his last visit to Ghana."⁷¹ They believed this water from their shaikh communicated the *baraka* of a living saint. Ryan asserts that extremists "deform" their societies, such as when Tijani "pose as "money-doublers, magicians, and other types of opportunists preying on the ignorant and poor" or when Wahhabis "preach community-disrupting hatred of fellow Muslims and fellow citizens of traditional [ATRs] and Christian faith."⁷²

---

67. Ryan, 211.

68. Ryan, 211.

69. In Sufi tradition, every earthly age has a human figure who serves as a mystical axis (*qutb*) of divine knowledge. Ryan, 214.

70. Vikor, "Sufi Brotherhoods in Africa," 450.

71. Ryan, "Mystical Theology," 219.

72. Ryan, 221.

The Mahdi Movement

As early as 1904, the Mahdi (meaning "divinely guided one") movement came to Ghana and gained traction among the Asante and the northern regions of Ghana through the Sudanese Muslim revivalist Malam Musa and his three assistants.[73] Islam at this time in the Gold Coast had stagnated and even retrogressed in some parts of the country. Due to the rivalries and various reactions and division created by the individual Islamic groups, a spiritual void was created among the general body of the Ghanaian Muslims that made way for revival. The arrival of Malam Musa brought a revival to Islam in Ghana, especially in the Asante and eastern part of the country, where many non-Muslims threw their idols away and were converted to Islam.[74]

The Ahmadiyya Movement

It was in the midst of this quest for revival that the Fante Muslims brought the Ahmadiyya movement to Ghana in 1921. Many Muslims who were formerly adherents of the Sunni group were converted to the Ahmadiyya movement, deemed to be the most charismatic Muslim group in Ghana. The Ahmadiyya movement became a great threat to the Sunni/Tijaniyya Muslim community and even Christianity in terms of their positive influence.[75]

The movement was established by Hazrat Mirza Ghulam Ahmad (1835–1908). Ghulam Ahmad was born in a pluralistic society in eastern Punjab, India. He grew up in an era when Christian missionary activities were competing for converts from the major religions of his area, Hinduism and Sikhism.[76] Ghulam Ahmad was influenced by this competition for souls, and his movement was marked by proselytizing and conversion. During a time of contemplation, he was said to have received a revelation that he was the *mujaddid*[77] from God. He declared himself in 1901 to be a prophet and the recipient of divine revelation, appointed by God as the Messiah and Mahdi to

---

73. Samwini, "Muslim Resurgence," 94.

74. Samwini, 91.

75. Samwini, 106.

76. Antoine, "Practice and Conversion," 74.

77. *Mujaddid* means "one who renews" and refers to the renewal of the Islamic faith. Abu Da'ud al-Sijistani (d. 275 AH/889 CE) in his Sunan, "one of the six compilations of the reliable hadiths esteemed by the Sunnis," stated that the Prophet has said, "Indeed God will send to this community at the beginning/end (*ra's*, literally "head") of every hundred years one who will renew for it its religions." The implication is that there shall be renewal or revival of the true

renew the religion of Islam. He asserted that he was the Mahdi and Messiah who was a spiritual manifestation of Jesus and his "heir." He believed he was ordained to bring sanity to an Islam that had gone astray from the orthodox teachings of the holy founder of Islam, Muhammad. He interpreted Islam as a peaceful religion that is more accommodating than other religious sects, so he gained prominence from other Muslims.

Because of his interpretation and redefinition of jihad, he was attracted to the British colonial government. Ghulam Ahmad stated that the Ahmadiyya movement "believes that the fight for supremacy over all other religions should be entirely spiritual, devoid of the use of material weapons [except] the use of the weapons of reason and arguments based on religious truths." Such an argument made jihad un-Islamic.[78] The Ahmadiyya movement then used its relationship with the British government as a tool to defend itself from other Muslim groups who saw the movement as a colonial ploy. After decades of persecution in Pakistan, the headquarters of the Ahmadiyya movement was moved to London in 1984. In 1974, the World Muslim League (*Rabita al-Alam al-Islami*) renounced the claim of Ghulam Ahmad as a prophet and reduced the Ahmadiyya movement to a sect. It prohibited adherents from entering the holy cities or taking the hajj, a mandatory pillar of faith for those who are financially able.[79]

The Ahmadiyya Mission in Ghana

In the central region of Ghana, two indigenous people, Benjamin Sam and Mahdi Appah, were key in the establishment of Islam. Benjamin Sam, who was then a Wesleyan Methodist catechist, got converted to Sunni Islam by Abubakar Sadique, a Hausa soldier of Nigeria origin in 1885.[80] Benjamin Sam used his Christian experience to establish a Muslim community made up of about five hundred indigenous Fante through whom the faith spread in the Fante land in the central region. He blended Christian values with Islamic practices and traditional customs of the people. Since Benjamin did not oppose the traditional customs of the people of the central region, he allowed

---

Sunnah of the Prophet to eradicate any form of dangerous innovations (*bid'a*) of the Sunnah. Esposito, *Oxford Encyclopedia*, s.v. "Mujaddid."

78. Effah, "Early History of Ahmadiyya," 1, cited in Antoine, "Practice and Conversion," 75.
79. Antoine, 75.
80. Antoine, 77.

the consumption of alcohol and valued Western education. His value for Western education became a noticeable feature among Fante Kramo.

Benjamin Sam's group led the initiative of the Ahmadiyya movement in Ghana. His members were the first to invite the Indian missionaries of the Ahmadiyya Muslim movement of the Qadiani Branch, which was headed at the time by Khalifat-ul-Masih E. R. Hakeem in the central region.[81] The first Ahmadiyya missionary arrived in Saltpond in the central region of Ghana in 1921 after receiving an invitation by Sunni Muslims and former Christians in the region. A group of Fante Kramo communicated with the supreme head of the Ahmadiyya movement, Bashir ud-Din Mahmud Ahmad I, who was then in Rabwa, India, before Pakistan was separated from India. They were unwilling to remain under the spiritual leadership of the Hausa and northern Ghana Muslims, so Ahmad sent Al-Hajj Maulana 'Abdul Rahim Nayyar as a missionary to preach to them. For the first decade, the movement was led by this Indian missionary through a Fante interpreter and the locals took up roles as imams.[82] By 1922, Al-Hajj Maulvi Fazlur Rahman Hakeen was posted to the Gold Coast as the successor of Al-Hajj Maulana 'Abdul Rahim Nayyar, and he adopted an aggressive evangelism approach. He established forty Ahmadiyya stations along the coastal areas and the Asante counted over three thousand converts by 1927.[83]

The Impact of the Ahmadiyya Mission

Hakeen was said to be scholarly and chose his preaching topics based on the audience. In Muslim dominated areas, he preached that "Jesus did not die on the cross nor is he sitting alive in the fourth Heaven at the right hand of God," while in non-Muslim areas his topic was that "the Bible shows Jesus did not die on the cross."[84] Likewise, he used both the Qur'an and the Bible in public preaching to diffuse the Christian notion of Jesus's second coming and the authenticity of the Bible. With many scholarly arguments, he succeeded in winning peasant Christians and ridiculed the church. Once the Ahmadiyya established a missionary society in 1927, it facilitated the rapid

---

81. Sarbah, "Critical Study," 38.
82. Antoine, "Practice and Conversion," 78.
83. Samwini, "Muslim Resurgence," 107.
84. Samwini, 107.

spread of such teaching in Ghana, which posed a great threat to both Sunni Muslims and Christians.

The Ahmadiyya group made a large impact on education, making meaningful contributions to the progress of Ghana. They set up the Ta'lim Islami (II) Ahmadiyya secondary school in Kumasi as early as 1950. Also by then, they had already established several primary schools in 1925 in Saltpond, Mumford and Gomoa, and Potsin. Justice G. E. K. Kins, a former Ghana Attorney General and retired Supreme Court Justice, was a proud product of the Ahmadiyya school in Saltpond. Besides him, Rt. Rev. Dr. Sam Prempeh, head of the Presbyterian Church of Ghana, and Maulvi A. Wahab Adam, the spiritual head of the Ahmadiyya Muslim Mission in Ghana, are also two of the many alumni of the Ahmadiyya mission schools. Their schools were opened to all regardless of belief, gender, nationality, or religious restrictions.[85] Due to their use of education as a tool for mission, the Ahmadiyya movement had much influence on the educated youth, who outnumbered the aged population of Ghanaians. The national missionary of the Ahmadiyya movement remarked that it was easier to win youth to Ahmadiyya than the aged.[86]

Politically, the group engaged in a number of issues that affected its relationship with non-Muslims and the Sunnis. Considered a heresy group, yet arrogating to itself the position of authentic Islam in Ghana, the Ahmadiyya's activities were fiercely opposed by the mainstream Sunni Muslims. The Sunni/Tijaniyya clerics were the main distributors of amulets and talismans in Ghana, especially among the Kumasi and Gonja, and the Ahmadiyya Muslims denounced the Sunnis for using such articles, which they claimed were the work of the devil.[87] While the Sunnis brought amulets and charms into Ghana, the Ahmadis built more schools and hospitals than mosques in Ghana. They laid emphasis on modern medical facilities and strategically denounced Sunni practices, such as divination and the "making or keeping of talismans as means of warding off evils or exercising luck."[88] Due to the Ahmadis' efforts in establishing educational and health centers in Ghana, they gained much recognition and influence among the people. The Ahmadiyya

---

85. Gyasi, "Ahmadiyya's Contribution."
86. Antoine, "Practice and Conversion," 81.
87. Samwini, "Muslim Resurgence," 112.
88. Antoine, "Practice and Conversion," 89.

Mission brought a paradigm shift in the negative sociocultural mindset in Ghana that Muslims are a backward and inferior people.[89] Ahmadis successfully targeted the Akans, who formed the majority ethnic group in Ghana, and made use of the most commonly used language in Ghana, Twi, as a medium for making converts. Unlike the Sunni Muslims whose background and educational system was purely dependent on the Makaranta school system, the Ahmadiyya's blended version of Western education and Islamic education attracted Ghanaian youth who generally considered the Sunnis to be uneducated.

The Ahmadiyya Muslims are now the fastest growing order of Islam in Ghana, due to its monolithic background and nature. Hakeen's words to the Ahmadiyya Mission in 1948 reveal the tremendous impact the group had on the churches in Ghana. In a letter to the headquarters, he stated this:

> In Abasa and Gomoo [sic] two wholly Christian towns, and especially in the latter town which is a great Christian center of Christianity in these parts, I had the good fortune to expose the untenability and hollowness of the Christian precepts and tenets [while] standing at the entrance of the central church of the town. The whole congregation listened to me attentively, and the Christian catechist in a vein [sic] effort to neutralize the effects which my speech had evidently produced upon the audience was badly discomfited.[90]

Hakeen's letter demonstrates the outcome of his polemic approach to Christians. To counter the work of Christians and the Tijaniyya, the Ahmadiyya Mission put in place society structures in each town and community where their presence is registered.

Shi'ism

The concept of Shi'a implies "followers, party, groups, partisans or supporters" (Qur'an 19:69; 28:15; 37:83) whose religious code and inspiration followed those of the descendants of Prophet Muhammad, the *ahl al-bayt* (the people of the house). Shi'ism's strongest claim of leadership rested on the descendants

---

89. Antoine, 84.
90. Hakeen, "Ahmadiyya Movement," 400, quoted in Samwini, "Muslim Resurgence," 109.

of 'Ali, and the succession of Muhammad was exclusively claimed by only the Prophet's direct descendants.[91]

After the Prophet Muhammad's death, the choice of leadership for the community determined the vision for the Muslim community. The majority of the Prophet's companions of northern Arab backgrounds trusted that the role of his successor would lead the Muslim community and safeguard first and foremost the political heritage, or the community's political character, and secondly, propagate the message of Islam beyond Arabia. However, very few of his companions from southern regions believed that the successor must as a priority safeguard the spiritual authority of Muhammad among other temporal functions; such functions were to become the responsibility of imams in the Muslim community.

Apart from the above sociocultural traditions, the exalted position of the members of the Prophet's family was crucial to determining a successor. Four key terms are used to describe the prophetic progeny in the Qur'an: *dhurriyah* (direct descendant), *al* (offspring, house, or dynasty), *ahl* (family, progeny), and *qurba*, (relation or nearest of kin). Mostly, these terms were interpreted as Muhammad's nearest of kin: "his cousin and son-in-law, 'Ali, his daughter Fatimah, [and] their sons Hasan and Husayn."[92] The Shi'a extend this *ahl al-bayt,* nearest of kin, to include Hasan and Husayn. The origin of Shi'a Islam is therefore traceable to Muhammad's days in Madina where his prominent companions recognized Muhammad's cousin 'Ali ibn Abi Talib as the *wasi* (legatee) of Muhammad and the imam to lead the Muslim community after Muhammad. The first supporters of 'Ali constituted the nucleus of the Shi'a Muslims. However, 'Ali himself later recognized the leadership of Abu Bakr, and the Shi'a tendencies lost their active and open manifestations. After the death of Umar, Shi'a sentiments rose again when Uthman was declared the third caliph. 'Ali was offered the opportunity to lead the community on the condition that he followed the heritage or precedents established by the first two caliphs, but he objected. 'Ali's refusal to follow the line of the first two caliphs became the foundation of the Shi'a Muslims' legal thought.[93]

---

91. Haider, *Shi'i Islam*, 3.
92. Esposito, *Oxford Encyclopedia*, s.v. "Shi'i Islam."
93. Esposito, s.v. "Shi'i Islam."

In the late 1980s, the Iranian mission began to promote Shi'ism in Ghana through the establishment of a few educational institutions and their sponsorship of Ghanaian students to Iranian universities. By 2001, the Iranian mission succeeded in establishing Ghana Islamic University through which a considerable number of Sunni Muslims were converted to Shi'ism.[94] Due to the offer of scholarships to study in Iranian universities, many Muslim youth members from Sunni adopted Shi'ism to get access to good and free education. The cultural and educational activities of the Iranian mission helped the Shi'a Muslims to make converts in Ghana.[95] In their confession of faith, the Shi'a or Shi'ites "testify there is no God but Allah and Muhammad is the Messenger of Allah and 'Ali is the Friend of Allah."[96] They consider 'Ali's son Husayn to be a martyr and commemorate his death on the Day of Ashura (the tenth day of the month of Muharram).[97] On this day, members of the Shi'a group march through the streets in a funeral procession and beat their chests symbolically to prove that they are atoning for the cruel murder of Husayn.[98] The Shi'a accuse the Sunni of using a corrupt collection of *ḥadīth* and claim the hidden meaning of the Qur'an is only known to their imams and representatives who are given the title *ayat-ul-llah* (sign or representative of Allah). Due to the value the Shi'a place on the intercession of saints (referred to as "friends of God") and the deification of 'Ali, they have tension with the Ahmadiyya and Sunni Muslims.[99]

Although Islam in Ghana continued to experience diversification, the main Islamic orders in Ghana are the Sunni and Ahmadiyya.

---

94. Kobo, "Promoting Good," 187.
95. Kobo, 186.
96. Azumah, *My Neighbour's Faith*, chap. 6.
97. The Day of Ashura can be compared in a way to the Christian Good Friday celebration held among certain denominations and Yom Kippur among the Jews.
98. Azumah, *My Neighbour's Faith*, chap. 6.
99. Azumah, chap. 6.

Understanding the Christian-Muslim Relationship in Ghana

Inter-Muslim Groups

The early days of the Muslim groups in Ghana were marked by bloody confrontations, intolerance, mutual suspicion, and noncooperation, especially on the part of the Ahmadiyya movement and the mainstream Muslims in Ghana. In a number of instances, the Sunni Muslims walked out from meetings because of the presence of the Ahmadis. There have also been misunderstandings, mainly over leadership issues, between the indigenous Ghanaian Muslims and Muslims of other neighboring west African regions. These misunderstandings have often led to violence during Friday prayers and the subsequent closure of some mosques by the Ghanaian authorities. Arab-trained Muslim missionary groups clash with the mainline traditional Ghanaian Muslims, popularly called the Ahl al-Sunnah group, which takes its inspiration from the Saudi Wahhabi. There is also confrontation between Tijaniyya-inclined Muslims and those who have an inclination toward Qadariyya.[100] The Tijaniyya group are supported by Iran, while the Qadariyya derive their support from Saudi Arabia.[101]

Among the three Islamic groups in Ghana, the Al-tijaniyya (Sufi), Ahl al-Sunnah Wa al-jama'ah (Sunni), and the Ahmadiyya, there are some incidences of Islamic radicalization and violence based on socioeconomic, political, doctrinal, and interpretive differences. The three groups use *da'wah*, "mission" that is characterized by a struggle for doctrinal preeminence and often leads to hostility, disagreement, and frequent ideological and verbal clashes. The resulting radicalization and violence is gradually endangering national security in Ghana, especially in the northern region where Muslim groups continue to have a marked impact on interreligious and intrareligious coexistence. Their impact is also felt in southern Ghana among the Asante and the Brong-Ahafo.[102]

---

100. Azumah, "Muslim-Christian Relations," 1–5.
101. Azumah, 1–5.
102. Aning and Abdallah, "Islamic Radicalization," 149–67.

Islamic Violence Based on Socioeconomic and Political Dynamics

The majority of the northern region of Ghana is Muslim and the southern region is predominantly Christian. There are noticeable disparities between the north and south in terms of socioeconomic living conditions. The north is generally poor due to an unfavorable climate for agriculture and the political and economic neglect of the north prior to Ghana's independence. Colonizers were interested in timber and gold which were not found in the northern regions, so the south received more investment. Colonial governments moved people of the north to the south as labor reserves without any meaningful economic investment in return. These migrants were not well-educated because they resisted formal education out of a fear of being indoctrinated by Christian missionaries. Together, these factors impoverished the north and underpinned the north-south divide in Ghana. While migration from the north to the south is ongoing, Muslim migrants from the north are still not well integrated into sectors of formal employment in the south because of their lack of education.

Ghanaian governments since independence in 1957 have tried to correct these socioeconomic disparities, but the situation persists.[103] When a little economic or educational support is given to Muslims in the north, it creates opportunities for religious and political alliances that serve as catalysts for radicalization and intrareligious violence in the nation. Generally, the Ahl-al-Sunnah and the Tijaniyya align with the National Democratic Congress (NDC) while their biggest rival, the Ahmadiyya (made up predominantly of Asante and Fante), are strong supporters of the New Patriotic Party (NPP).[104]

Doctrinal and Interpretational Differences

All the three Islamic groups in Ghana – the Al-tijaniyya (Sufi), Ahl al-Sunnah Wa al-jama'ah (Sunni), and the Ahmadiyya – believe in the five pillars of Islam and consider the Qur'an and the $ḥadīth$ as sources of doctrinal authority. However, they disagree on the interpretation of theological issues, such as the finality of the Prophet Muhammad as the seal of the prophet, the crucifixion of Jesus, the meaning of jihad, and many other innovative faith

---

103. Aning and Abdallah, 151–53.
104. Aning and Abdallah, 153.

practices, including the wearing of charms and the consultation of *malams* (spiritualists).[105] While the Tijaniyya and the Alh-al Sunnah continue to adopt parts of ATRs in their expression of Islam, the Ahmadiyya condemn the use of certain elements of ATRs. This does not mean the Ahmadiyya are more orthodox, however. Notably, the Ahmadiyya claim Muhammad was not the seal of the prophets and consider Hadrat Mirza Ahmed Ghulam (1835–1908) the Messiah and the Madhi of Islam.

While the Tijaniyya are supported locally, Ahl-al-Sunnah and Ahmadiyya Muslims receive external support from other countries, including Saudi Arabia, Libya, Egypt, and Kuwait, which enhances their proselytization efforts. Youth members who receive support for their university education through their religious affiliation return after graduation to champion the proselytization agenda of others through *da'wah*. The *da'wah* methodologies of the three groups involve character attacks that directly or indirectly insult each other, which give rise to hot arguments and confrontations.

Though Ghana has not experienced a major radicalization of youth, some Muslim youth in Ghana still hold concepts of jihad that threaten national security and peace. Such concepts say that jihad is "to die in defense of Islam," "to establish Sharia Law in Muslim dominated states," or "to kill a non-Muslim for making derogatory remarks against Prophet Muhammad."[106] When such concepts are promoted amidst Ghanaian Muslim youth struggling with unemployment, alienation, ethnocentrism, and the north-south divide, this proselytization becomes a real security threat.

Additionally, Ghanaian Muslims are divided by scholarly traditions and the school of thought they follow besides the Qur'an and the Sunnah of the Prophet Muhammad. The Suwari tradition, traceable to Al-Hajj Salim Suwari, is one of the main schools of thought followed by Ghanaian Muslims, especially the Tijaniyya. Al-Hajj Salim Suwari's teachings were mainly transmitted through two of his disciples, Muhammad al-Buni who went to the Dyula and Yusuf Kasana who went to the Jakhanke. Suwari adopted a liberal attitude toward non-Muslims, unlike his contemporary Muhammad b. Abd al-Karim al-Maghili (d. 1503/4).[107]

---

105. Aning and Abdallah, 155.
106. Aning and Abdallah, 160.
107. Wilks, "Juula and Expansion of Islam," in Levtzion and Pouwels, *History of Islam*, 97.

Suwari's position concerning non-Muslims is that *kufr* (unbelief) does not result from wickedness but rather from *jahl* (ignorance). According to his school of thought, God's overarching design for the world is that some people remain in *jahiliyya* (the state of ignorance) longer than others. Thus, true conversion to Islam can only occur at God's appointed time. Engaging people by force or proselytization to accept Islam would imply an interruption of God's perfect will. He considered jihad against non-Muslims as an unacceptable way of making converts. He stressed that jihad of the sword is only permissible for self-defense and when the very "existence of the Muslim community be threatened by unbelievers."[108] He encouraged Muslims to accept the authority of non-Muslim rulers so far as their leadership principles did not infringe on the Muslims' religious rights or prevent them from following their own way of life in accordance with the Sunnah of the Prophet. The Suwarian school of thought posits that Muslims must set an example to non-Muslims in character so that when their time of conversion comes, they can emulate the exemplary faith life of Muslims.[109]

Thus, this school of thought was "pacifistic and quietist in content," promoting tolerance, peace, and respect toward non-Muslims.[110] Suwarian Muslim clerics kept the political class at arm's length, resisted the temptation to assume political office, and avoided direct interference and control by rulers.[111] In this way, they kept a prophetic voice that enabled them to speak to power. This explains why Ghanaian Tijani can scarcely be found among Muslim extremists. This type of Islam was what Dyula traders brought to Ghana and was adopted by most folk Muslims in Ghana. It was a peaceful Islam cooked in a traditional Ghanaian hospitality pot.

The Hausa who originate from Nigeria, like other Nigerian Muslims, follow the Dan Fodio school of thought. Shaikh Uthman ibn Muhammad ibn Uthman ibn Salid (c. 1754–1817) was a Nigerian religious leader and reformer popularly known to the Hausa people as Shehu Usuman Dan Fodio. According to the Oxford Encyclopedia of the Islamic World, he belonged to a family of Fulani Muslim clerics who taught Sunni, Maliki Islam, after having

---

108. Wilks, 97.
109. Wilks, 98.
110. Samwini, "Muslim Resurgence," 38.
111. Azumah, "Historical Survey of Islam."

abandoned a nomadic lifestyle. He is known for inciting the Muslim Fulani community to engage in the jihad *al-qaw* (the preaching jihad) against the Hausa aristocracy in Gobir, present-day northern Nigeria, due to their syncretic form of Islam that was mixed with ATRs. Although he demanded that these syncretic Muslims leave behind that way of life and practice orthodox Islam, they refused. Their refusal to follow his preaching jihad led to hostility between the Fulani and the Hausa Muslims in 1804, so Shehu Usuman transitioned to a "holy war of the sword" (jihad). The battle was led by his brother Abd Allah ibn Muhammad, a field commander and hardened legalistic Muslim inclined to Shari'ah law. When British imperialism took over Nigeria in the twentieth century, it inherited a Muslim society governed by Shari'ah law.[112] Through the actions of Shehu Usuman and his brother Abd Allah, Nigerian Islam changed from a "tolerated minority religion into the official religion of the state. . . . [This] elevated the Islamic scholars from their previous position as mere advisers of polytheistic rulers . . . to a place as the sole custodians of political power and the arbiters of social behavior."[113]

Shehu Usuman declared that "there should be no friendship, counsel, or living together between an unbeliever and a believer even if they are blood relations. On the contrary, believers must bear ill-will towards them [infidels] and fight them on account of the faith."[114] He took this idea from the Maghilian school of thought. Abd al-Karim al-Maghili (d. 1505) was against *muwâlät*, maintaining friendly relations with non-Muslims. Maghili cites a host of qur'anic verses and traditions to conclude that "every true believer must be severe against the unbelievers," for "it is one of the signs of love for the Prophet that we should hate those who are hated by God or the Prophet and become hostile to those who are enemies of God and the Prophet." Thus, fighting and killing rulers and their supporters who did not enforce the Shari'a, in the words of al-Maghili, is permissible "even if they pray, fast, and pay zakat and perform the pilgrimage." In this sense, he viewed jihad against pagans as obligatory for Muslim rulers.[115] Ghanaian Muslims who were Maghili and Shehu Usuman's disciples copied the same ideology in Ghana, and it continues

---

112. Esposito, *Oxford Encyclopedia*, s.v. "Dan Fodio, Usuman."
113. Esposito, s.v. "Dan Fodio, Usuman."
114. Azumah, "Historical Survey of Islam."
115. Azumah, "Historical Survey of Islam."

to breed tension between some Muslims groups in Ghana today. For instance, the Ghanaian Tijanis did not break completely from their historic past and could not sacrifice all their cultural past for Islamic practices. Shehu Usuman was of the view that "African arts in the form of singing, drumming and dancing are forbidden in Islam and declared everything of the 'ignorant' *ajam* as *bid'a.*" His mission was "de-traditionalization and Islamization" and his school of thought was exclusivist and intolerant in nature. He threw overboard every traditional principle of "accommodation and compromise" necessary to enhance mutual respect and acceptance that could lead to the celebration of diversity among Muslims.[116] Although Islam was historically conceptualized in Arabic culture and continues to express itself within the Arabic context, Ghanaian Muslims are specific Muslims within a particular cultural context. Completely separating Ghanaian Muslims from their cultural roots will continue to cause tension and interreligious clashes. For lasting religious tolerance and continued peaceful coexistence among Muslims in Ghana, Ghanaian Muslims and Muslim scholars must revisit the African library of the Islamic school of thought that is void of foreign influence, among which the Suwarian school of thought is paramount.

Christian-Muslim Relations

Except for the conflicts that arise when Muslims or Christians attempt to convert each other, Christians and Muslims have enjoyed a cordial relationship in Ghana. Until recently, Ghanaian Christians did not engage Muslims in evangelism. The *da'wah* – the Muslim equivalent of Christian evangelism – is executed with much more effectiveness than Christian missions. As discussed, Islam missions have built schools and mosques all over the country and provided numerous welfare services to villages, especially in the northern part of the country, as a tool to spread the Islamic faith. In contrast to such proactive initiatives, Christians continue to hold averse attitudes toward Muslims in Ghana and mostly view them in a derogatory way, such as labeling them terrorists. This negative tendency toward Muslims has bred mistrust and a host of missed evangelism opportunities.[117]

---

116. Azumah, *Legacy of Arab-Islam*, 139.
117. Nuekpe, "Muslim Christian Encounter," 195.

The root of the conflict between Muslims and Christians in Ghana is not only religious but also political, international, and external. Muslim countries such as Iran, Lybia, and Saudi Arabia, under the guise of offering financial support to various Muslim organizations, transport their Islamic political and religious rivalries into the country. Such actions sow seeds of discord, as evidenced in the Tijaniyya-Qadariyya controversies in Ghana.

Three things have been used to maintain peace between Christians and Muslims: "cultural community, cooperative education, and political alliance." Over the years, Ghanaians adopted an integrated communal lifestyle as a means of forging healthy relationships with Muslims. Most Ghanaians consider first their Ghanaian, or tribal identity, before their religious identity; thus, they relate to Muslims first of all as brothers and sisters from the same country. This prioritization of communal identity in the marketplace, farms, funerals, and other Ghanaian festivities continues to draw people together. The single sound of the *muezzin* usually awakens both the Ghanaian Christians and Muslims alike for prayer, the Christian for his morning devotion and the Muslims for the *fajr* (dawn prayer). Sometimes members of the same family share different faiths; one goes to the mosque while the other goes to a Christian chapel. The Ghanaian Christians host their Muslim neighbors during Christmas, Easter, weddings, naming ceremonies, and child dedications, and the Muslims in turn freely invite their Christian neighbors to their festivals of Eid al-Fitr and Eid al-Adha. It is not uncommon to find Muslims at a church during the ordination service of a priest in their community. The obligation to attend depends mostly on their tribal or communal identity rather than their religious identity. The cooperative education system in Ghana makes room for both Muslim and Christian students to attend the same high schools where all are exposed to ATRs, Christianity, and Islam. This also helps to reduce religious tensions among Christians and Muslims in Ghana.

The Ghanaian practice of integrating both Muslims and Christians into elite government positions has enormously contributed to the peaceful coexistence of Christians and Muslims in Ghana.[118] Mustapha Abdul-Hamid has noted that in 1954, the Muslims in Ghana formed the Muslim Association Party (MAP), a political party with Islamic agendas. However, the spirit of

---

118. Nuekpe, 196.

communal identity allowed them to ingraft two well-educated Christian leaders, Bankole Awoonor Renner and Cobbina Kesse, which has promoted peace. Since this event, the presidential and vice-presidential positions in Ghana have always been strategically held by a Christian and a Muslim, or vice versa.[119] The Ghanaian politic of integrating both Muslims and Christians into elite government positions helps solve the challenges associated with a new trend in Muslim-Christian relations, which Mbillah calls "religious tribalism," "a wind blowing across the African continent that tends to categorize African heads of state according to their religious affiliations, especially Christian and Muslim."[120]

The Christian-Muslim conflict, however, continues to arise in Ghana when either faith tries to make converts. The emergence of some Christian groups who try to convert Muslims to Christianity, without adequate knowledge of the effective methods of engaging Muslims, has led to fierce anti-Christian polemics by Muslims, which mars the peaceful relationship in Ghana. The most popular among these Christian groups is the Converted Muslims Christian Ministry and the COP as the local version of Pentecostalism in their mission to Muslims in Ghana.

Historical Development of the Church of Pentecost's Missions to Muslims

As already stated in the introduction of this work, the COP is the local version of Pentecostalism and the leading member of the Pentecostal movement in Ghana. For this reason, its ministry and relations toward Muslims is representative of the Pentecostal ministry to Muslims in Ghana. The COP began its evangelistic activities toward the northern and upper regions of Ghana in the 1940s. The COP classified the churches in these areas as internal missions on account of the low socioeconomic development of the area.[121] People in these parts of the country are from more than forty different ethnic backgrounds, and due to the tropical savannah, grasslands nature of the landscape, living conditions are predominantly difficult compared to the southern part of Ghana. In 1940 when the COP launched its evangelistic

---

119. Abdul-Hamid, "Christian-Muslim Relationship," 29.
120. Mbillah, "African Churches," quoted in Fredericks, "Let Us Understand," 268.
121. Markin, "Spirit and Mission," 129.

activities among the people of northern Ghana, the area was not yet considered a Muslim-dominated area. The evangelistic strategies used then were not in any way different from those used in the other parts of the country, and there was no specific focus on Muslim evangelism. The various pastors sent to the northern region used their discretion in spreading the Christian gospel among the people.

In 1952, John Spencer Trimingham was sent by the Church Missionary Society and the Wesleyan Methodist Missionary Society to tour west Africa and make recommendations on how west African churches should work among Muslims. He reported that the northern territories were not yet predominantly Muslim; however, if the missionaries neglected the traditionalists in the north, Islam would eventually win them over.[122] As predicted, Islam claimed northern Ghana and spread south.

Even though the COP registered its presence in the north as early as the 1940s, there was no significant focus on Islam until 1997 when a COP pastor of northern descent, Patrick Aseyero, initiated the northern outreach ministry of the COP. Based on a survey conducted by the Ghana Evangelism Committee in 1989, it was discovered that due to the search for greener pastures, there were more northerners in southern Ghana than in the north, and most of them were Muslims. The population of Muslims living in the south was higher in number than the total population of the three northern regions of Ghana (northern, upper east, and upper west) put together: 30 percent of the population in the Brong Ahafo region, 35 percent of the Ashanti region, and 21 percent of Greater Accra were migrants from the north who were predominantly Muslims, although a few of them were Muslim Christians or converts from other faiths.[123] Based on this survey, the COP in January 1997 finally launched a mission toward the northerners living in the south. The main objective was to reach out to them through literacy classes, vocational training in the vernacular, and the establishment of local congregations that were culturally and linguistically friendly toward the people of the north.[124] However, there was no specific agenda toward the engagement of Muslims. The aim was to create a culturally conducive environment for northerners

---

122. Dovlo and Asante, "Reinterpreting the Straight Path," 218.
123. Markin, "Spirit and Mission," 130.
124. Anank, "Impact of Northern Outreach," cited in Markin, "Spirit and Mission," 130.

to mingle with their own people for the purpose of social and economic support. Besides the use of the various ethnic groups' vernacular from their home regions, there was no training or strategies to engage them on the basis of their Islamic faith.

Reverend Patrick Aseyero pioneered the work of the Northern Outreach Ministry, which started with 420 members in three local or ethnic assemblies in Accra. He was assisted by twenty-five lay leaders. Due to the attractive ethnic and linguistic elements of the services, the congregations grew and spread in other parts of Accra, including Nungua, Ashiaman, Timber Market, Nima, Madina, Ablekuma, and Dome. Between 2001 and 2005, the concept spread to Kumasi, the second largest city in Ghana, and pastors were appointed by the COP leadership to supervise these ministries. By 2010, the Northern Outreach Ministry reported 4,859 adult members, 2,155 child members, and 277 leaders operating in sixty-six local assemblies all over the country. The membership grew to 11,500 among 105 local congregations by the end of 2013.[125]

After twenty years of existence, the focus on the Northern Outreach Ministry was discontinued. Among the main factors that contributed to the dissolution of the ministry was the larger church body's perception of Muslims and people of northern descent, the challenge of supervision by pastors who were mostly untrained in Islamic studies, and the feeling of segregation experienced by some of the members. In a report presented by a review committee on 2 January 2013, the Northern Outreach Ministry was dissolved and the members were asked to integrate into the main church.[126] Currently, the COP operates an integrated system where people of all tribes and people groups worship together without particular attention paid to the background of the members. Given this, there may be a need for a specialized ministry. Muslims have a specific worldview, especially in Ghana where folk Islam is common.

The evangelism committee of the church at the local level was tasked with supporting the northern outreach activities. However, there was no specific strategy or model for engaging these people outside of the traditional model of rallies, campaigns, and personal evangelism backed by social interventions.

---

125. Markin, "Spirit and Mission," 131.
126. Markin, 132.

Generally, the COP adopts aggressive forms of evangelism and has been characterized by an evangelistic outreach. However, as remarked by Anderson, most Pentecostals are notorious for aggressive forms of evangelism.[127]

The COP employs the local model of mission. After water baptism and Holy Spirit baptism, evidenced by speaking in tongues, every member is expected to share their new faith in whatever way practicable. This model is the democratization of priesthood and mission that allows every member to theologize, contextualize, and formulate methods of sharing the gospel through songs and prayers backed by the Holy Spirit.[128] The church views this as personal evangelism, or evangelism on a one-to-one basis where the proclaimer uses personal skills, including sharing personal testimonies backed by Scripture (John 1:12; 6:37, 47; Rom 3:23; 1 John 1:7; Rev 3:20). The venue for this evangelism can be door-to-door, to prisons, beaches, hospitals, or hotels, through media, on the street, or in any place an opportunity presents itself. However, not many members at the local level of the church possess the requisite knowledge to share the gospel. The church also employs the model of mass evangelism. This model makes use of individual members and the local church in addressing more than one person at a time through street and open-air preaching, campaigns, rallies, crusades, conventions, gospel dinners, prison visitations, radio or television broadcasts, film shows (cinema evangelism), electronic and print media, gospel nights and music festivals, funerals, and many other social functions.[129]

The COP also provides social services as a means to evangelism. Currently, it has expanded its social services by offering medical services and has established a hospital in the city of Accra and built educational facilities, including Pentecost University, a leading private university in Ghana. A particular ministry to chieftaincy is established to evangelize chiefs using lay leaders with chieftaincy backgrounds or church leaders who were once chiefs in their communities. The church has also launched country-wide environmental campaigns and assisted the government of Ghana by building police stations and prisons to decongest the conditions of the crowded prisons in the

---

127. Anderson, *Introduction to Pentecostalism*, quoted in Onyinah, "Movement of the Spirit," 187.

128. Tsekpoe, "Local Species," 70.

129. Church of Pentecost Evangelism Ministry, "21st Century Church," 1–96.

country.[130] The church continues to expand its social services as a launching pad to share the gospel with Ghanaians.

The COP uses direct mentoring as a model of discipleship in mission, engages the young unbeliever directly, and assists in answering their questions. James McKeown, the founder of the church, had used the concept of direct mentoring as his model of discipleship in mission. The COP has since used his approach to share the gospel. Mentoring has been defined as "a relational experience in which one person empowers another by sharing God-given resources and a lifelong relationship, in which a mentor helps a protégé reach his or her God-given potential."[131] This process involves developing a closer relationship with a particular person and demonstrating to that person Christlike love until he or she is won and grounded in the Christian faith. McKeown carried out direct mentoring by intentionally bringing young Ghanaians closer to himself and, in some cases traveling with them, supporting and providing for their basic needs, and introducing them to Christian maturity resources. A close relationship provides these people with an opportunity to observe his life as a child of God and be drawn to Jesus. Members develop their methods of sharing the gospel as they watch leaders at different forums sharing the gospel. While the COP uses different models of sharing the gospel, there are no specific models tailored toward the needs of folk Muslims in Ghana.

The Converted Muslim Christian Ministries

The Converted Muslim Christian Ministries (CMCM) was begun in Kumasi in the 1980s by a Muslim convert and operated in many parts of the country. The members were public anti-Islamic polemical preachers whose aim was to convert Muslims in the country. Their methods involved sharing testimonies during public rallies and conventions, and these testimonies often involved exaggerations and direct attacks on Islam that undermined peace. Christians in Ghana became alert to the influence of Islam in Ghana in the 1990s, realizing the challenge the faith posed to Christianity through its competition to convert the traditionalists and Christians, and through its attempts to prevent

---

130. Tsekpoe, "Local Species," 256.
131. Hilborn and Bird, *God and the Generations*, 170, quoted in Tsekpoe, "Local Species," 96.

Christians' efforts to convert Muslims.[132] Even though Christians were alert about the influence of Islam in Ghana, the major churches and parachurch organizations did not have any distinctive nonaggressive mission to Muslims. Among the parachurch organizations committed to engaging Muslims with the gospel was the CMCM.

Reverend Ahmed Agyei is the founder of the CMCM. He was born in 1960 and raised in a Muslim family; his father was the chairman of the Ghana Muslim Mission. Reverend Agyei practiced the Islamic faith until his conversion in 1982.[133] He ascribes his conversion to certain verses in the Qur'an that provoked his thought (Qur'an 3:55; 57:27). Contrary to what he had been taught, Rev. Agyei concluded that the mission and authority of Jesus has not ended and that those who follow Jesus do not blaspheme. He was shocked to learn that the followers of Jesus are people imbued with compassion and mercy of heart and will be made superior to those who disbelieved. From Qur'an 3:45, Rev. Agyei became convinced that Jesus was the Messiah as proclaimed by Christians: "And when the angels said: 'Mary, God gives you the glad tidings of a Word from Him, to be called the Messiah, Jesus son of Mary, highly honored in the world and the Hereafter, and one of those near-stationed to God.'"[134] Based on these three texts, Rev. Agyei admitted the following:

> That Jesus's mission and authority are still valid until the day of resurrection which is yet to come; that Jesus has followers who are made superior above those who disbelieve and in whose heart Allah has placed compassion and mercy, that Jesus is referred to as the Word from Allah to Mariam his mother and also he is referred to as the Messiah (al-Masih).[135]

Reverend Agyei had been taught that the name of Muhammad was mentioned in John 14:6 as the "Comforter" but through study with Christians, he became convinced that the Comforter was instead the Holy Spirit. His experience led him to fast and pray for God's self-revelation to him. On one night, Rev. Agyei claimed he heard a small voice telling him to "surrender

---

132. Dovlo and Asante, "Reinterpreting the Straight Path," 217.
133. Dovlo and Asante, 223.
134. Unal, *Qur'an with Annotated Interpretation*, 134.
135. Dovlo and Asante, "Reinterpreting the Straight Path," 224.

yourself to Jesus Christ to avert any disaster" and this voice finally led to his conversion to Christianity.[136]

His father denounced him but he held to the faith. Many Christians in his area of Kumasi were interested in his conversion experience but were unable to assist him materially when he was rejected from his father's house. This kind of testimony among Muslim converts in Ghana was not uncommon, especially in southern Ghana where there is much indifference toward Muslim converts in churches. They are referred to with derogatory names linked to their tribal identity and ethnicity as people from the northern part of Ghana. Jean-Marie Gaudeul confirms, "Whether at the beginning of the conversion process or at the end, Muslims called to be Christians find themselves on their own."[137] Reverend Agyei's experience inspired him to engage in mission to Muslims in Ghana. He succeeded in converting his sister Sakina and his brother Ishmael, and together they embarked on personal evangelism to Muslims. His converts became the basis for the formation of the Converted Muslim Christian Fellowship in Ghana. Their aims were:

> Bringing together newly-converted Muslims for mutual fellowship; praying for one another concerning the plight of rejection by their families; encouraging one another to stand firm in Christ and share their faith with other Muslims; praying for families of converts for their salvation and also that they might fulfil their responsibilities towards converts; acting as a mouthpiece for converted Muslims in religious and national issues; helping one another to complete their schooling since Muslim parents had refused to pay their fees.[138]

On 11 May 1987, the fellowship was inaugurated with the new name of CMCM. Headed by Rev. Agyei, the membership grew from four to eighty-five people. The aims were readjusted to focus purely on evangelism and discipleship of Muslims and to ensure that they fully integrated into the Ghanaian Christian community.[139]

---

136. Dovlo and Asante, 224.
137. Gaudeul, *Called from Islam*, 267, quoted in Dovlo and Asante, "Reinterpreting the Straight Path," 225.
138. Dovlo and Asante, 225.
139. Dovlo and Asante, 226.

The CMCM used open-air crusades in Muslim suburbs as a method of reaching out to Muslims in Ghana. An open-air crusade is a type of meeting that is normally held at night in a public square. The preacher stands on a high platform, aided by a public address system, and directly proclaims the gospel message for the hearing of the community and the members gathered there. At these meetings, Rev. Agyei used both the Bible and the Qur'an. His presentations were polemic in nature and attracted the displeasure of the Ghanaian Muslims. At a crusade organized by the Methodist Church in Kumasi Suame, Rev. Agyei was reported to have publicly "blasphemed against Islam," which led to a mob attack and distorted Christian-Muslim relations in the community. Even though Rev. Agyei made offensive remarks about the holy Qur'an in his preaching and the CMCM was characterized by such incidents, the CMCM was generally known in Ghana as the distinctive face of Christian ministry in direct mission to Muslims. As mentioned, until the emergence of the CMCM, Ghanaians were not much engaged in mission to Muslims but sought to coexist peacefully.[140] Besides the open-air crusades, the CMCM adopted "mobile open air preaching" by means of a van with loudspeakers that went to areas unannounced and preached to the people who gathered around the van. This method left little room for an organized mob attack on the preachers.

Person-to-person evangelism and workshops were also used. The CMCM first trained its members in some essential Christian doctrine, such as the messiahship of Jesus, his sonship, issues concerning the Trinity, and the concepts of sin and forgiveness. Once a member understood these concepts, they proceeded to do a comparative study of the Bible and the Qur'an to equip the CMCM members to confront Muslims in evangelism. These methods, according to Rev. Agyei, proved effective. However, despite the few converts made, the issue of confrontation in evangelism continued to pose a threat to Muslim-Christian relations in the country as some main churches attempted to adopt the CMCM's approach to Muslims.

The Ghana Evangelism Committee made use of the CMCM to equip other churches through a training called the "Awareness Seminars for Effective Evangelism." In addition, they printed evangelism tracts and made audio cassettes for use by Christians to engage Muslims. An attempt was made to

---

140. Dovlo and Asante, 227.

go on the FM radio with the gospel to Muslims; however, they were banned by the Muslim community in Ghana from using the Qur'an during their proclamation on the radio, since this was generating many controversies and confrontations.[141] Elom Dovlo and Alfred Ofosu Asante assert that though Ghanaian Muslims resisted the claims of the CMCM and were defensive, the Muslims themselves had little knowledge of the Qur'an. According to Dovlo and Asante, knowledge of the Qur'an and the Bible must be the foundation of good Muslim-Christian relationships to share the gospel.[142]

Educated Muslims saw nothing wrong in Christians trying to convert Muslims, since both Muslims and Christians have mandates to make converts. The educated are of the opinion that even if Christians make attempts to convert Muslims, Allah would protect and defend his religion on the premise of Qur'an 15:9: "It is we who revealed the Qur'an (Message), and we will certainly preserve it." However, the Muslims using the CMCM as an example are worried about the approach used by Christians in their mission to Muslims. A leading Muslim intellectual in Ghana, Shaikh Ishaak Ibrahim Nuamah, remarks in his book entitled *Islam, the Misunderstood Religion in Ghana*:

> Of late, we have been witnesses to instances of incessant derogatory verbal attacks on Islam and Muslims in Ghana by some Evangelical groups in Christendom. Without mincing words, we are greatly shocked by these unwanted developments in view of the fact that Ghana, has for years been regarded as a land of peace, civilization and hospitality despite the existence of multifaceted religious dogmas. . . . Upon analyzing these attacks, it became quite conspicuous that they are part of a cunning but failure-bound strategy aimed at swaying Muslims away from the noble religion of Islam. This strategy finds expression in the following approaches. a) Diving [sic] Muslims towards worldly pleasures; b) Wrong analysing of Qur'anic quotations through the following methods: misrepresentation, misinterpretation, employing the art of creativity; c) Casting of insinuations at Islam and Muslims; d) Attacking the personality of the Holy

---

141. Dovlo and Asante, 227.
142. Dovlo and Asante, 227.

Prophet Mohammed (P.B.U.H.); e) Using some Qur'anic quotations to support their fabricated stand of Jesus.[143]

Besides this statement, Nuamah notes that he personally witnessed Christians preaching in Kumasi and referring to Muslims as fools and even saying Muhammad died like a pig. There have been many instances of clashes in Ghana that resulted from these kinds of polemic methods of sharing the gospel with Muslims. The missionary in charge of the Ahmadiyya Mission in Ghana, Ameer Maulvi A. Wahab, identified the CMCM as the brain behind these polemic methods that have brought conflicts between Muslims and Christians in Ghana. He labelled the CMCM members as "illiterates" of the Qur'an who are ignorant of the claims and comparisons they make, leading to verbal and physical clashes. The Muslim community in Ghana has reacted to the activities of the CMCM's literary work of Rev. Agyei through counter tracts and books, such as *Muhammed the Comforter*, written by Muhammad Braimah Youseph on behalf of the Al-Haqq Society.[144] Furthermore, Dovlo and Asante assert that churches were not able to meet the spiritual needs of the few converted Muslims, as churches were unable to identify the spiritual needs of converts with a Muslim background.

Though the CMCM aimed at reaching out to Muslims, their approaches have rather aggravated Muslim-Christian relations, and there is still the need to identify appropriate methods of engaging Muslims with the gospel and integrating them into Christian communities in Ghana. To that end, I agree with Mbillah that:

> Whatever the case, religious diversity has become the lot of the human race. God-given freedom allows free human beings to choose the religious path they wish to tread [a Quranic verse also affirms this (Qur'an 2:256)]; the churches in Africa and like elsewhere therefore, cannot be impatient with the religious diversity around them since arguably, religious variety will remain the lot of the human race until the end of the time. A credible question for the churches to ask therefore, is not how to eradicate religious diversity, (for that will mean attempting

---

143. Nuamah, *Islam, the Misunderstood Religion*, quoted in Dovlo and Asante, "Reinterpreting the Straight Path," 235.

144. Dovlo and Asante, 236.

to eradicate the God-given freedom of human beings) but how to constructively relate with religious diversity.[145]

Summary

The people of west Africa have been exposed to Islam since the eighth century through north African traders and missionary teachers. Islam was reintroduced to Ghana in the fourteenth century in a dispersive manner. A combination of factors, including the actions of British colonial power, led to the spread of Islam in west Africa. Dyula Muslim traders who practiced Sufism visited Ghana for the gold trade and introduced this type of mystical Islam to Ghana. As Africans, they identified with the traditional cultural values of the people, so they integrated into the royal system and quickly intermingled with Ghanaians. As the Islamic faith spread through them, the Tabons returning from Brazil and other Muslim migrants also brought Islam to Ghana. The encounter between Islam and ATRs in Ghana produced a new brand of Islam, which transformed according to the various cultural milieu that surrounded it. Thus, the Ghanaian expression of Islam became a syncretic or folk Islam.

Muslim revivalist movements in Ghana attempted to purify Islam from unorthodox practices. The majority of Ghanaian Muslims formed part of the mainstream Islam, which is characterized by a unique ethnic and doctrinal diversity. They were the main custodians of the Sunni tradition. Ghanaian Muslims until 1921 were organized along ethnic groups with specific ethnic tags, and not on the basis of doctrinal beliefs. The Sufi orders in the country are the Tijaniyya and Qadariyya orders. The Ahmadiyya Mission in Ghana is the most charismatic and the fastest growing Muslim group in the country and has great influence.

In terms of Muslim-Christian relations, the people of Ghana enjoy relative peace and good relationships, culturally and politically. Three things have been used to maintain peaceful coexistence: the cultural community, cooperative education, and an integrative political alliance that includes both Muslims and Christians in elite government positions. However, conflicts continue to arise in Ghana when Christians make efforts to proselytize or

---

145. Mbillah, "African Churches," quoted in Fredericks, "Let Us Understand," 261–74.

share the gospel with Muslims. This is true especially of Pentecostals' missions to Muslims. The cases of the COP and the CMCM have been discussed. Although a leading denomination, the COP only recently launched evangelistic activity toward Muslims in 1997 but could not sustain it, thereby discontinuing evangelistic activity by 2003. Even though evangelism remains a core element of the COP's tenets, it presently has no specific or effective method for engaging Muslims, and this has led to its adoption of traditional, often polemic, methods. The CMCM, the pioneer group in mission to Muslims in Ghana, succeeded in their mission to Muslims, but their evangelistic approaches have led to religious confrontations. There is, therefore, the need to understand folk Islam and its practices in Ghana to engage Muslims with the gospel through appropriate methods that will not result in conflicts. Chapter 4 further discusses this point.

CHAPTER 3

The Influence of Animism on the Beliefs and Practices of Ghanaian Folk Muslims

The religious acts of ordinary Muslims all over the world seem to be identical, because the expression of their statement of faith and the five pillars give a unified outward image to the Islamic faith. There are, however, divergent meanings of the five pillars among orthodox Muslims and folk Muslims. Islam comes from the Arabic root word s/l/m, which means peace (*salam*), soundness, and safety. The term Islam implies submission or surrender[1] – a person's total submission to the will of God that results in peace and safety in the present age and an escape from divine retribution in the life to come. However, most folk Muslims believe in surrounding evil forces, invisible spiritual beings whether imagined or real, and constantly struggle to fight these evil, unseen powers through various traditions and practices. Thus, understanding the real plight of folk Muslims is an antidote to meeting them on their level when engaging them with the gospel.

Core Beliefs

Like Jews and Christians, Muslims generally are monotheists and believe in one God who is "the creator, sustainer, ruler and judge"[2] of the entire universe, including humans and creatures. Besides the Prophet Muhammad, Muslims believe in all other biblical prophets in both the Old and New Testaments,

---

1. Ayoub, *Islam*, 8.
2. Esposito, *Everyone Needs to Know*, 4.

such as Abraham, Moses, Jesus, and John the Baptist. They believe in heaven, hell, the day of judgment, and angels and acknowledge that God revealed himself in the Torah, the Psalms, and the Gospels as indicated in the Qur'an: "We sent Jesus the son of Mary, confirming the Torah that had come before him: We sent him the Gospel in which is guidance and light, and confirmation of the Torah that had come before him, a guidance and an admonition to those who fear God" (5:46).[3] In Muslims' understanding, the Prophet Muhammad received his revelations from God through the angel Gabriel to correct all human errors that have corrupted the Judeo-Christian Scriptures and belief systems. It is popularly understood that Islam is the newest monotheistic religion among Judaism, Christianity, and Islam. However, Muslims believe according to the Qur'an that Islam is the oldest and final revelation of God to Abraham, Moses, Jesus, and Muhammad. "He established for you the same religion as that which He established for Noah, that which We have sent to you as inspiration through Abraham, Moses, and Jesus, namely that you should remain steadfast in religion and make no divisions within it" (Qur'an 42:13).[4]

Muslims order their religious and community life through practices and faith symbols, which are devotional duties that help them to enhance their worship and communal identity. Popularly known as *ibadat*, they include the five pillars (*arkan*) of Islam, which is the common denominator that unites all practicing Muslims. The observance of these pillars is an absolute requirement for every Muslim, irrespective of their sect, ethnicity, politics, geography, or culture, and unites them with a group identity as a single worldwide ummah. This observance of pillars gives them spiritual fulfillment and assurance of God's ongoing presence in their lives. Though similar in form, the *ibadat* carries different meanings for folk Muslims. As Abu Hamid al-Ghazali says, "every act of worship has both an outer and an inner aspect, a husk and a kernel."[5]

The formal or "official Islam" (orthodox, high, or normative Islam) focuses on high Islamic ideologies of human existence, ultimate realities, and religious duties. Formal Islam is identified with the "six articles of *iman* (belief), the five pillars, jihad (the Muslim struggle 'in the way of God'), the efforts

---

3. Esposito, 4.
4. Esposito, 5.
5. Al-Ghazali, "Inner Dimensions," quoted in Hillenbrand, *Introduction to Islam*, 89.

to emulate the lifestyle of Muhammad, and other beliefs."[6] Folk Islam (low Islam) originates from primal religions that have mixed with Islam in particular cultural settings. Folk Muslims, while making efforts to comply with orthodoxy, engage in practices that are outside formal Islamic practices. For example, the Qur'an asserts that God is nearer to every human being "than his own jugular vein" (50:16) and that God is "the Light" of the heavens and the earth (2:255).[7] However, in practical terms, folk Muslims struggle to see the nearness of God in a way that overcomes their fear of *jinn* (spirits) or to see how light brightens their daily paths and the dark world around them. The nonorthodox practices they engage in seem to give them the assurance or security that they may not feel from a God who is professed to be close but seemingly far away.

Thus, folk Islam addresses the "here and now" problems of Muslims who experience troubled lives and unresolved life questions. In some regions, the *ḥadīth* have endorsed folk practices, because Islam gradually integrated with pre-Islamic local traditions. Any given Muslim culture contains three religiocultural components, namely "the normative Islamic features, Hadith-based Muslim traditions, and pre-Islamic traditions."[8] The mixture of these three religiocultural components of Islam comprise the faith expression of folk Muslims. It is not uncommon to see such Muslims engaging in ritual prayer five times a day while still consulting local shrines in their communities.

Ghanaian folk Islam, like ATRs, does not have prescribed, rigid rules, or doctrines but varies according to the practitioners. Adherents have no specific temples, mosques, or systematic procedures for worship. Some missiologists view it as "religious schizophrenia caught rather than thought."[9] Due to its potential to attract the uneducated and peasant classes, folk Islam is referred to as low or popular Islam, which emphasizes that the orthodox form of Islam has been altered. Folk Islamic practices, which Musk refers to as "the Unseen Face of Islam,"[10] did not simply occur overnight but as the result of several centuries of Islam's adaptation to the traditional and cultural milieu.

---

6. Kim, Travis, and Travis, "Relevant Responses," 240.
7. Ayoub, *Islam*, 156.
8. Kim, Travis, and Travis, "Relevant Responses," 240.
9. Twumasi, "Understanding Folk Islam," 59.
10. In the title of the book of this name: Musk, *Unseen Face*.

Arkan: The Five Pillars

Shahada: Declaration of Faith

The first and most important of these practices is the Shahada, the profession of faith that states, "I testify that there is no god but God. I testify that Muhammad is the Messenger of God,"[11] and must be said in Arabic, "*La ilah illa Allah, Muhammad rasul Allah.*" The confession is generally prefaced with a statement of intention[12] and should be said before eye witnesses at least three times to affirm one's submission to God and belonging in the Islamic faith. Most Muslims begin their daily prayers with this type of confession of faith, which contains two important elements: the pronouncement of the uncompromising oneness of God (monotheism) and the affirmation of Muhammad as a prophet or messenger of God. Muhammad is referred to as the "Seal of the Prophets," affirming that he is God's final prophet whose revelation confirms and completes all other revelations beginning with Adam's.[13] The oneness of God (*tawḥid*) is a crucial tenet of Islam affirmed by the Qur'an: "Say, 'He is the One, God the eternal. He begat no one nor was He begotten. No one is comparable to Him'" (112:1–4).[14] The inscription "There is no god but God" is said to be the most frequent Arabic inscription found in the prayer niches of mosques and has been engraved on coins issued by Muslim dynasties for centuries.[15] Many Islamic countries place this creed on their flags and government seals as a sign of commitment to Islam. The importance of the Shahada is seen in its prevalence; it is reported to be the first words that greet a new born baby and the last words that a dying soul hears before his/her departure from this life.[16] The daily repetition of the Shahada is a constant reminder of the oneness of God and an injunction not to bow down to any other god; to ascribe divinity to anything but God is idolatry and the one unforgivable sin. This emphasis is revealed throughout the Qur'an: "God: there is no god but Him, the Ever Living, the Ever Watchful" (2:255); "God does not forgive anyone for associating partners with Him, while he does forgive whomever

---

11. Hillenbrand, *Introduction to Islam*, 89.
12. Rippin, *Muslims*, 87.
13. Esposito, *Everyone Needs to Know*, 18.
14. Hillenbrand, *Introduction to Islam*, 91.
15. Hillenbrand, 91.
16. Twumasi, "Understanding Folk Islam, 53.

He wishes to for anything else. Anyone who gives God associates [partners] has invented an awful sin" (4:48).[17]

However, in the mind of folk Muslims, the words of the Shahada and the phrase "in the name of God" (*bismillâh*) possess power to drive away evil. The belief in the only God degenerates into the magical use of the various names of God. It is generally believed that there are ninety-nine Beautiful Names (*al-îmâ' al-husnâ*) of God in the Qur'an, which folk Muslims believe are written on the hands of each human being. The crease of the left hand contains eighty-one names (the Arabic numerals for eighty-one are ٨١), and the right hand has eighteen (١٨ in Arabic numerals), making the two hands ninety-nine. Folk Muslims may evoke some of these names to compel God to act in their favor. Prayer beads (*subha*) are specially designed to assist Muslims in recounting the ninety-nine names, but among folk Muslims, the beads are used as a medium of divination known as *is-ikhâra*. The evocation of the names of God among folk Muslims is not for the purpose of submitting to God but as a way of manipulating God for their personal benefit.[18] Similarly, the Qur'an is believed to be a repository of *baraka* and is used among folk Muslims in *is-ikhâra*, just like the prayer beads. Various verses are known for solving problems like "headaches, fevers, swellings, aches, blindness, insanity, toothaches, and the protection of property." Thus, throughout the folk Muslim world, the Qur'an is used as a charm.[19]

Salat: Ritual Prayer

The second most important expression of faith in Islam is the salat, which is a ritual prayer that requires specific body movements and recited words that must be said in Arabic. According to Muslims, "to pray and to be a Muslim are synonymous."[20] From the age of seven, all Muslims are expected to pray at least two kinds of prayers: *du'a*, the private prayer, which has no strict posture and is prayed by an individual at any time on topics that vary from person to person; and salat, the ritual prayer in a prescribed form and at a prescribed time, which is carried out five times a day throughout the Muslim world as

---

17. Esposito, *Everyone Needs to Know*, 16.
18. Musk, *Unseen Faces*, 210.
19. Musk, 213–14.
20. Hillenbrand, *Introduction to Islam*, 92.

a regular habit of prayer.[21] The prescribed movement reveals the Muslim's submission to God and the recited words serve as a constant reminder of their devotional duty to God.

The salat must be said in a state of ritual purity (*tahara*). Otherwise, the prayer is said to be invalid. For this reason, fountains and ablution basins are found in every mosque. There are two forms of ablutions: *wudu* and *ghusl*. *Wudu* is the minor ablution that often "involves the washing of face, hands, arms as far as the elbow, and the feet, including ankles, and wiping part of the hair with water."[22] However, if a person engages in sexual activity or any act that is deemed ritually unclean, such as a woman in her menses or who has given birth within the past forty days, that person must perform a major ablution, *ghusl*. Both men and women are expected to wear clean clothing during salat. A man must not expose his body from his navel to his knees and a woman must not expose any part of her body except her face and hands. The ablution is an outward symbol that reminds Muslims of the spiritual need for a clean mind before prayer. In the mind of Muslims, "if a man says all his prayers during this ablution, his sins will have departed from all parts of his body, a seal has been set upon his ablution."[23]

Similarly, the place of prayer must be clean, so mosques frequently sweep their carpets and provide clean rugs to each individual. Where there is no running water or water at all, as when travelling in the desert, sand may be substituted to perform the ablution. The whole world is considered a mosque to Muslims, and wherever the hour of prayer catches them, there they pray.[24] The prayer is said facing *qibla*, the direction of the Ka'bah in Mecca, and that direction is commonly marked in mosques by a niche referred to as the *mihrab*. Facing the direction of Mecca symbolically means the Muslim faces his creator even though Muslims admit God is everywhere.[25] Five times a day – at dawn (*fajr*), midday (*zuhr*), afternoon (*asr*), sunset (*maghrib*), and nightfall (*'isha*) – the salat is said under the summon of the *muezzin*, or in a

---

21. Lewis and Churchill, *Islam*, 13–14.
22. Hillenbrand, *Introduction to Islam*, 93.
23. Hillenbrand, 94.
24. Hillenbrand, 94.
25. Osman, *Islam*, 65.

contemporary world, through a loudspeaker from a mosque's minaret. The words of invitation to prayer, *adjan*, are recited in Arabic in this manner:

> God is most great. (4x)
> I testify that there is no god but God.
> I testify that Muhammad is the Messenger of God.
> Hasten to salat (2x)
> Hasten to salvation (2x)
> God is most great (2x)
> There is no god but God.[26]

Muslims are expected to make up any prayer time they miss. An exception is made when travelling; the midday and the afternoon prayers can be combined into one, and the sunset and nightfall prayers can also be combined. No intermediary like a priest is needed for the prayers, except on Friday afternoon when an imam leads the prayers. The Friday worship is important to Muslims, because the day is said to have been ordered by the Prophet Muhammad himself as indicated in the Qur'an: "Believers! When the call to prayer is made on the day of congregation, hurry towards the reminder of God and leave off your trading – that is better for you, if only you knew" (62:9).[27]

Salat is viewed by folk Muslims as a protective instrument against evil forces in the spirit world. A particular process of ablution may help to remove demonic pollution in folk Muslims. A particular part of the *hadīth* that deals with the "Purging of Sins with Ablution Water" says that Muhammad recommended washing the nose before prayer, because the devil spends the night inside people's noses. Muslims believe their sin is washed away in the process of ablution; thus, folk Muslims lay more importance on the ablutions than the prayers.

Zakat: Almsgiving

Almsgiving is the third pillar. Two forms of donations are identified in Islam: voluntary donations known as *sadaqah* (charity), and the required or obligatory donation, zakat. For people who do not possess much, a minimum threshold of wealth, called *nisab*, should be reached before they give zakat.

---

26. Hillenbrand, *Introduction to Islam*, 94.
27. Hillenbrand, 99.

Payment of zakat generally reminds Muslims that they are stewards of God and their wealth belongs to God; thus, giving of their personal resources is a form of thanksgiving to God for his goodness and beneficence toward them. The zakat also serves as a means of purifying oneself from the greed of the world and becoming acceptable to God. The term itself means "something that purifies," and therefore has a cleansing effect on the souls and possessions of the Muslims who practice zakat.[28] For folk Muslims, almsgiving has a magical implication. They believe almsgiving brings special *baraka* to Muslims. Since they believe that beggars generally possess evil eye,[29] giving zakat to beggars promotes *baraka* for donors.[30]

Within the Muslim community, the payment of the zakat is obligatory, and the motivation to pay it is to avoid the dreadful judgment of God on the day of judgment. The Qur'an requires Muslims to be generous with their wealth: "You who believe, give charitably from the good things you have acquired and that We have produced for you from the earth" (2:267). Usually, giving in secret is recommended as the Qur'an states, "If you give charity openly, it is good, but if you keep it secret and give to the needy in private, that is better for you, and it will atone for some of your bad deeds" (2:271). It is a form of worship to God and a means of providing for the poor in the Muslim community. "Alms are meant only for the poor, the needy, those who administer them, those whose hearts need winning over, and to free slaves, and to help those in debt for God's cause, and for travelers in need. This is ordained by God" (Qur'an 9:60).[31] Today, the official rate fixed by Sunni Muslims for zakat is 2.5 percent of one's wealth while the Shi'ite emphasize a 5 percent tax on income called *khums* (a fifth) based on Qur'an 8:41: "Know that one-fifth of your battle gains belongs to God and the Messenger, to close relatives and orphans, to the needy and travelers."[32] Thus, the zakat brings the community together and enhances community solidarity and social welfare, providing some social equilibrium between the haves and have-nots.

---

28. Osman, *Islam*, 71.

29. The concept of evil eye is discussed in the next section, but it can briefly be described as a curse that can be cast through a "dirty look" of remote eye contact.

30. Musk, *Unseen Faces*, 217.

31. Hillenbrand, *Introduction to* Islam, 100.

32. Hillenbrand, 101.

Sawm: Fasting

The fourth pillar of faith is *sawm* (fasting). During the ninth month of the Islamic lunar calendar, every Muslim is expected to fast during daylight hours as a part of their devotional duty toward God. The ninth month is known as Ramadan; it is valued by Muslims across the globe as a month of blessing and renewal of commitment to God. Fasting is a ritual obligation that has a deep spiritual implication, so it has both inner and outer dimensions. The outer dimension concerns abstinence from food, drink, sexual intercourse, and other pleasures during daylight whereas the inner dimension involves a refraining from lust, envy, greed, and all that pollutes the heart.[33] It is emphasized by the Qur'an, "You who believe, fasting is prescribed for you, as it was prescribed for those before you, so that you may be mindful of God" (2:183). Commemorated on 26–27 of Ramadan is the Night of Power (*laylat al-qadr*) when the qur'anic revelation was given to the founder of the faith, the Prophet Muhammad. "We sent it down on the Night of Power. What will explain to you what that Night of Power is? The Night of Power is better than a thousand months" (Qur'an 97:1). For this reason, when fasting during Ramadan, folk Muslims believe the heavens open as prayers are offered and that the destinies of adherents can be changed.

Every able-bodied Muslim is expected to fast during daylight hours in abstinence from pleasure, including food, sexual intercourse, and music, but a few exceptions are made for nursing mothers, travelers, and the elderly. If a person is unable to participate in fasting, he/she is required to make up for it by feeding the poor. "Fast for a specific number of days, but if one of you is ill, or on a journey, on other days later. For those who can fast only with extreme difficulty, there is a way to compensate – feed a needy person" (Qur'an 2:184).

Hajj: Pilgrimage

From the end of Ramadan until the twelfth and final month of the year (*Dhû'l-Hijja*), Muslims are enjoined to undertake pilgrimage to Mecca, which is the fifth pillar required by the Qur'an: "Pilgrimage to the House of God is a duty owed to God by people who are able to undertake it" (3:97). The significance of the pilgrimage is linked to Abraham, because Muslims generally believe that God commanded Abraham to build a stone structure in Mecca, known

---

33. Osman, *Islam*, 67.

as the Ka'bah, in the present region of Saudi Arabia. In their understanding, Abraham was a *hanif* (a true monotheist) who initiated the hajj as indicated in the Qur'an: "We showed Abraham the site of the house, saying, 'Do not assign partners to Me. Purify My House for those who circle around it, those who stand to pray, and those who bow and prostrate themselves. Proclaim the pilgrimage to all people'" (22:26–28).[34] To Muslims, seeing the Ka'bah in this life is an assurance of seeing the face of God in the afterlife. The Ka'bah serves as a reminder to keep faith with God to inherit heaven. The hajj affords Muslims an opportunity to reflect upon the future day of judgment and be prepared through the strict practice of the five pillars. According to Islamic tradition, God instructed Abraham to take his second wife Hagar and the son Ishmael to Arabia and leave them there to avert the jealousy of the first wife Sarah. While in the land of Mecca, Ishmael became thirsty and Hagar tried in vain to get him water to drink, running seven times between the hills of Safa and Marwa outside Mecca. In the process, the angel Gabriel miraculously struck the ground with his wing and provided water for Hagar to quench the thirst of Ishmael. This miraculous water comes from the Zamzam well and is a site along the pilgrimage.[35] Muslims view Zamzam water as sacred or as a blessed gift. They fill their bottles with it and give it to people as a present from the pilgrimage.[36]

Folk Muslims consider the site of the Ka'bah to be an open heaven where intercessory prayers are heard and accepted. The *multazam* (the place of clinging) is the span between the door of the Ka'bah and the black stone. The pilgrim attempts to unite with the Ka'bah by rubbing themselves on the wall, *multazam*, which is purported to release *baraka*.[37] A part of the pilgrimage process is referred to as the "stoning of Satan," where symbolic pillars of Satan are subjected to stoning, usually on the morning of sacrifice. Three pillars known as the "the first," "the middle," and "the last," commonly called *al-Shaytânu'l-Kabîr* (the Great Devil), represent the spots where the devil is purported to have appeared to Adam, Abraham, and Ismael under the pretext of being a shaikh. At those times, he was forced away by stoning.

---

34. Hillenbrand, *Introduction to Islam*, 106.
35. Hillenbrand, 107.
36. Ayoub, *Islam*, 77.
37. Musk, *Unseen Faces*, 218.

In the mind of folk Muslims, Satan is always present and active, appearing sometimes as a respected religious elder who must be dealt with. Pilgrims draw water from the Zamzam Well and believe it offers *baraka* and refreshment when it is sent back home for sick relatives or other people.[38] There are three major mosques for pilgrimage, the mosques in Mecca, Madina, and al-Aqsâ – where Muhammad was said to have ascended to heaven, leaving an imprint of his foot in a *sakhra* (rock) on the Temple Mount in Jerusalem. This symbolic footprint becomes a focus of veneration for Muslims during pilgrimage. The hajj in any pilgrimage is viewed as endowed with extra power and *baraka*; thus, the hajj is considered among folk Muslims as conferring more authority on practitioners of the faith.[39] However, the religious pilgrimage to Mecca by able folk Muslims in Ghana is not to fulfill a religious obligation but to get some form of supernatural power and *baraka* that enables them to meet their socioeconomic needs. Some also believe they are able to mediate for their communities in solving spiritual problems and have power to curse their enemies as well.

The Everyday Life of Folk Muslims in Ghana
Folk Muslims' World of Spirits

Sanneh asserts that the religious life of Islam in Africa, including Ghana, was characterized by "accommodation or, more correctly, by a dualism or a parallelism of the old and the new." Thus, most of the Ghanaian traditional religious practices found their way into Islam and fought against any idea of Islamic exclusiveness.[40] Phil Parshall notes that:

> Muslims who are influenced by animism syncretize a very basic and inadequate knowledge of Islam with a fear and worship of the unseen spiritual and naturalistic forces of the cosmos. They are seeking to respond to felt needs. To the best of their simple understanding, they are trying to interact with the power that they perceive to be resident in the universe.[41]

---

38. Musk, 221.
39. Musk, 221.
40. Trimingham, "Phases of Islamic Expansion," 100.
41. Parshall, *Bridges to Islam* 76, quoted in Twumasi, "Understanding Folk Islam," 59.

While most Westerners make distinctions between the "natural world" and the "supernatural world," Africans do not make such distinctions. Among folk Muslims, such a distinction is rather nonexistent. In their understanding, the world of the living is linked with the world of the dead, and the natural world is a continuation of the supernatural world. Folk Muslims understand the entire universe within the frame of the Qur'an's concept of creation, which involves the unseen world connecting with the physical world. This concept is expressed in Qur'an 55:31 and understood in most Muslim traditions as the duality of the world of mankind and the world of jinn.[42] Thus, folk Muslims perceive innumerous unseen spiritual beings that menace their natural or physical wellbeing.

The framework provided by Paul Hiebert can be used to understand folk Islam's practices. The distinction between folk Islam and orthodox Islam can be seen in the difference between personal beings and impersonal powers or forces of darkness, the distinction between the otherworld and this world. Folk Islam is mostly concerned with experiences of this world, a world in which personal beings – "the prophets (in Paradise), dead saints, ancestors, Iblis (chief *jinni* or the Devil), all other *jinni* (with several names), etc." – are part of the unseen or supernatural world.[43] With the exception of Allah and his angels, personal beings can be an object of human manipulation, experience, and engagement. Impersonal forces and personal beings in folk Islam are interconnected. Impersonal local forces are in the category of this world and they include "magic, sorcery, astrological forces, divination, *baraka*, merit of dhikr, evil eye, evil tongue, curses, talisman, amulet, reading of the Qur'an, drinking of the qur'anic writings, etc."

Jinn and Spiritual Forces

Folk Muslims believe in jinn, which they consider a separate species of spirit created from smokeless fire (Qur'an 15:27; 55:15) in contrast to the creation of human beings from dust (Qur'an 22:5). Jinn are viewed as spirits that constantly seek to destroy human beings and are therefore referred to as *shayatin* (devils). Jinn reportedly perform different activities and are labeled in Arabic with different words that reveal the type of activity. For instance,

---

42. Kim, Travis, and Travis, "Relevant Responses," 240.
43. Kim, Travis, and Travis, 242.

they are referred to as *ghûl* (to destroy), *khâfi* (concealed), and *afrît* (to roll in the dust).⁴⁴ It is believed that when jinn are mentioned by name, they are usually incited to perform harm; therefore, folk Muslims speak about jinn by allusions. In the Arab world, the common word used for them is *hâduk al-nâs* (those people there), but in Iran, they are often designated as *az mâ bihtarân* (those better than ourselves).⁴⁵ It is commonly believed they have the ability to change shape and form. Because jinn are considered a species of creation parallel to the human race (Qur'an 55:33), they have the ability to marry, produce offspring, and possess human beings and animals. Folk Islam attributes death, barrenness, curses, paralysis, and dangerous illness to jinn and view jinn as an avowed enemy of man (Qur'an 17:53).⁴⁶ They are said to rebel against God, but some who heard Muhammad's recitation of the Qur'an were converted to Islam (Qur'an 72:1–5).

Caleb Chul-soo Kim notes that Islamic supernaturalism is characterized by practices associated with jinn, which vary from person to person. Practices associated with jinn are found among Muslims during rituals for birth, child naming, marriage, death and burial, sowing season, moving house, travelling, and laying the foundations of new buildings.⁴⁷ In each of these instances, the Islamic tradition provides the theoretical foundation for the belief and practice among folk Muslims.

Folk Muslims have developed different solutions to their daily encounters in life, frustrated by their inability to access God. Because the doctrine of *tawḥīd* places God far away from ordinary Muslims, folk Muslims consult dead saints, angels, and jinn as spiritual reinforcement for *baraka* for daily survival. Most accounts in the *ḥadīth* depict jinn as evil and not to be associated with. They are described as entities that even Muhammad feared and sought protection from by using Qur'an 38:35.⁴⁸

For example, folk Muslims believe exposing one's nakedness to jinn can be harmful; therefore, when folk Muslims visit the toilet, they must recite "In the name of Allah besides whom there is no other god" as protection

---

44. Musk, *Unseen Faces*, 39.
45. Musk, 39.
46. Kim, Travis, and Travis, "Relevant Responses," 243.
47. Kim, *Islam among Swahili*, 80.
48. Kim, 90.

against jinn harm. In addition, a hole is believed to be the dwelling place of jinn; therefore, folk Muslims are not expected to urinate in a hole. Jinn are also believed to be associated with certain animals. A black dog is believed to be a jinni and avoided at all costs among folk Muslims, and since jinn can take the form of a snake, a snake must be warned three times if it enters a folk Muslim's house. If the snake returns, it is proof that it is an evil jinni and must be killed.

Yawning is believed to be from jinn, but sneezing is favored by Allah (al-Bukhari 4:509; 8:242; 8:245).[49] A good dream is believed to have come from Allah while a bad dream stems from a jinni (al-Bukhari 4:513; 9:113–15). According to their beliefs, jinn can be seen by both human beings and animals. For instance, when a cock crows or a donkey brays, it is believed that they are conscious of the presence of jinn; thus, Muhammad said, "When you hear the crowing of cocks, ask for Allah's Blessings for they have seen an angel. Furthermore, when you hear the braying of donkeys, seek refuge with Allah from Satan (for their braying indicates) that they have seen a Satan" (al-Bukhari 4:332).[50]

Folk Muslims believe that jinn are sensual and desire women. Women must, therefore, conceal themselves when they go out, and men must avoid staying with a woman other than their wives. Additionally, jinn are capable of harming human offspring during sexual intercourse. For this reason, folk Muslim couples need to pray for Allah's protection when they engage in sexual relations with their wives (al-Bukhari 4:503; 7:94).[51] Jinn also possess human qualities, such as emotions, intellect, reasoning power, and they eat, drink, give birth to children, and die like human beings. They have no bodies; therefore, they express their will through human bodies, known as spirit possession, and their main headquarters are in the ocean.

Most Muslims believe all pre-Islamic spirits are jinn and that "Satan reaches everywhere in the human body as blood reaches everywhere in one's body" (al-Bukhari 3:140). Due to their harmful effect on human beings, ordinary Muslims are more jinn-conscious than Allah-conscious and depend on local Muslim jinn experts (*malam*) to develop methods to overpower jinn and their

---

49. Al-Bukhari, *Translation*, cited in Kim, 92.
50. Kim, 93.
51. Kim, 92.

evil attacks. According to Kim, the phenomenon of jinn or spirit possession, especially during healing rituals, is an accepted fact among Muslims, even though folk Muslims fear or dread jinn. A folk Muslim healer, in order to overpower the jinn that troubles a sick person, voluntarily enters into a state of spirit possession and invokes stronger jinn upon the patient to ensure his or her deliverance. In the state of jinn possession, a magical medicine is prescribed to ward off the jinn and ensure healing of the sick person. Amidst chanting, songs, and dancing, the jinn are said to climb or rise up to the head of the patient. The patient thus loses his/her consciousness and is controlled by the jinn. Often the person enters into ecstasy and becomes uncontrollable in behavior, beating the chest, jumping violently, and moving up and down.

The emotional and physical pain that results from jinn possession is often enormous enough that although the person is sick and requires spirit possession to be healed, the sick person usually feels reluctant to seek healing.[52] The practice within the African context is evident in the Swahili therapeutic cults of jinn possession for healing and divination that Kim illustrates.[53] These supernaturalistic assumptions or beliefs pervade folk Muslims' worldview, so this jinn- and fear-induced worldview has led to the development of different degrees of folk theories and practices in the African context.

Folk Muslims also believe in the existence of spiritual forces that, unless controlled or appeased through ritual sacrifices, are harmful to human beings. Some humans are believed to possess spiritual forces that can transfer *baraka,* curses, or spells on others. These types of forces can cause one to prosper in business or fail. The fear of spiritual forces leads folk Muslims to continuously desire *baraka* or some form of power to counteract evil effects:

> A mysterious and wonderful power, a blessing from God granted to certain people, places, and things; a divine grace and mercy as opposed to justice, protection from danger and trouble, charisma for leadership, and power to protect and heal; a gift from Allah who always dispenses it as a blessing which can be passed on to others.[54]

---

52. Kim, 175–79.

53. Kim, 186.

54. Rheenen, *Communicating Christ*, 199–200, quoted in Twumasi, "Understanding Folk Islam," 87.

Thus, folk Muslims purchase strong charms, amulets, and talismans or pay for consultations with local shamans, healers, exorcists, or other powerful people in the local community.[55]

They may also visit the tombs of dead saints with the hope of obtaining *baraka*.[56] They perform varied ceremonial rituals at special times, dates, or months that they believe have some spiritual implication; if they fail to observe the spiritual activity within the right time, they believe it leads to spiritual calamity. This feeling alone puts much stress and unrest on folk Muslims. They endeavor to rigorously apply diligence to everything folk tradition determines – certain directions and positions for prayer, rules, and regulations – to avert spiritual calamity or secure their welfare in the face of hostile spirits. Folk Muslims are constantly in fear of the unknown, fate, the unseen realm of reality, angry ancestors, failure, sickness, and death. Their world is filled with endless dos and don'ts, the application of which are extremely inconvenient or impossible for normal human beings. Therefore, they need an alternative that responds to their felt needs.

Religiomagical Practices

In Ghanaian tradition, no one dies a natural death and nothing happens by a natural cause. Everything that happens to people, whether good or bad, has a spiritual origin, and understanding these origins is a great burden to folk Muslims in Ghana. It is therefore common to see Muslim clerics "prophesying" over folk Muslims and making use of various elements to provide guidance and reveal causality behind events. In other instances, Muslim medicine men copy verses of the Qur'an deemed as powerful for a cure or solution on a special board. The board is then washed with water and the water collected, bottled as a concoction, and sold for its magical power.[57] Adherents of folk Islam believe the use of such water can cure certain diseases that defy scientific methods, can help students pass their exams, and can enable barren women to conceive a child. By sprinkling such water on commercial vehicles, they believe that the vehicles will be protected from fatal accidents and the owner will receive special *baraka*. Because folk Muslims believe that *baraka*

---

55. Kim, Travis, and Travis, "Relevant Responses," 371.
56. Kim, Travis, and Travis, 373.
57. Twumasi, "Understanding Folk Islam," 86.

is transferable from one person to another, *baraka* is sometimes purchased and then sold to others who desire it. *Baraka* can also be obtained through penance, and this concept of *baraka* through penance is mostly found among the Dagomba of Ghana.[58]

Folk Muslims in Ghana are generally plagued with a fear of witchcraft that is seen as a threat to the entire society. This fear, fundamentally linked to the fear of death and insecurity, results in the consultation of fetish priests and the wearing or placing of various charms in their farms, inside cars, and at work places. At the market place, women sometimes put a red pepper inside their product to ward off evil spirits and to overcome actions of witchcraft against them. Amulets are used to "curse, protect, cure, pass exams, win competitions, protect lovers, or maintain relationships and marriages."[59] Among the folk Muslims in Kumasi, some amulets are prepared for the protection of soldiers on the battlefield and others for the treatment of "smallpox, bed-wetting, sexual impotency, leprosy, headaches, and difficult childbirth."[60] Below are translations of instructions for preparing some charms and amulets in Ghana.

The instructions below are for easy childbirth:

A special magical seal *khatim* was required;

- write 3 times the prayer "O God! The God of Jibril, Mikha'il and the Prophet Musa and the Prophet Muhammad (Peace be upon them) and of Harun";
- write 3 times the incantation "cause it to come out from mother's stomach "Musaisa, Musaisa";
- it was instructed that the written statement be washed into a solution and given to the expecting mother to drink.

To protect a difficult pregnancy, the Quranic passages (Qur'an 2:55; 17:111; and 18:1) were to be combined with the ground-up root of a tree. The medicine was to be drunk or inserted.

In order to gain multiple health benefits and win favors from women, the following instructions were recommended for making an amulet:

---

58. Twumasi, 87.
59. Twumasi, 85.
60. Ansah, "Prayer, Amulets and Healing," 482.

> Write the *du'a* (incantation) "God, He is not a father and He is not a son. There is no power without God. O! You who permits. You are the one. There is no god but Him. The Living. You who created the skies and the earth. The infallible."
>
> The above was to combined with a *khatim* and made into a talisman. This same prayer, if written 6 times, washed into a solution and mixed with water for bathing, the user will never be harmed.

In order to experience happy marriages, an amulet could be prepared with the following instructions:

> To find a wife and secure marriage,
>
> On Wednesday, write Surat al-Yusuf (Q. 12). Wash the material that has been written into a solution. On Thursday, before sunrise, wash the previously written material, sit on a stone and wash yourself with it. After washing with it, continue sitting on the stone till sunrise. The result will be prosperity during the year. The amulet is also useful in the recovery of lost slaves; and therefore in ensuring the permanency of marriages.
>
> Make [the] amulet, write the recommended passages on your right foot, rub some meat on the led [sic] and give it to either the slave or wife to eat. By this process, the amulet is internalized and therefore effective.

Owusu Ansah has written of charms constructed to cure smallpox or protect against the spread of diseases:

> For curing *judari* (smallpox), the construction of a seal *khatim* was the sole content suggested; the seal was to be washed and solution used to cook food. When eaten, the afflicted would be cured if God willed it. Another *khatim* was instructed as protection against epidemic. The prescribed material was to be used for bathing.[61]

Folk Muslims thus engage in a series of practices rooted in ATRs and pre-Islamic *jahiliyya* (period of ignorance). These "charismatic Muslims" apply

---

61. Ansah, 482–83.

prophetic *ḥadīth* and qur'anic verses as a source of *ruqya* (words, incarnations, or chants performed for spiritual protection to ward off evil powers and beings).[62] Their use of specific instructions with qur'anic passages mixed with African religiomagical practices for healing, deliverance, *baraka*, or protection is similar to what some Pentecostals practice today in Ghana in breaking bondage, binding, loosing, and casting out demons, and praying for deliverance by using biblical texts. Folk Muslims practice *khalwa* (spiritual retreat), which sometimes involves ritual performances that require several days of fasting and contemplation. Sufi Muslims especially share commonalities with Pentecostals' practices of long periods of fasting and prayer for spiritual power. These commonalities of primal religion as a bedrock of spiritual practices can serve as a bridge to engage folk Muslims in Ghana with the gospel.

Ghanaian folk Muslims, especially those from the Tijaniyya Order, engage in *boka* ("traditional healing and divination techniques involving the spiritual"),[63] which involves divination, casting out of jinn and spiritual beings, and preparation of *rubutu* (liquids). They also seek *sekan aduro* (knife counteragent) to protect themselves from harm during riots or physical attacks. Such religiomagical practices are considered part of *malam adwuma* (the duties of the male Islamic scholar) and *ibadat* (acts of worship). *Malams* who engage in such practices, especially from the zongo, prove their efficacy in *sekan aduro*, healing, deliverance, and exorcism. Benedikt Pontzen observes in an ethnographic narration:

> The *malam* wanted to demonstrate the efficacy of his prayers. He took out a ring from his pocket, uttered a prayer over it and dry spat on it. He then stretched out his arm, slipped the ring on his right ring finger, then loosened his grip and continued the movement upwards, sliding his left hand up his arm to the elbow – all in one seamless movement. Then, he took a machete and a razor blade from a corner and offered them to me to cut his arm. As I refused, he took the machete himself and – with me exclaiming "No" – swung it with full force at his arm, from which it rebounded without leaving a scratch. He hit himself with the machete three times before taking the razor blade to

---

62. Ansah, 483.
63. Pontzen, *Islam in a Zongo*, 182.

slice his arm, although I asked him not to do so. Then, he displayed his arm, which did not bear any mark of what had just happened, and he took off the ring. "Come on over here," he called to a boy playing in the courtyard, and the boy came to the door, his mother behind him. As she watched, the *malam* slipped the ring on the finger of the boy after he had uttered the same prayer over it. The other women and children present in the courtyard gathered around us. The *malam* took the razor blade and attempted to cut the boy's arm, but the blade could not penetrate the flesh. While the women intoned songs in praise of God and their *malam*, thanking God for his blessings and protection, the baffled ethnographer asked to take his leave.[64]

While these mystical practices serve to boost folk Muslims' confidence in Ghanaian Islam, they are not always reliable; in a few instances, they fail practitioners and their supplicants. Pontzen, who had experienced such practices in Ghana several times, reflects on one such occasion:

[The *malam*] took a butcher's knife, and sharpened it. After uttering some prayers, putting on his lāyā and rubbing his left forearm, he raised the knife and struck his arm. The first stroke resulted in a minor scratch, but the second one cut deep into the flesh and left a gaping wound. At this moment, one could see from his face that his ways of making sense of the world had gone awry. This did not make any sense to him. We drove to the local hospital so a doctor could suture the wound, but the conundrum of why the knife had cut him remained unanswered, as the medical treatment could deal only with the "physical" wound.[65]

Regardless of the folk practice, the result *In sha Allah* (all depends on God). There are still vacuums to be filled and unanswered riddles of life in the mind of Ghanaian folk Muslims. Pentecostals must, therefore, find answers to these riddles of life when sharing with folk Muslims in a way that meets their quest for *baraka*, protection, power, healing, and deliverance from evil.

---

64. Pontzen, 182.
65. Pontzen, 183.

The Evil Eye

The concept of the evil eye is one that evokes fear in the lives of folk Muslims. It is also known as bad eye or unclean eye, and they believe it has power and influence to devastate lives. It is believed that important people and things are vulnerable to attack and destruction through the projection of envy or jealousy in the eyes of another person. Folk Muslims see envy (*hasad*) as a force that is tangible and represents the opposite force of *baraka* derived from God.[66] *Baraka* must be received by a touch, but *hasad* has power to destroy blessing through remote eye contact.

The central place that the evil eye occupies in Muslims' lives may suggest that the concept is an integral part of the formal faith of Islam. Many Muslims believe the Qur'an speaks about the concept of evil eye; however, it only mentions human envy twice in 113:5 and 2:103.[67] It is the *ḥadīth* that places emphasis on evil eye and adds that Muhammad instructed the use of incantations against the effect of the evil eye. To counteract the effect of evil eye, often the folk Muslim is given water to drink in which some specific verses of the Qur'an have soaked.[68]

The evil eye concept varies from place to place. For instance, folk Muslims in Iran believe in a form of evil eye known as "the salty eye" that has a permanent effect. This kind of evil eye is transferable to a child while the mother is pregnant. The child then becomes very dangerous and may stop tractors or even topple a building with a mere glance. The commonest form of the evil eye is known as the "bad eye," and this results from an envious and prideful life. The effect is not deemed as dangerous as that of the incurable "salty eye." A third form of the evil eye is known as the "unclean eye." This type occurs when the person who casts it happens to live in a state of ritual uncleanliness after failing to perform a purifying bath after intercourse. Other types of evil eye, like "the eye that wounds," "the narrow eye," and "the hot eyes," exist in other cultures.[69] These concepts of the evil eye reveal folk Muslims' perpetual fear of evil forces and the spiritual world around them. They are worried about all forms of causalities and live with insecurity about their

---

66. Musk, *Unseen Faces*, 26–27.
67. Musk, 29.
68. Musk, 28.
69. Musk, 28.

daily life, such as marriage, good business, household protection, children's success on exams, childbirth, etc. In order to combat this fear, they resort to various magical acts, including visiting the tomb of saints for *baraka* and reading the Qur'an. To protect the house from the activities of evil eyes and guarantee a strong foundation, cards containing qur'anic verses are dropped into the foundation of the building. All over the world, Muslims use varied protective rites to battle against evil eyes. A frequent phrase used for protection in daily life is *"ma sha allah,"* implying that God has willed.[70]

Divination or Pathfinding

"Practices of divination or fortune-telling are widespread and much sought after by ordinary Muslims"[71] with the aim of unveiling the details of an uncertain future. Having a glimpse of future events can put their hearts at peace by reducing the fear of the unknown or help them alter or regulate present actions to their advantage. Folk Muslims may consult diviners to determine the sex of a child or to give the child a name. The cause of sickness or the death of a loved one may also be sought through divination practices. A parent may consult diviners to ascertain whether it is appropriate to give a daughter in marriage to a particular family, even though this may be contrary to orthodox Islamic teaching.

The practice of divination and fear of evil eye as part of folk Islamic practices in Ghana is more common among the Tijaniyya. Because folk Muslims feel threatened by evil eyes, they engage in what is popularly known in Ghana as *abisa* (unveiling of the hidden). *Abisa* is a divination concept of discovering the causation of diseases or causalities. A correspondence between the Asantehene of Kumasi and the Imam of Gonja in the nineteenth century reveals this practice, which is still ongoing among Ghanaian folk Muslims. Below is the correspondence of the Asantehene and the reply from the Imam of Gonja:

> The reason for this letter is that I, the great Sultan, ask you to pray for all our body. A prayer for the ailment that flows in all our body. A prayer against the Satan, Iblis who visits people at night. A prayer for sickness that is known and sickness that is

---

70. Musk, 29.
71. Musk, 67.

unknown, sickness that is hidden in our body. A prayer for sickness at night. A prayer for the sickness of arms and legs. I say, ask you to pray for the new house; that never will the plague, the bad disease and misfortune enter our house. For all the people in our land and in all the land of others. I say, ask you, protection from the evil eye. I, the great Sultan, ask you to foretell [the future] for me, and let me know whatever is foreseen concerning my lifetime. Then send me a report of what you saw in this divination. I beseech you not to conceal anything of your divination.

Concerning our sultan, the Sultan of Ashanti, may Allah give him long life until old age in good health. He has to give out the best of sheep with four thousand cowries and forty kola nuts. He should ask to read prayers for the Prophet, that is, Dala il al-Khayrat [a famous collection of litanies for the Prophet of Islam] in its entirety, concerning this world and the hereafter. Then he may ask Allah whatever he wishes for himself, and whatever he wishes for his posterity and whatever he wishes of this world's needs. His necessities will be provided promptly.[72]

Among folk Muslims in Ghana, especially those in the zongo, the practice is part of *boka* that *malams* perform.[73] The Kramo use the *tasbih* (Islamic prayer beads) as an instrument for divination. The *malam* prays over the *tasbih* on the ground and requests the supplicant to pick it up and give it to him. The *malam* will then count the beads while reciting specific prayers and declare the particular jinni that needs to be dealt with to deliver the supplicant from evil.[74]

Veneration of Saints

Most folk Muslims engage in the veneration of saints, which is believed to have originated from the Muslims' concern for honoring Prophet Muhammad through the celebration of his birthday, *Mawlid al-Nabî*.[75] Saints play an important role in the worldview of Muslims and have different designations:

---

72. Azumah, "Historical Survey of Islam."
73. Pontzen, *Islam in a Zongo*, 178.
74. Pontzen, 270.
75. Musk, *Unseen Faces*, 49.

"*shâfi* who plays the role of an intercessor, shaikh (leader), *pîr* (elderly person considered as wise), [and] *murâbit* (one who has joined himself to God)."[76] Muslims depend on the *pîr* for personal or communal guidance on major decisions. Shehu Uthman dan Fodio was recognized as a *pîr* in northern Nigeria, and a female saint, Bilikisu Sungbo, was venerated in west Nigeria. In Ghana, folk Muslims have their own local saints designated to bring them *baraka* and guidance. It is worth noting that in Africa, dead saints are mostly venerated instead of living ones. However, whether alive or dead, saints are deemed to possess great power that enables them to solve difficult problems, including the healing of chronic diseases, removing barrenness, and discerning present and future events.

Ancestral Worship

A combination of ancestor veneration and saint veneration is rampant among African folk Muslims. In describing the practice among east Africans, Kim notes that the Waswahili visit their ancestors' graveyards and the tomb of departed Muslim saints to pray for *baraka*.[77] Kim has also confirmed the practice of healing and foretelling among folk Muslims and the use of Arabic magic in east Africa. While some Muslim clerics view these practices as unorthodox, the Swahili clerics believe them to be compatible with Islamic teaching and not "unfaithfulness to Allah nor the sin of infidelity." It is, however, not easy to place a clear demarcation between strictly ideological Islam and popular Islam within the African context due to the animistic and shamanistic tendencies embedded in African Islamic practices.[78]

Most folk Muslims in Ghana also engage in the practice of ancestor worship. They believe the ancestors are living dead who can give *baraka* and protect them from spiritual harm. Because of this, some folk Muslims bury the corpses of family close to their houses with the aim of keeping a close relationship. Food is offered to them on special days, and when children are born into the community, the ancestors are consulted through a Muslim soothsayer to discover which of the ancestors has returned back to earth. Children are named after these ancestors so that the child can receive *baraka*

---

76. Musk, 50.
77. Kim, *Islam among Swahili*, 64.
78. Kim, 65.

from the returning ancestor and maintain spiritual contact with them.[79] At the tomb of ancestors, special prayers called *dhikr* (remembrances)[80] of God are offered by repeating selected names from the ninety-nine names of God. Some, especially of the Tijaniyya, believe their ancestors pass on to them the ability to perform miracles and render services such as the "reversal of curses, protection from blows, gunshots and knives, [and] treatment of sexual weakness."[81]

Some Ghanaian folk Muslims believe they cannot come before God's presence with their petitions because of a failure to strictly keep the ritual prayers or because of their sins. The ancestors then serve as intercessors or intermediaries between them and God (which is not allowed by orthodox Islam). Folk Muslims believe that their tribal or ethnic saint or their ancestors are at the door of Muhammad. Since the ancestors know them very well and are able to sympathize with them, the ancestors will bring their petition to Muhammad who is believed to be at the door of God. Through the ancestors, Muhammad becomes the final advocate and intercessor.[82] This concept of ancestor worship among Ghanaian folk Muslims fuses ATRs ancestor worship and some elements of Islamic faith. However, the Qur'an asserts that there can be no intercessor except one appointed by God as it is written: "None shall have the power of intercession, but such a one as has received permission from God most gracious" (19:87).[83]

Rites of Passage

In Ghana, marriage and funeral ceremonies constitute the most important pre-Islamic African rites of passage that often blend with Islamic practices. One example is the ritual cleansing of the bride that is sometimes practiced in northern Ghana. The bride, covered only at her loins with a piece of cloth, is made to sit on a wooden mortar in a public square, surrounded by a host

---

79. Twumasi, "Understanding Folk Islam," 95.

80. *Dhikr* is a Sufi practice of chanting divine names or qur'anic phrases (Qur'an 18:24; 33:41; 62:10) repeatedly for blessing. One such phrase is, for instance, *la ilaha illa Allah* (no god but God). It is an interior sob or cry of yearning accompanied sometimes with music and dancing. Esposito, *Oxford Encyclopedia*, s.v. "Dhikr."

81. Pontzen, *Islam in a Zongo*, 139.

82. Shenk, "Islamic Mysticism," cited in Azumah and Sanneh, *African Christian and Islam*, 255.

83. Shenk, 255.

of women. The ritual bathing specialist (*aliwanka*) takes his place at the center of the circle with the bride. In the full view of the community, he pours cold water mixed with herbs on the bride's nakedness while chanting some incantations. The incantations appeal to the bride's ancestors to protect her from all evil and make her womb fruitful, and the herbal concoction drives away evil eye that may interfere in the bride's childbearing. It also serves to purify the bride and present her acceptable to her future husband. The onlooking crowd of women engage in singing songs composed for such occasions, which are often sexually profane. They take turns dancing around the bride in a seductive manner in rhythm with the drums and xylophone played in the background. The bride's peers dance and tease her by touching the vital parts of her body with wooden pestles. Together "the combination of profane lyrics, body rhythm, and the sexual symbolism of the pistil [*sic*] and the mortar reinforced the ritual's deliberate profanity."[84]

It is normally prohibited to publicly expose sexual organs or even mention them in the Ghanaian community, but during this marriage ritual bathing ceremony, the prohibition is deliberately suspended in order to allow the public to participate in the bride's transition to the world of marriage. The teasing and profane acts are deemed therapeutic for the bride to instill courage and take away her fear and timidity, preparing her to act boldly in marriage. This ritual is also intended to ward off evil forces that could destroy the marriage and is a means to attest the bride's ritual purity.

As part of this ceremony, the bride needs to publicly demonstrate her state of virginity, and this state is ascertained by requiring the newly married couple to sleep on a white bedspread during their first contact. The breaking of the hymen would soil the bed as a testimony of innocence and ritual sanctity. If the bride is found innocent and "unspoiled," the stained bedsheet is used in a public procession with drumming and dancing to demonstrate the bride's worthiness and attract future suitors to a trustworthy family. If the bride is found to be a "spoiled" bride, the entire family and progeny suffer sociocultural stigma that marks them as unworthy. For this reason, the ceremony became a defining factor of the fate of the bride and her family within the *Ahl al-Sunnah* movement.

---

84. Kobo, "Promoting Good," 195.

While the origin of the practice is unclear, it is said to have been sanctioned by Islam's proscription of premarital abstinence among west African Muslims where folk Islam is predominant.[85] Although the practice violates Islam's prohibition on sexual promiscuity and profanity, Muslim scholars are unable to condemn it because it serves as a means of ensuring chastity before marriage.[86] Shaikh Yussif Afajura did condemn the practice as un-Islamic, but the elderly women of Dagbani protested and accused him of promoting promiscuity. The ritual continues as a formality in many conservative cultural environments like Dagbon, where most family want to prove the sanctity of their women. They may even stain the bedsheet and perform the ritual themselves. However, the ritual has become obsolete in other areas due to the effects of urbanization that has allowed many of the young brides to mingle with the multicultural and cosmopolitan towns where they seek jobs.[87]

The funeral rite is another meaningful ceremony among folk Muslims in Ghana. The death of a member of the community is the concern of the entire community. Both men and women gather in the bereaved family's house to express their condolences, and usually, the men will help dig the grave, prepare the burial attire, participate in the prayer for the dead, and accompany the corpse to the graveside. While they wash the corpse, the crowd commonly chants the *kalimat al-Shahada* until the corpse is brought out for the funeral prayers. The officiating imam will usually ask the crowd if the deceased is indebted to anyone to ensure that the deceased did not owe anyone anything in the community. In case there is a person who has any outstanding debt, the family are required to settle it. The imam leads the entire community in a procession and they chant until the corpse is laid to rest. At the cemetery, the imam gives a brief sermon during which he cautions other Muslims about the inevitability of death, the need to do good while alive, and the practice of the five pillars of faith. The crowd finally returns to the house of the bereaved family for an elaborate prayer session. The *afenema* (clerics) are requested to recite special prayers for the deceased and the family. Mourners give alms and ask for God's forgiveness for the departed souls. The alms collected are shared at the end of the session among the officiating *afa* (cleric) and his

---

85. Kobo, 197.
86. Kobo, 197.
87. Kobo, 197–98.

people. While the burial ceremony ends on the day of the funeral for most Muslims, the Tijaniyya organize *dua* on the third, seventh, and fortieth days after burial and collect donations to aid the bereaved family.[88]

Summary

Even though all Muslims engage in the ritual practices of the five pillars, Ghanaian folk Muslims attribute different meanings to these general practices and see them as tools for liberation. The various practices reveal the felt needs of folk Muslims. As Musk describes,

> The ideal [orthodox] Islam has few resources for dealing with the everyday concerns and nightly dreads of ordinary Muslims; popular Islam, on the contrary, knows an abundance of remedies. Each local community recognizes practitioners who can provide the charms or ceremonies necessary to effect peace of mind and to restore equilibrium. It operates in the realm of human beings with needs and fears that inform and are informed by their outlook on life.[89]

The fear of evil eyes, the fear of the unknown, the fear of evil spirits and powerlessness before the power of jinn, the insecurity of the future, the need for healing and power to overcome evil forces, and the meaninglessness of life itself engulf folk Muslims. For these and other reasons, they worship saints and ancestors and rely on the numerous ritual practices and charms of local clerics. The issue of power, not the knowledge of the Qur'an, remains the most essential concern of folk Muslims.[90] Musk asserts that "the intellectual discussions about the historicity of the crucifixion may not communicate well with the Muslim who believes that because his local magician has been to Mecca on hajj, that man's magic has greater power." He notes that "beneath the surface of conventional religious behavior, huge needs expose the disequilibrium many Muslims know in their lives."[91] Most Muslims long for

---

88. Ibrahim, "Tijaniyya Order in Tamale," 89.
89. Musk, *Unseen Faces*, 238.
90. Musk, 204.
91. Musk, 248.

direct connection with the divine (power) because of sin, breakdowns in family relationships, and a vacuum in their hearts.

Folk Muslims, whose trust is in the incense burner, the local healer, and the diviner, need a stronger antidote to their fears. The diviner can predict an accident on a particular road and warn his folk Muslims to avoid that road, and the accident actually happens. Such supernatural occurrences enforce the fears and practices of folk Muslims, and they must be engaged at that supernatural level to gradually grow in faith in Christ. In view of the many spiritual needs of folk Muslims, the fear of jinn and evil forces, their quests for physical and spiritual healing, and their desire for blessing, there is an opportunity for Pentecostal Christians to respond by sharing the gospel. How to effectively do this will be the focus of the following chapters.

CHAPTER 4

Existing Methods of Sharing the Gospel with Folk Muslims

The Direct Approach

Islam contains truth as well as serious weaknesses that may lead to controversy when sharing the gospel with Muslims. Sam Schlorf has noted that:

> The amount of truth which is included in the Religion of Islam has . . . commended it to the acceptance of vast multitudes of our fellow-creatures. The errors, superstitions and falsehoods with which these doctrines are mingled have deceived the followers of the "Arabian Prophet" to their ruin. The evil results which have followed are everywhere patent.[1]

Due to the mixture of truth and errors in Islam, attempts over the century to share the gospel with Muslims have ended up in hot debates and confrontations that did not yield much result. For example, Henry Martyn started a Protestant missionary approach to Islam from 1781 to 1812, during which time he wrote three polemical tracts in debate with Muslims in Persia who defended Islam. These debates, referred to as "Mohammedan Controversy," usually took the form of aggressive polemics.[2]

---

1. Schlorff, *Missiological Models*, 4.
2. Schlorff, 4.

However, by the turn of the twentieth century (c. 1900–1930), Protestant missionaries had to rethink the polemical approach to Islam.[3] A direct approach was adopted by most missionaries, since a concern for the proper Christian attitude toward non-Christian religions started to preoccupy the missionary enterprise during the World Missionary Council held at Edinburgh in 1910.[4] The report of the conference admitted the absoluteness of the Christian faith but maintained that the Christian attitude toward non-Christian religions should be that of understanding and sympathy through knowledge and charity. It affirmed that all non-Christian religions exhibit fundamental needs of the human soul that only Christianity can meet.[5] Thus, a direct presentation of the gospel message should help people encounter the truth of God in his word while demonstrating his love through both the hands of God's people and the demonstration of God's power. Then people may see, feel, touch, smell, and taste these things for themselves to the discovery that Christ is the Lord. This implies deliberate efforts to respect, tolerate, and lovingly persuade Muslims in a way that is not offensive. There are different classes of folk Muslims with different levels of understanding, so to reach out to them, Christians should apply the principle of being all things to all men (1 Cor 9:19–22). By demonstrating love and care, Christians may end up winning Muslims for Christ.

J. Christy Wilson Sr. (1891–1973), a Presbyterian missionary to Persia, was a representative of the direct approach in an Islamic context. He observed that anyone who would like to share a direct presentation of the gospel with Muslims must be an expert in avoiding argument.[6] Argumentation, defense, and confrontation are common grounds from which most Muslims engage Christians; therefore, a Christian who engages Muslims in a confrontational or argumentative way is fighting on Muslims' own ground, and this must be avoided. Christian-Muslim relations are generally marked by mistrust, fear, and hostility embedded in historic roots of bitterness that are as old as Islam itself. The challenge for Christians remains appropriately approaching and responding to various classes of Muslims.

---

3. Schlorff, 7.
4. Schlorff, 8.
5. Schlorff, 8.
6. Wilson, "Christian Message to Islam," cited in Schlorff, *Missiological Models*, 13.

Some Muslims, especially militant Muslims, are aggressive, but others are peaceful. The reactions of these two categories revolve around different perspectives in the interpretation of Qur'an 2:256; 4:89; and 47:4. Using a polemic or aggressive Christian attitude toward non-Christian religions, including folk Muslims, is unlikely to win any souls for Christ. Just like Wilson who warned against polemics, Walter T. Fairman (1874–1941) was a missionary who favored the simple, loving, "full preaching of the Gospel of Jesus Christ" devoid of all polemic. He has observed that "there are no Moslem lands today where something is not being attempted to win Moslems to Christ. Yet relatively, and actually, very little has been accomplished. . . . The failure is on our part, and its secret must lie in the method we have hitherto adopted."[7]

The Indirect or Fulfillment Approach

In the nineteenth century, Islam was considered to have a latent power on which missionaries could build a presentation of their gospel. Thus, in the twentieth century, the attitude of Christian missionaries in sharing the gospel with Muslims underwent a turnabout as Christians began to see some elements of truth in Islam. A group of Islamicists and missionaries reasoned that if Islam contains some truth, then the errors could not have completely invalidated the truth; thus, Islam should not be evaluated by its errors and the good truth swept under the carpet.[8] They asserted that the positive elements in Islam could be used as a basis to unveil the gospel message. As described by L. Bevan Jones, within the context of the indirect or fulfillment approach, if Islam contains some truths, then these truths might have been the result of the work of the Holy Spirit:

> How else are we to account for the innumerable fragments of truth to be found in other religions except on the ground that God's Spirit is quietly at work in the hearts and minds of men, notwithstanding human opposition and imperfection? So then we require patience, understanding and sympathy in our study,

---

7. Fairman, "Approach to Moslems," 9.
8. Bevan, *People of the Mosque*, cited in Schlorff, *Missiological Models*, 15.

and with these, faith to believe that there is something of real worth to the Kingdom of God at the heart of Islam.⁹

In this view, Islam is genuinely struggling toward the goal of God in spite of the human elements that distort the whole truth of God.

Jones asserts that the spiritual experience must be appealed to in preaching the gospel to Muslims.¹⁰ Just as Jewish Christians, despite their prejudices, have come to faith in Christ because of their spiritual experience through the Holy Spirit, so also Muslims can come to faith by means of the work of the Holy Spirit. It is, therefore, important to exercise patience in dealing with Muslims. They must be lovingly invited to experience the work of the Holy Spirit who is able to convict them and bring them to a saving knowledge of Christ. This spiritual experience can satisfy the deepest needs of Muslims that Islam is unable to satisfy.

The Dialogical Model

Liberal theologians and those in the ecumenical movement adopted an indirect approach, which was positive in the sense that it affirmed the good elements of Islam. Evangelicals used the direct approach, which was considered to be a negative approach, because they directly opposed the elements of Islam that were not congruent with their evangelical position. However, both the indirect and the direct approaches had their pitfalls, which led to the abandonment of polemical methods. Those who were inclined to the positive elements of Islam saw themselves alienated from biblical authority, and those who had negative attitudes toward Muslims based on their commitment to biblical authority failed to distinguish the similarities between the gospel and the Islamic culture.¹¹

---

9. Bevan, 15.

10. Bevan, "Christianity Explained to Muslims," cited in Schlorff, *Missiological Models*, 16.

11. Schlorff, *Missiological Models*, 19.

Interreligious Dialogue

An Anglican bishop, Kenneth Cragg (b. 1913), was the first to lay a theological background for dialogue with Islam.[12] He actively contributed to the field of Christian-Muslim relations and served as a role model for those who wanted to remain faithful to their traditions while showing honesty and sympathy in dialogue with Muslims.[13] Dialogue with Muslims as it is today was developed by the World Council of Churches (WCC) or the ecumenical movement. After a series of meetings in the 1990s, the WCC released a statement (1997) condemning proselytism as a "scandal and counterwitness." In it, they defined proselytism as "the encouragement of Christians who belong to a church to change their denominational allegiance, through ways and means that 'contradict the spirit of Christian love, violate the freedom of the human person and diminish trust in the Christian witness of the church.'"[14] The WCC is right in saying that authentic witness involves respect and understanding for other Christian traditions and confessions by speaking the message of the gospel with respect, speaking the truth in love (Eph 4:12), treating others as we would like them to treat us (Matt 7:12), and respecting people of other faiths.[15] However, the WCC seems not to leave any room for evangelism that leads to conversion, soul-winning, or baptism of Muslims into Christianity. The condemnation of proselytism or conversion is in contravention to the missionary spirit of both Christianity and Islam and tends toward relativism. Disciple-making and Islamic *da'wah* (evangelism) are essential parts of the two faiths, and neither has ever renounced the practice.

Still, Ah Young Kim points out that many Muslims today are conscious that an attempt to do away with another religion through the aggressive *da'wah* strategies leads to failure. Furthermore, the "arrogant and triumphalist rule of one religion over other religions is nearly dead."[16] Adherents of many religions are becoming aware of the need for dialogue, peaceful coexistence, respect, and mutual tolerance. In keeping with this idea, Christians can make a theological appeal to Muslims on the basis of the Qur'an through peaceful

---

12. Schlorff, *Missiological Models*, 20.
13. Odem, "Reviewed Work(s)," 74.
14. World Council of Churches Central Committee, "Towards Common Witness."
15. World Council of Churches Central Committee, "Towards Common Witness."
16. Kim, "Muslim Presence in Korea," 205.

dialogue and conversation as an appropriate method of engaging them with the gospel.

Both Islam and Christianity are missionary religions struggling for human souls. Islam possesses a "defense mechanism" that stands against the core elements of the Christian doctrine, and this makes theological dialogue with Muslims a hard, often frustrating, effort.[17] Due to the controversial nature of the innermost core of Islam, one must see folk Muslims the way they see themselves. Muslims consider themselves to share the same spiritual heritage with Christians; both are united by faith in God and look forward to an eternity following death and resurrection. Muslims and Christians have assurance that God has certainly sent prophets to communicate a divinely revealed word that is recorded in the sacred books. Adherence to the revelation makes them believers. However, the faiths differ in the nature of the revelation and the character or the form of the sacred books. Christians who are aware of the essential theological divergences and convergences of Muslim and Christian doctrines will be able to share the gospel with Muslims and, in this case, folk Muslims. Developing this understanding will be a bridge to engaging folk Muslims in a truth encounter.

Muslims' Understanding of Jesus
God's Self Revelation and Oneness

The first complex issue between Muslims and Christians is the nature of God and how God has revealed himself. Both religions are emphatically monotheistic, affirming the ultimate truth that there is only one God. This ultimate realization of the monotheistic nature of Christianity and Islam led a mixed group of scholars from both religions to produce a joint book entitled *We Believe in One God: The Experience of God in Christianity and Islam*.[18] However, the faiths disagree on the nature of this oneness. The heart of Islamic doctrine expresses the oneness of God as *tawḥīd*, which intimates that God is one person because he is not made up of parts. In contrast, Christians believe that God is one in three persons, which is the doctrine of the Trinity. The Qur'an condemns this view of God, stating "disbelieved have those who say

---

17. Kim, 221.
18. Schimmel and Falaturi, "We Believe," cited in Kim, 223.

God is the third of three; there is no deity except one deity" (5:73). In effect, Muslims criticize the Trinity as a belief in three gods, but Christians also condemn tritheism as heretical. This final revelation according to Christians is fulfilled in Christ. "And the Word became flesh and dwelt among us, and we have seen his glory, glory as of the only Son from the Father, full of grace and truth" (John 1:14).

Aside from this, both faiths hold a similar view of the nature of God. Islam asserts "God as eternal, personal, sovereign, powerful, wise, holy and just" as revealed in the Qur'an:

> Allah is He, than Whom there is no other god; Who knows (all things) both secret and open; He, Most Gracious, Most Merciful. Allah is He, than Whom there is no other god; The Sovereign, the Holy one, the source of Peace (and Perfection), The Guardian of Faith, the Preserver of Safety, the Exalted in Might, The Irresistible, the Supreme: Glory to Allah! (High is He) above the partners they attribute to Him. He is Allah, the Creator, the Evolver, the Bestower of Forms (Colors); To him belong the Most Beautiful Names. Whatever is in the heavens and on earth declares His Praises and Glory: And He is the Exalted in Might, the Wise. (59:22–24)[19]

The power, sovereignty, holiness, and eternal nature of God are all reference points that Christians also appeal to (Ps 111:1–5). The Qur'an admits that the God who revealed himself to Moses and Jesus, and is worshiped by both Jews and Christians, is the same God Muslims worship – the same God who revealed the sacred Qur'an to the Prophet Muhammad. Montgomery W. Watt has remarked that:

> Both Mohammed and those among his followers who are reckoned orthodox had and continue to have just and true notions of God, and his attributes (always excepting their obstinate and impious rejecting of the Trinity) appear so plain from the Koran itself and all the Mohammedan divines, that it would be loss of

---

19. Kim, 224.

time to refute those who suppose the God of Mohammed to be different from the true God.[20]

In spite of these shared ideas, dwelling on the theological issue of the oneness or unity of God is not an ideal way to share the gospel. The doctrine of the Trinity itself is subtle and abstruse to the understanding of most ordinary Christians; they simply accept it by faith without the ability to actually explain it. However, Christians can help Muslims understand the concept by first understanding the rationale behind their rejection of the Trinity. In the pre-Islamic context of *jahiliyya*, traditional Arabian pagan gods supposedly got married and gave birth to children. Muhammad considered the notion of pagan gods giving birth to be polytheism and, against this background, rejected any concept of God being three or having a son. The Trinity is reprehensible to Muslims because God cannot marry or have children (Qur'an 5:75; 6:100–101). Trinity, therefore, should be explained to Muslims through love, respect, and dialogue.

Christians must be clear that the word "trinity" does not exist in the Bible. It is a word that was introduced into the Bible two hundred years after Jesus by Tertullian, a north African theologian, in an attempt to explain the human experience of God. It is an expression of God's love with inadequate human language. The Trinity implies that in God there is "communion, fellowship, loving relationship, and unity."[21] Since God is love, he came down to meet humanity in loving service and invitation to mankind. God revealed himself and his love to mankind by means of Jesus the Messiah and invites mankind to participate in his loving relationship, which is exemplified in Jesus the Messiah. God through the Holy Spirit empowered mankind to love one another just like Jesus loves. Although Muslims object to the idea that Jesus is an associate of God (Qur'an 4:171), the same surah makes reference to the Spirit of God and calls the Messiah the Word of God. This mention of the Spirit of God and the Messiah is an open door by which the Trinity can be explained to Muslims. They must be lovingly pointed to the truth that the Son of God does not imply God married and gave birth but represents the Word of God in human form. John 14:8–10 explains the oneness of the Messiah and the

---

20. Watt, *Islam and Christianity Today*, 45, in Kim, 225.
21. Shenk, *Journeys*, 163.

Father, and through the Messiah, we are invited to join the family of God to become adopted sons and daughters (Eph 1:5).[22]

Christian evangelism aims to illuminate the nature of Christ so that people are able to confess Jesus as Lord and Savior. Muslims refer to Jesus as Isa, the son of Mary, and have a high view of him[23] as a prophet and the Messiah. Whereas Muhammad is referred to as "the Seal of the Prophets" (Qur'an 33:40), Jesus is sometimes referred to as the "the Seal of the Saints." They honor him as one of the greatest prophets who ever existed, and some Muslims even name their children after Jesus. Even Muhammad, tradition claims, covered the Virgin Mary and her son with his coat when he got to them while cleansing the Ka'bah of idols in 630 CE. Fifteen surahs of the Qur'an and ninety-three ayat speak about Jesus,[24] but the qur'anic understanding of Jesus is quite different from what the New Testament says about him.[25] Jesus's miracles and specific acts are told without much detail in the Qur'an, which constitutes a difficult task when Christians try to aid Muslim encounter in the gospel.[26] Nevertheless, since Muslims already have a particular understanding of Jesus, Christians first need to understand what Muslims believe about him to lead them from the known to the unknown.

The Birth and Life of Jesus

Muslims acknowledge the birth of Jesus and join Christians in commemorating Jesus's birth at Christmas. Some go to the extent of sending Christmas cards expressing good wishes to Christian neighbors. Although Muslims consider Jesus to be the son of the Virgin Mary, they do not consider him to be the Son of God as Christians do. The Quran's version of Jesus's birth and life bears some similarity to the Gospel of Luke, albeit there are important differences.

According to the Qur'an, Mary was committed to God for divine protection, and lots were cast to determine her guardian, Zachariah (3:37, 44). When she had grown up, God divinely provided Mary with food in the sanctuary

---

22. Shenk, 167.
23. Larson, "Jesus in Islam," 327.
24. Kim, "Muslim Presence in Korea," 239.
25. Woodberry, "Muslim Understanding," 173.
26. Kim, "Muslim Presence in Korea," 240.

where she lived (Qur'an 3:37). When visited by an angel, she was told that she was chosen and made pure, preferred above all women of creation (Qur'an 3:42). The Bible does not affirm this backstory of Mary, but the angel Gabriel, who delivers the news of Jesus's birth, does tell her that she is favored by God, and her cousin Elizabeth calls her blessed among women (Luke 1:30, 42).

The annunciation of the birth of Jesus to Mary occurs in two places in the Qur'an: the first version in surah three claims an angel delivered the news, and the second in surah nineteen states that "God's spirit messenger"[27] (Qur'an 19:19) took the form of a well-shaped man and told Mary God would bestow upon her a pure boy. In surah three, the angel's response to Mary's question of how a chaste woman could bring forth a boy is "God creates what he wills by simply decreeing it" (3:45–47); in surah nineteen, God's spirit replies that "it was easy for God and that he would be made a sign for mankind, a mercy from God, and a thing ordained" (19:16–22).[28] In both accounts, Jesus is portrayed as a created being, but due to his unusual birth, Muslims set Jesus above ordinary human beings. The Qur'an thus closely parallels the narrative of Luke's Gospel (Luke 1:26–38): Mary is visited by an angel and inquires how she can conceive as a virgin.[29] However, the Bible states that Jesus's birth results from the Holy Spirit coming upon Mary (Matt 1:18; Luke 1:35). "And Mary said to the angel, 'How will this be, since I am a virgin?' And the angel answered her, 'The Holy Spirit will come upon you, and the power of the Most High will overshadow you; therefore the child to be born will be called holy – the Son of God'" (Luke 1:34–35).

According to Muslims, Jesus spoke like an adult while in the cradle and is a miracle worker who "forms birds out of clay and gives them life" (Qur'an 3:46, 49; 5:110; 19:30). They grant that Jesus healed the leper, gave sight to the blind, and brought forth the dead, but only as a man with God's permission.[30] The Bible confirms that Jesus healed the lepers (Mark 1:40–42), gave sight to those born blind (John 9:1–7), and raised the dead to life (John 11:38–44), but there is no indication that he spoke in the cradle. The qur'anic Jesus was the son of Mary, a prophet who bore a gospel to direct and admonish the children

---

27. Some scholars translate God's spirit as an angel and add [Gabriel].
28. Kim, "Muslim Presence in Korea," 24.
29. Larson, "Jesus in Islam," 328.
30. Woodberry, "Muslim Understanding," 174.

of Israel and performed miracles upon God's permission. To Muslims, the miracles of his birth and healing ministry confirm the truth of his prophethood and are *aya* (a sign) of God's peace and mercy.[31] The Bible, in contrast, draws a crucial distinction about these miracles in relation to Jesus's identity. The biblical Jesus is himself God who performed miracles as proof of his deity as the Son of God (Mark 1:1) who can forgive sins (Matt 9:6; Mark 2:9–11).

The Crucifixion and Death of Jesus

In addition to the virgin birth, the crucifixion, death, burial, and resurrection of Jesus are essential parts of the gospel proclamation (Matt 27:32–28:20), yet Muslims deny his crucifixion. Qur'an 4:157 implies that the claim of Jews to have "killed Jesus the Messiah, the son of Mary, the messenger of Allah" is untrue.[32] According to the Qur'an, Jesus only appeared to be crucified and did not die. While Muslim commentators affirm on the basis of Qur'an 4:157–58/156 that Jesus was not crucified, they are unable to say what happened to him. Muhammad, and many scholars after him, chose the interpretation that it was not the actual Christ who was crucified but rather someone who closely resembled him, because it is inconceivable for a prophet of God to suffer such an ignominious death.[33] This explanation is congruent with ancient gnostic views that a substitute died in place of Jesus: "his body was crucified while the true Jesus did not suffer."[34] Likewise, Kenneth Cragg explains that according to the qur'anic consensus, "to Jesus at the Cross death did not happen"; "it need not happen, and it should not happen." Theologically, there is an agreement among Muslim scholars that, redemptively, Jesus could not die, and, morally, he should not and need not die.[35] In interpreting Qur'an 4:157–59/156–57, Muslims claim Jesus went to heaven without undergoing crucifixion. They, therefore, expect the return of Jesus and his death before resurrection day. Muslims thus consider Christians' witness of the death of Jesus as *kufr* (disbelief). When eschatologically considering the ministry of Jesus, the Qur'an states, "On the Day of Judgment he will be a witness against

---

31. Kim, "Muslim Presence in Korea," 245.
32. Woodberry, "Muslim Understanding," 175.
33. Parshall, *New Paths*, 139.
34. Woodberry, "Muslim Understanding," 174.
35. Cragg, *Jesus and the Muslim*, 178.

them" (4:159) – meaning the people of the Book, Christians, who indulge in the conjectures of human doubt (Qur'an 4:157).

While Muslims commonly refute the crucifixion and the death of Jesus, some qur'anic accounts expressly affirm Jesus's death, which poses an intertextual contradiction. Qur'an 19:34 references a "statement of truth" about Jesus in Qur'an 19:33: "Peace be upon me the day I was born, the day I die, and the day I shall be raised up to life."[36] This reveals that Jesus talked about his own birth, death, and resurrection. Thus, some Muslim scholars observe that Jesus did die and cite Qur'an 3:55; 48, which speaks of "the real death of Jesus." Al-Tabari (d. 923) inspired the thought of three ancient authorities who interpret the text as the actual death of Jesus, namely Al-Razi, Ibn Kathri, and Al-Baydwi.[37] Al-Razi (d. 1210) cited Wahb B. Munabbih's statement that Jesus was received in death for at least three hours before his resurrection, while Ibn Kathri (d. 1373) referred to Wahb b. Munabbih to note that God caused Jesus to die for three days, after which he resurrected him and raised him.[38] Ibn Ishaq asserts that Jesus died for seven hours. Likewise, Al-Baydwi (d. 1284–1316) emphasized that God caused Jesus to die for seven hours before raising him from death, and that is why Christians believe this truth. Ibn Anas notes that "God received Jesus in death when he raised Jesus to heaven."[39] Jesus's death is therefore a contradiction in the Qur'an, and the Muslim authorities who spoke about it only differ in views concerning the time of death.

In spite of this, Muslims generally disbelieve the crucifixion. Those who speak of Jesus's death claim that his body died, but his soul did not die (Qur'an 2:154/149) as emphasized by the New Testament: "Do not fear those who kill the body but cannot kill the soul" (Matt 10:28).[40] Since the crucifixion is essential in Christian witness, it becomes a challenge to lead Muslims to an understanding of the nature of Jesus's crucifixion and its purpose as it pertains to the sinner. Christians see Jesus as the Savior, and the cross was necessary for Christ to atone for the sin of all sinners; the shameful death was intended for

---

36. Kim, "Muslim Presence in Korea," 246.
37. Woodberry, "Muslim Understanding," 175.
38. Woodberry, 175.
39. Woodberry, 175.
40. Woodberry, 176.

the eternal redemption of sinners. Thus, Christians believe that God's power was demonstrated after the cross by raising Jesus from death, not before the cross. Muslims, however, do not profess a need for a savior but desire a guide to knowledge; they believe humanity's problem is ignorance and not sin or evil as the Bible portrays it (Rom 3:23; 6:23). The Qur'an refers to salvation (*najat*) only once (Qur'an 40:41/44).

Although this poses a significant challenge in evangelism because of Muslims' disbelief in Jesus's actual death and their traditional view that Jesus was raised before the event on the cross,[41] Christians can address this challenge by respectfully allowing the Bible to speak for itself and using a portion of the Qur'an, like Qur'an 3:55; 5:17; or 19:33, to clearly speak about the death of Jesus when speaking about the death of Christ.

The Nature and Sonship of Jesus

Christians view Jesus as the Son of God and exclude any form of physical paternity from the notion of sonship, but Muslims view Jesus as a man and not as God incarnate. Islamic tradition portrays Jesus and the mother Mary as the only people that Satan could not touch at birth. With this view, it is blasphemous to say that Jesus is the Son of God and dishonoring to claim that wicked men crucified him. Muslims respect Jesus as a prophet, but the theological frame Muslims place Jesus in is so removed from the Christian faith that their understanding seems to reinvent his personality.[42]

For Muslims, Jesus's deity poses a threat to Islam's view of the oneness of God. The Qur'an states God cannot have an offspring, "Say: "He is God, One; God, the Eternal; he brought not forth, nor hath he been brought forth; co-equal with him there hath never been any one" (Qur'an 112). Many verses in the Qur'an categorically reject any form of sonship or acquisition of a son:

> They say, "God has begotten a son." (10:68)

> He to Whom belongs the dominion of the heavens and the earth: no son has He begotten; nor has He a partner in His dominion: it is He Who created all things, and ordered them in due proportions. (25:2)

---

41. Woodberry, 176.
42. Larson, "Jesus in Islam," 327.

> That they should invoke a son for [Allah] Most Gracious. For it is not consonant with the majesty of (Allah) Most Gracious that He should beget a son. Not one of the beings in the heavens and the earth but must come to [Allah] Most Gracious as a servant. (19:91–93)
>
> Had Allah wished to take to Himself a son, He could have chosen whom He pleased out of those whom He creates. (39:4)[43]

Furthermore, referring to Jesus as the son of God according to the Qur'an is a form of *shirk,* an imitation of Arabian paganism or the unbelievers of old as stated in Qur'an 9:30–31:

> The Jews call Uzair a "son of Allah," and the Christians call Christ "the Son of Allah." That is a saying from their mouth; [in this] they but imitate what the Unbelievers of old used to say. Allah's curse be on them: how they are deluded away from the Truth! They take their priests and their anchorites to be their lords in derogation of Allah, and [they take as their Lord] Christ the son of Mary; yet they were commanded to worship but One God [Allah]: there is no god but He. Praise and glory to Him: [far is He] from having the partners they associate [with Him].[44]

This presents a challenge for Christian-Muslim engagement, because the center of the Christian gospel is that Jesus is God incarnate. Take Christology out of the gospel proclamation, and you will be left with nothing to witness about, for Christ's deity is the condition for his sinless nature by which he could make atonement for humanity.[45]

Thus, Parrinder notes that the easiest way to open conversation with Muslims about the gospel is to point them to the Christ of the Qur'an because "Jesus is always spoken of in the Qur'an with reverence; there is no breath of criticism for he is the Christ of God."[46] Instead of using the Son of God, Christians can use "Spirit, Prophet, Apostle, Preeminent One, Example, Sinless One, [or] Miracle Worker," which are other ways Muslims refer to

---

43. Kim, "Muslim Presence in Korea," 249.
44. Kim, 251.
45. Woodberry, "Muslim Understanding," 177.
46. Parrinder, *Jesus in the Qur'an,* 16.

Jesus. Jesus is known as the Al-Masih (Messiah) in the Qur'an (3:45; 4:157, 169–70; 5:17, 75; 9:31), and Christians understand the Messiah to be the anointed one of God for the work of redemption (Dan 9:25–26; John 1:41; 4:25).[47] Jesus was a respected prophet from birth (Qur'an 19:21), and the Bible also confirms him as a prophet (Matt 13:57; Luke 1:76; 4:24; John 4:19). While Muslims consider Jesus one of many prophets, the Bible portrays him as the ultimate prophet, "the culmination of the line of prophets" (Deut 18:15, 18; Luke 24: 25–27; John 6:14).[48] Everything he did validates his claim of being the Christ, the Son of God, who would give his life (John 20:30–31).[49]

Although the Qur'an asserts that all prophets sinned and needed forgiveness, including Noah (11:49), Abraham (26:80–82), Moses (28:15), and Muhammad himself (40:57; 47:21; 48:1–2), Jesus's sinlessness is confirmed by both the Qur'an and the Bible (Qur'an 19:9; John 8:46; 14:30; Heb 4:15; 7:28).[50] The sinless nature of Jesus the Messiah thus becomes a starting point to engage Muslims with the gospel, since God is the only one who is sinless.

Using the qur'anic designation of Jesus as "the Word" is another way Christians can bridge the gap in proclaiming the gospel to Muslims. Jesus is referred to in the Bible as the "logos" (John 1) that creates (Gen 1; Ps 33:66; Col 1). Though the Qur'an denies the divine sonship of Jesus (72:3), it gives Jesus the title of "God's Word" (3:39; 4:171; 19:35).[51] Christians believe Jesus is the "Word" made flesh, the perfect representation of God (Heb 1:1–3) who dwelt among men and offers salvation to all who believe in him (John 1:1–4, 12, 14). Jesus is also referred to as the Injil from God (Qur'an 3:45). Thus, Muslims can be made to understand that the Injil is in the person of Jesus, who is the good news, the Word of God in human form. The gospel is not a book but God in human form.[52]

However, some qur'anic references will not help Christians share the gospel. When referring to Jesus, Muslims use the proper name Isa, but this reference does not help in witness as it obscures the biblical meaning of Jesus as the one who saves and Immanuel (God with us) (Isa 7:14; Matt 1:21, 23).

---

47. Larson, "Jesus in Islam," 330.
48. Larson, 329.
49. Larson, 329.
50. Larson, 331.
51. Parshall, *New Paths*, 139.
52. Shenk, *Journeys*, 169.

Muslims say the name Isa was imposed on the Prophet Muhammad by the Jews, who also referred to Jesus as Esau because of their hatred toward him. Additionally, the Qur'an refers to Jesus as the "son of Mary," which some Christian apologists in the Middle Ages regarded as humiliating. Within an Arab context, ancestry is only traceable to a father and not a mother.

Addressing the person of Christ in the Qur'an is a central task and a suitable bridge in Muslim evangelism because the Qur'an talks much about Jesus. From the known, Muslims can be brought to the unknown; what was once relative information can be known as the "absolute truth that Jesus Christ is God incarnate,"[53] the Messiah and the anointed one of God. The vacuum created by the obscure thought of Jesus and his title as the Messiah in the Qur'an can be filled with the truth of the gospel.

Jesus's Return

Christians believe Jesus will return not to die again but as the judge of both the living and the dead, and this constitutes an essential part of their proclamation in evangelism (Acts 1:11; 2 Tim 4:1). All Muslims believe that "Isa will return to this earth" to uniquely demonstrate his power and authority.[54] However, Muslims' opposing views regarding Jesus's return causes a severe challenge for Christian-Muslim encounters in evangelism.

In interpreting Qur'an 4:159/157, al-Tabari asserts that the people of the Book will believe in Jesus between his return and death, and they shall be united with Muslims under Islam. The implication is that Muslims believe Jesus will return, but they believe that he will return and live on earth for forty years before he dies and resurrects to kill the antichrist as a just judge. Then there will be great security so that "lions will lie down with camels and wolves with sheep while youth play with snakes without harm" (Qur'an 4:159), which the Bible also teaches (Isa 11:6–8). Qur'an 43:61 is also used to support Jesus's return but without clarity in meaning, because some use "it shall be a known sign" referring to the Qur'an, and others say "Jesus shall be a known sign":[55]

---

53. Parshall, *New Paths*, 144.
54. Parshall, 139.
55. Al-Tabari, *Commentaire du Coran*, 14–17, quoted in Woodberry, "Muslim Understanding," 176.

> And he [Isa (Jesus)], son of Maryam (Mary) shall be a known sign for (the coming of) the Hour (Day of Resurrection) [Isa's descent on the earth]. Therefore have no doubt concerning it (i.e., the Day of Resurrection). And follow Me (Allah) (i.e., be obedient to Allah and do what He orders you to do, O mankind)! This is the Straight Path (of Islamic Monotheism, leading to Allah and to His Paradise). (Qur'an 43:61)[56]

Ibn Khaldun asserts that Jesus will return to "the minaret of Umayyad Mosque in Damascus," get married, bear children and finally die after forty years.[57] There is some level of understanding among folk Muslims that Jesus will return. Because folk Muslims in Ghana generally have no deep knowledge of the scriptures (both the Bible and the Qur'an), the biblical story may still prove helpful to point out exactly what the Bible says about Jesus's return.

Pentecostals' Theological Medium to Approach Folk Muslims

Jesus as an Ancestor in the Ghanaian Folk Context

Jesus means different things to different people (Matt 16:13–20; Mark 8:27–30; Luke 9:18–21). As discussed in chapter 3, folk Muslims in Ghana believe in saints and worship ancestors who they believe are closer to God and able to intercede on their behalf. The ummah among folk Muslims goes beyond the living and is extended to the living dead, hence the veneration of the ancestors. This concept can become a bridge for sharing the gospel to folk Muslims. Kwame Bediako asserts:

> Strange as it may seem, theological affirmations are meaningful ultimately, not in terms of what adherents say, but in terms of what persons of other faiths understand those affirmations to imply for them. In other words, our Christian affirmations are validated when their credentials and validity are tested not only in terms of the religious and spiritual universe in which Christians habitually operate, but also – indeed especially – in

---

56. Khan and Al-Hilali, *Interpretation of Meaning*, 966.
57. Khaldun, "The Muqaddimah," 194, in Woodberry, "Muslim Understanding," 177.

terms of the religious and spiritual worlds which persons of other faiths inhabit. For it is in those "other worlds" that the true meaning of Jesus Christ becomes apparent and validated. Christian history shows that as Christian faith engages with new cultures, new insights about Jesus Christ emerge.[58]

The Christian theological understanding of Jesus Christ can only be meaningful to folk Muslims if this understanding is made relevant to the cultural understanding of folk Muslims. A journey through the book of Hebrews with folk Muslims may be a good start. This Injil reveals Jesus as an ancestor par excellence, the perfect medium or link between the living and the dead in terms of "ancestral relationship." Jesus qualifies beyond all Ghanaian ancestors as a member of the folk Muslim clan and as the universal savior. He is "a Spirit father," an "Elder brother," a friend, an intercessor for the family (Rom 8:34; Heb 2:10–18; 1 John 2:1), the "Revealer of truth" (John 16:7), and a mediator (1 Tim 2:5).[59] Bediako explains that the essential message of Hebrews is that Jesus embodies God's fullest self-disclosure to humanity in the person of Jesus, a revelation that is superior to all revelations.[60] The epistle points to Jesus as completely sufficient for salvation. In it, Jesus is superior to angels (Heb 1:4; 10:8), superior to all leaders (Heb 3:1–3), superior to priests (Heb 4:14–7:28), and offers better sacrifices sufficient for the remission of sins (Heb 9:11–10:18).[61] Folk Muslims' quest for ritual washing and purification finds fulfillment in the "ritual purification of the blood of Jesus," which in Hebrews is a better sacrifice. In Hebrews, God spoke to our forefathers in many ways and at many times by means of the prophets of old, including Moses whom Muslims affirm to be a messenger of God. However, God has now communicated through Jesus.

> Long ago, at many times and in many ways, God spoke to our fathers by the prophets, but in these last days he has spoken to us by his Son, whom he appointed the heir of all things, through whom also he created the world. He is the radiance of the glory of God and the exact imprint of his nature, and he upholds the

---

58. Bediako, "Christianity, Islam and Kingdom," 6.
59. Bediako, *Jesus and the Gospel*, 25–26.
60. Bediako, "Christian Faith," 45–57.
61. Veerman, "Introduction to Hebrews," 26–32.

universe by the word of his power. After making purification for sins, he sat down at the right hand of the Majesty on high, having become as much superior to angels as the name he has inherited is more excellent than theirs. (Heb 1:1–4).

Mbiti notes that ancestors are those who play the role of parents for their living kinsmen and the living consult them to determine their destiny and wellbeing.[62] They are the pathfinders of the living community, the great ummah of folk Muslims. Death is not annihilation or even separation in the African context; thus, the ancestors remain "the living dead." They are responsible for channeling the life force within the community and able to exert influence on the vitality of the community.[63] Given this context, Bediako writes,

> Purification rites and sacrificial offerings to achieve social harmony are ineffectual. It is a death with eternal sacrificial significance that deals with our mortal failures and infringements of social relationships. Christ's death heals our wounded and soiled consciences and overcomes once and for all and at their roots, all that in our heritage brings us grief, guilt, shame, and bitterness. As a true Elder Brother and Saviour he is in the presence of our Father and displaces mediatorial function of our natural "Spirit-fathers."[64]

Ghanaian folk Muslims offer prayers to their ancestors with the hope that they will connect them to Muhammad for *baraka*. However, in the Ghanaian context, Muhammad would not have met all the needed requirements to become a true ancestor because his hands were stained with blood. Among the qualifications is the ability to live a long life, live an exemplary life worthy of emulation, and be a "hero ancestor" who "died young defending the community and thus may not have fulfilled the traditional requirements for ancestorhood."[65] Traditionally, hero ancestors are revered and memorialized through specific rituals because of their level of sacrifice and self-denial for the good of the community. Jesus was a hero ancestor because he died a

---

62. Mbiti, *Concepts of God*, 230.
63. Nichols, "African Christian Theology," 27–35.
64. Bediako, *Jesus and the Gospel*, 27.
65. Jawanza, "Reconceiving the Doctrine," 150.

tragic death defending his community, Israel (Luke 4:18–19). The cross was the ultimate example of self-denial and self-sacrifice Jesus showed on earth (Matt 10:38). He was not married, did not have physical offspring, and died a good death as traditionally required of normal ancestors. Because he demonstrated a high level of moral decency, a sinless life that no other ancestor has ever attained in Ghana, Jesus became the ancestor par excellence within the folk context. His commitment to his community and his self-sacrifice were necessary to preserve and protect the values and religious beliefs of the community. From a Ghanaian folk perspective, therefore, Jesus has power to mediate between God and his community (1 Tim 2:5) and offer protection from existential evil in the community.[66] Presenting him to folk Muslims as such will prepare the way for the gospel. It is a way to bring folk Muslims to Jesus who need to be supported with truth encounters in the gospel through a systematic or gradual process of loving discipleship.

The experience of the Ghanaian folk Muslims could be likened to those in Hebrews 5:11–14 where the writer urges the readers to move onto spiritual maturity, "leaving behind the elementary truths which brought them into Christianity and with which their former beliefs and practices were largely compatible, and establishing a deeper spiritual foundation for their faith."[67] There is always a point of entry in every religion. There is a time to rely on ritual practices and a time to transition from a reliance on material rituals and regulations to sustain faith to rely on Jesus as the only sustenance of faith. Folk Muslims may need to come to faith through these ritual practices but must be gradually helped to transition to real faith in Jesus to receive "mercy and find grace to help in time of need" (Heb 4:16). Just as the audience in Hebrews had to transit from their Judaic context to Christianity so also folk Muslims will transit from their folk context to Christianity and from Abraham to Jesus as a common ancestor.[68] This must be done through discipleship and loving follow-up.

---

66. Jawanza, 155.
67. Green, "Guidelines from Hebrews," 240.
68. Green, 240.

The Holy Spirit as a Bridge to Folk Muslims

Folk Muslims are concerned with the real challenges of this world and this must be the terrain on which Christians meet them. Muslims believe in the work of *Agya no Sumsum* (the Spirit of the Father). The Qur'an speaks about the Holy Spirit at least four times and the Spirit about seventeen times. Muslims have been taught that the Holy Spirit refers to the angel Gabriel. However, a careful look at the Qur'an shows that Islam has a similar understanding of the Holy Spirit with Christian thought.

S. P. Steinhaus groups the Qur'an's verses on the Holy Spirit into four categories: the Holy Spirit referring to angel Gabriel (16:102; 17:85; 19:17; 26:193; 40:15), the Spirit as breathed into man in the process of creation (15:29; 32:9; 38:72), the Spirit that has the function to strengthen and indwell Jesus and believers (2:87, 253; 5:110; 58:22), and the Spirit mentioned in cases that are hard to interpret (4:171; 12:87; 16:2; 42:52; 66:12; 70:4; 78:38; 97:4).[69] Although the Qur'an does not have one uniform description of the Holy Spirit, Muslims are likely to heed to stories on the works of the Holy Spirit in the Bible. Qur'an 2:87 and 2:253 both state, "we strengthened Jesus with the Holy Spirit," and Qur'an 5:110 states of Jesus, "I strengthened thee with the holy spirit so that thou spakest unto mankind in the cradle as in maturity." Qur'an 58:22 says, "As for such, He hath written faith upon their hearts and hath strengthened them with a spirit from Him," implying that the Holy Spirit not only strengthens but also provides miracle-working power.

Pentecostals have Bible verses that can be used as bridges to explore the Spirit's work in sustaining folk Muslims. For instance, Ephesians 3:16 states, "I pray that out of his glorious riches he may strengthen you with power through his Spirit in your inner being" (NIV). The Holy Spirit is the unseen actor who provides power for speaking/preaching (Acts 1:8), signs and wonders (Acts 2:17), visions (Acts 7:55), directing and guiding (Acts 8:39), encouraging (Acts 9:31), anointing (Acts 10:38), appointing leaders (Acts 20:28), prophecy (Acts 21:4), etc. Jesus will "give the Holy Spirit to those who ask him" (Luke 11:13).[70] Steinhaus has noted that opening a conversation with Muslims to

---

69. Steinhaus, "Spirit-First Approach," 20.
70. Steinhaus, 28.

share on the person of Jesus makes Muslims rebuff dialogue. However, when the Holy Spirit is used, Muslims are often attracted and yield to discussion.[71]

The Holy Spirit is not only the source of spiritual power that confronts jinn (spirits) but also the source of righteous life, good character, increased spiritual devotion to Allah, and the assurance of salvation. Folk Muslims may struggle to fill the letter of the quranic laws and are often left frustrated by their inability to meet all the requirements of the Sunnah. They look to the letter of the law (Qur'an) without the Spirit and have no other source of power, except the Qur'an and their devotional practices. Their ardent quest for right living or holy living can be likened to the Pentecostal emphasis on holiness. The struggle for holiness, therefore, can become a bridge by which Pentecostals can present Jesus to folk Muslims. Pentecostals posit that none can live holy without the enabling power of the Holy Spirit (Gal 5:16) and can present the Holy Spirit to folk Muslims as the power source for right living, to stay clean, and fulfill the letter of Allah's laws. Steinhaus observes:

> [Folk Muslims] may be doing everything right but they still lack the assurance that God will find them pleasing. Moreover, they struggle with the battle against the flesh. Lust, greed, malice and other such vices rage in their hearts even though they know they should not. Yet after years of struggling against them, the battle rages on.[72]

Jesus's manifesto in Luke 4:18 reveals Christ's appointment to deliver people from the oppression of Satan by the Holy Spirit, and Luke 11:13 reveals that this Spirit is available to all. Specific biblical examples (in the Injil) can be used to show how the Holy Spirit responds to those that have struggled to live rightly. In this sense, the example of Paul's struggle in Romans 7 and the solution through the sustaining power of the Holy Spirit in Romans 8:2–9 is an applicable example to open Muslims' hearts to the gospel.

Pentecostalism's mission strategy embraces healing and deliverance through the Holy Spirit. Clinton El Arnold notes that the writers of the synoptic Gospels meant for the healing and deliverance performed by Jesus to serve as a pattern for subsequent mission practice. He prepared his disciples

---

71. Steinhaus, 24.
72. Steinhaus, 26.

for this kind of ministry in the world, to cast out demons, and to heal every disease and affliction (Matt 10:1; Mark 3:14–15; Luke 9:1–2).[73] Pentecostals believe that authority over demons and deliverance of the oppressed was not limited to the twelve disciples of Christ but was passed down from the seventy (Luke 10:1–20) to modern-day missionaries.[74] They believe the Holy Spirit has been poured upon God's new covenant people of this age, anointing and empowering them to proclaim the good news of the kingdom of God, to proclaim liberty to the captives and the oppressed (Luke 4:18), and to enable sight to those who are blinded by the god of this age (2 Cor 4:4). Pentecostals reference the extraordinary miracles and healing that took place in Paul's ministry through the power of the Holy Spirit (Acts 19:11).[75] Pentecostals view Satan as a strong man against people, but believe he can be overcome by the Holy Spirit: "But no one can enter a strong man's house and plunder his goods unless he first binds the strong man. Then indeed he may plunder his goods" (Matt 12:29; Mark 3:27; Luke 11:22).[76] Folk Muslims face similar oppressive situations, and the Holy Spirit's power within the mission of the kingdom of God is available to folk Muslims who turn to Jesus.[77]

The Power of Lifestyle and Character

Michael W. Goheen observes that mission is the "participation of God's people in God's mission to renew the whole creation and the whole lives of all its peoples and cultures."[78] The Holy Spirit is the agent of that renewed life and character that reflects God's kingdom principles. "God's mission involves God's people living in God's way in the sight of the nations"[79] with the implication that Christian living attracts the world to Christ. It means living a remarkable life as a countercultural community, living publicly in a way that reflects God's character in Christ.[80] For example, in Antioch, the disciples

---

73. Arnold, "Kingdom, Miracles," 169.
74. Arnold, 169.
75. Arnold, 169.
76. Arnold, 171.
77. Arnold, 169.
78. Goheen, *Introducing Christian Mission Today*, 117.
79. Wright, *Mission of God's People*, 22–23.
80. Peskett and Ramachandra, *Message of Mission*, 123, cited in Goheen, *Light to the Nations*, 25.

were called Christians because they abandoned their former ways and became followers of Christ's way (Acts 11:26).[81] Life without the Holy Spirit is a carnal or worldly life (Gal 5:16) that drives people away from Christ instead of bringing them closer. Many moral failures can occur when missionaries are not filled with the Holy Spirit; they can fall prey to worldly temptations, including greed, pride, and sexual sin. Wolfgang Vondey points out that the Holy Spirit's baptism as evidenced on the day of Pentecost is an experience necessary for an effective Christian life and the transformation of a believer's character.[82]

Wherever folk Muslims are, their presence is visible through their practices, the call for prayer, and the sound of the minaret. Azumah observes that in Africa, Muslims "eat" Islam daily, because by default, they have monopolized the meat industry and ritually slaughter the animals in line with the Qur'an. Thus, "a visible and a public Christian presence in a Muslim neighborhood is vital as a witness to Muslims."[83] Jesus used leaven, light, salt, and a city on a hill to describe his followers (Matt 5:14–16). Paul states, "You yourselves are our letter, written on our hearts, known and read by everyone" (2 Cor 3:2 NIV). A Christlike lifestyle is crucial to sharing the gospel to Muslims, because in some contexts, Muslims are warned never to touch the Bible or read it because it is corrupt. Therefore, it is crucial for Christians to reach out to Muslims by visibly living lives congruent with the gospel. Christians can demonstrate to folk Muslims that they are able to live exemplary lives because of Jesus.

The Power of Oral Word Proclamation

Shenk suggests that the first word in the Qur'an is the command "recite," so the very meaning of the Qur'an is "recite." Muslims believe that the Qur'an is a recitation of the revelation that God sent through Muhammad (Qur'an 13:39). The implication of this is that Muslims will be more attracted by oral proclamation, since the Qur'an was intended for recitation. Based on this awareness, Christians can present the gospel to Muslims. The word of God itself is powerful enough through hearing to bring faith (Rom 10:17),

---

81. Peterson, *Apostles*, 356.
82. Vondey, *Pentecostal Theology*, 84.
83. Azumah, "Christian Witness," 14.

transformation, and conviction into the heart of listeners regardless of their religious background. This is because, unlike the Qur'an, the Bible is not just a book but God incarnate. "For the word of God is living and active, sharper than any two-edged sword, piercing to the division of soul and of spirit, of joints and of marrow, and discerning the thoughts and intentions of the heart" (Heb 4:12). Paul also expresses confidence that the gospel itself is the power of God to transform and save: "For I am not ashamed of the gospel, for it is the power of God for salvation to everyone who believes, to the Jew first and also to the Greek" (Rom 1:16). Based on the power of God foretold in the prophets (Rom 1:2), Paul challenged the philosophies, religious leaders, and religions of his time that vied for attention. The power here implies the intrinsic efficacy of the gospel, which is able to provide solutions to humanity's deepest needs.[84] Thus, faithful proclamation of the word of God can bring about faith in Muslims.

Dudley Woodberry has also noted that oral communication strategies, such as chronological Bible storytelling, dramatized audio of Bible stories or video clips through mobile phones, and charting, are workable strategies in most Muslim communities.[85] Muslim communities in Ghana possess a mostly oral culture. In Ghana, open-air rallies and public crusades are permitted by the government, so Christians who want to engage folk Muslims can launch crusades or rallies close to Muslim communities and proclaim the gospel through speakers. In Muslim-dominated areas in Ghana, such as Nima and Madina, former Muslims often testify of being converted to Christianity through open-air crusades or rallies where the gospel message was proclaimed in public and an altar call was made. The Jesus Film projected in a local dialect has also proven effective. Converts later sneak to nearby churches and are gradually integrated into the Christian community. It is, however, important to respect the Muslim community leaders by giving them notice of the rally or crusade and even inviting them to the program. Due to the community life in Ghana and the good relationship between Christians and Muslims in Ghana, one can always find Muslims standing from afar to listen to messages. One thing to note during these evangelism events is that the choice of

---

84. Harrison and Hagner, "Romans," 41–42.
85. Woodberry, *From Seed to Fruit*, 30.

terms is very important.[86] Since Muslims hold Muhammad in high esteem, no derogatory remarks are to be made about the Qur'an or Muhammad.

It is popularly observed in Ghana that most people dance to gospel music and enjoy music during some festivals and public events. Music is a core part of Africans' culture; therefore, gospel music strategically composed with the gospel message can attract Ghanaian folk Muslims, especially the Sufi, to Christ. Even though music and the playing of musical instruments is banned in mosques, you can hear Muslims outside the mosque singing in praise of Allah.[87] Muslims attend Christian funerals and some festivals where gospel music forms a significant part of the ceremony, so this shared love of music is an added advantage to Christian-Muslim engagement.

The Grace, Love, and Truth of Jesus to Folk Muslims

Another way folk Muslims in Ghana can be reached is through the message of God's grace. Although folk Muslims often refer to Muhammad as the most gracious, deliverance for Muslims is based on works and merit, which explains their strict adherence to the pillars of Islam as devotional duties. The grace in Christianity by simply trusting Jesus can appeal to folk Muslims if they become aware that they cannot be delivered through endless works. Jesus demonstrated his love and grace toward the world that "while we were enemies" (Rom 5:10), he died for us. After what he suffered from his enemies on the cross, he said, "Father, forgive them, for they do not know what they are doing" (Luke 23:34 NIV). Through the cross, Christians believe Jesus offers salvation that cannot be earned by human works and is only received by grace through faith in Christ (Eph 2:8–9) to all who believe, as demonstrated toward the criminal crucified at Christ's right hand (Luke 23:39–43). Jesus proclaimed peace and love and showed grace, even to the point of freeing Judas who betrayed him and all who opposed him (Matt 5:44; Luke 23:34). According to the Scriptures, Christ died for humanity's sins, was buried, and, on the third day, resurrected (1 Cor 15:3–4).

The Qur'an admonishes Muslims that "there shall be no compulsion in acceptance of the religion" (2:256).[88] Jesus revealed himself as "the way, and

---

86. Kure, "Evangelism among Muslims," 18.
87. Parshall, *New Paths*, 207.
88. Shenk, *Journeys*, 159.

the truth, and the life" (John 14:6) but never forced people to believe in him. The decision for or against faith is left to individuals. In contrast, Qur'an 8:39 encourages Muslims to fight non-Muslim believers until there is no more *fitnah* (disbelief). The Prophet Muhammad said he was sent with the sword so that Allah alone might be worshiped. He boasted that "I have been made victorious by terror."[89] In Islam, God only extends mercy to people who first make a step to God in repentance.[90]

The gospel of Jesus is grace-centered, so Christians must appeal to Muslims based on Jesus's grace. Jesus, as the Messiah, seeks for the sinner and sacrificed his life for the sinner's redemption (Matt 9:11, 13). Jesus conquered the world through the cross, not by sword or hatred, and is known as the "Prince of Peace" (Isa 9:6). He never encouraged his followers to kill people who disbelieve his message. Thus, the love and grace of Jesus, in light of Qur'an 2:256, can be an effective tool to attract Muslims to Christ. Jesus is the Word made flesh who lived among men "full of grace and truth" (John 1:14), so he calls all believers to bear witness about him in grace. "Be completely humble and gentle; be patient, bearing with one another in love" (Eph 4:2 NIV); "Live a life filled with love" (Eph 5:2a NLT).[91]

Jeff Liverman asserts that the commitment to work in the local language and culture are very essential to engaging Muslims effectively.[92] Folk Muslims must be reached in their own cultural practices, and what they identify with is a culture of fear. They cry, "Who shall roll away the fear of death and dangers of everyday life?" Folk Muslims, unlike orthodox Ghanaian Muslims, have need of salvation from fear instead of from sin.[93] Sin means little to folk Muslims, so the emphasis must be on the grace of God, the love of God, and the power of God to save from fear and danger. Forgiveness, salvation, and everlasting life must be presented as a free gift of God's grace to those who believe in Jesus. The emphasis must be placed on Jesus who gives grace and who saves from fear and death itself because of his demonstration of power over death through the resurrection.

---

89. Shin, *Dividing Worldviews*, 92.
90. Shenk, *Journeys*, 159.
91. Ripken, "Grace and Truth," 370.
92. Liverman, "Unplowed Ground," 15.
93. Woodberry, "Refurbished Chair," in Dudley, Van Engen, and Elliston, *Missiological Education*, 194.

I posit that removing the gap of ignorance between Christians and Muslims will enable Christians to share the gospel with folk Muslims sympathetically and lovingly. Instead of looking at Muslims as brutal and violent people, knowledge about the Qur'an and a peaceful approach to engaging Muslims will yield a positive result. By using the Qur'an in engagement, I have experienced a paradigm shift in relationship with Muslims. During a doctoral seminar in Islamic studies at Torch Trinity Graduate University, I acquired knowledge that was tested in relationship with my brother-in-law, a folk Muslim called Rama (pseudonym). Rama and my sister were deeply in love and married without first considering their religious differences. Pauline (pseudonym) was a Christian but agreed to marry Rama, a Muslim, because she felt she had waited for a partner and found a sign of a good and loving partner in Rama. Rama, from the beginning, ignored his religious stance as a Muslim and went ahead to ask Pauline's hand in marriage. Pauline had in mind to convert her husband to Christianity, but no sooner had they gotten married than Rama and his parents insisted that Pauline follow her husband into Islam. In a quest for peace, she accepted that after the marriage, she would bring her husband to Christ. Therefore, she went through the Islamic marriage rituals and confessed to the Shahada, but later broke faith with Islam and continued her Christian journey. She tried several times to win Rama, but unfortunately, he did not give in. As a result, there was a communication breakdown and separation for some years. The entire family was divided and bitter as a result of the separation.

My doctoral studies offered an opportunity to engage my brother-in-law with the gospel by using the Qur'an over a telephone conversation. After a simple exchange of greetings, I asked permission to share a portion of scripture from the Qur'an with him. Since it was the Qur'an and not the Bible, he consented. Quoting from Qur'an 2:256, I pointed out to him that the Qur'an admonishes Muslims that "there shall be no compulsion in acceptance of the religion," which implies he must not abandon Pauline because of her religion. Although she follows Isa (Jesus), the Qur'an testifies that Jesus is the Messiah, the good news (3:45). I suggested that if he recognizes Isa's authority in the Qur'an, then he must reconcile with his wife and speak to her according to what is said in Qur'an 16:125: "Invite all to the way of thy Lord with wisdom and beautiful preaching and argue with them in ways that are best and most gracious: For thy Lord knoweth best, who have strayed from His path and who receive guidance."⁹⁴ Even though the discussion with Rama did not make him accept Jesus, he called his wife the following day and has since renewed communication with her. In this way, appealing to Muslims based on their scriptures serves as a bridge to share the gospel with Muslims.

Sharing the gospel with folk Muslims is a call to be a witness and not an advocate or a judge. When engaging folk Muslims, care must be taken not to stand in judgment of their beliefs and practices or condemnation of their Prophet Muhammad. The Bible clearly states the role of the believer in his engagement with outsiders, including folk Muslims: "You will receive power when the Holy Spirit comes on you; and you will be my witnesses in Jerusalem, and in all Judea and Samaria, and to the ends of the earth" (Acts 1:8 NIV). The role of the believer is to testify of what has been seen, felt, heard, and touched concerning Christ, a simple witness about his death, resurrection, and ascension. John Azumah describes this through a court room illustration:

> In a courtroom, some of the principal characters include the judge, advocates/lawyers, witnesses and, of course, the accused and accuser. The duty of the advocates or lawyers is to argue the cases in order to seek conviction or acquittal, the witnesses are simply called upon to testify to what they have seen, heard, or experienced while the judge has the task of passing judgment as well as the sentence.⁹⁵

God is the judge, the Holy Spirit is the advocate, and the believer is called upon to act as a witness (John 14:26; Acts 1:8). In sharing the gospel with folk Muslims, the core truth must be presented and the conviction left to the Holy Spirit.

Based on his experience with African Muslims, Samuel Ajayi Crowther remarked, "After many years' experience I have found that the Bible, the sword of the Spirit, must fight its own battle, by the guidance of the Holy Spirit . . . The average African Christian knew the Bible better than the average African Muslim knew the Qur'an because of the translatability of the

---

94. Aning and Abdallah, "Islamic Radicalization," 157.
95. Azumah, "Christian Witness," 5–21.

Bible."⁹⁶ Engaging Muslims through polemical debate is like playing with a football team on their own playing ground. They are very familiar with the terrain and the corners from where they can easily score a goal effortlessly. Crowther recalls his own experience:

> As a fervent young evangelist, keeping school in a village where there were numbers of Muslim receptives, Crowther found a boy wearing a charm. Crowther cut it off, telling the boy to take it home, as such superstitions were not permitted in a Christian school. This brought the father with a wrathful complaint. Crowther offered to answer him in front of the Muslim elders, and duly appeared with his Bible and Sale's Koran. At the end of his long life, he could still recall the humiliation of that encounter. All his well-marshalled arguments were useless. For Muslims, there was only one argument: God did not have a son.⁹⁷

Like Crowther, several Christian leaders today engage Muslims in debates that lead to polemical confrontations, which result in lost opportunities to engage Muslims. Polemical approaches cannot produce the desired result of transformation in folk Muslims and historically have not done so. According to Andrew F. Walls, in Charles Wesley's mind "Muhammad was above all the great imposter, or, in Charles Wesley's phrase, 'the Arab thief, as Satan bold' whose doctrine should be chased back to hell."⁹⁸ Such antagonistic expressions must be avoided at all cost. Argument and criticism of Muhammad based on his weaknesses only lead to violent opposition. It is like a young man in love with a beautiful lady. When he first approaches the lady, all he can tell her are the bad things about her parents and family and proposes she to come to him for a better life and security. No lady would agree to a man who accuses her parents to her face. In a like manner, no Muslim will be pleased to follow a Christian who accuses Muhammad.⁹⁹ Raymond Lull (ca. 1235–1316)

---

96. Crowther, "Experiences with Heathens," 28, quoted in Walls, *Cross-Cultural Process*, 162.
97. Crowther, 143.
98. Osborn, "For the Turks," 137, quoted in Walls, *Cross-Cultural Process*, 137.
99. Azumah, "Historical Survey of Islam."

poetically wrote, "interreligious discourse, rather than military crusades, was the high road to evangelization of persons of other faiths."[100]

In his mature years as a missionary in Niger, Crowther sought common ground at the nexus of the Qur'an and the Bible to engage Muslims through loving and friendly relationships. He approached Muslims by presenting Jesus as a great prophet, Jesus's miraculous birth, and Gabriel as the messenger of God – whom Muslims believe cannot make a mistake. Qur'an 3:42–47 and 19:16–21 confirm Gabriel's announcement of the miraculous birth of Jesus. The Jesus whose birth Gabriel announced proclaimed himself to be the "way, the truth and the life" and commanded his followers to teach about him to all nations (Matt 28; John 14). Instead of using the title Son of God which Muslims reject, the Son of Man before whom "all nations shall assemble" can appeal to Muslims (Matt 25; Luke 12:39).[101]

In such ways, the gospel can be shared with folk Muslims on the basis of the full conviction of the core Christian message without diluting or hiding any element. It must be presented just as it is with grace, love, respect, humility, and patience, as it is said, "Always be prepared to give an answer to everyone who asks you to give the reason for the hope that you have. But do this with gentleness and respect" (1 Pet 3:15 NIV). Woodberry has observed,

> Our approach must start with what phenomenologists of religions call empathy – trying to enter into the religious experience of Muslims. This means, performing mental ablutions to cleanse away preconceived ideas and sitting at the feet of Muslims to learn from both scholars and common people.[102]

Nik Ripken has noted that more Muslims are eager to give their ears to these discussions than is generally supposed. Moreover, the Qur'an itself encourages openness of Muslims to Christians.[103] As mentioned earlier in chapter 2, Ghanaian folk Muslims first see themselves as Ghanaian and are

---

100. Lull, "Historical Paradigms of Mission," 25, quoted in Park, "MI 9300."

101. Crowther, "Experiences with Heathens," cited in Walls, *Cross-Cultural Process*, 143–44.

102. Woodberry, "Refurbished Chair" in Dudley, Van Engen, and Elliston, *Missiological Education*, 193.

103. Ripken, "Grace and Truth," in Woodberry, *From Seed to Fruit*, 369.

thus able to open up in nonconfrontational conversations on the basis of a Ghanaian brotherhood.

Folk Muslims in the Ghanaian context generally lack in-depth scriptural knowledge of their own faith, so a patient discursive approach or a gracious meeting for understanding will help them to trust in the Christian gospel of grace. Richard D. Love has noted that the following list of scriptures prove effective in engaging folk Muslims:

> The Son of God appeared for this purpose, that He might destroy the works of the Devil (1 Jn. 3:8); You know of Jesus of Nazareth, how God anointed Him with the Holy Spirit and with power, and how He went about doing good and healing all who were oppressed by the devil; for God was with Him (Acts 10:38); For He delivered us from the domain of darkness, and transferred us to the kingdom of His beloved Son, in whom we have redemption, the forgiveness of sins (Col. 1:12–14); When he had disarmed the rulers and authorities, he made a public display of them, having triumphed over them through him (Col. 2:15); Since then the children share in flesh and blood, He Himself likewise also partook of the same, that through death He might render powerless him who had the power of death, that is, the devil (Heb. 2:14). He raised Him from the dead, and seated Him at his right hand in the heavenly places, far above all rule and authority and power and dominion, and every name that is named, not only in this age, but also in the one to come. And He put all things in subjection under His feet (Eph. 1:20–22); Through the resurrection of Jesus Christ, who is at the right hand of God, having gone into heaven, after angels and authorities and powers had been subjected to Him (1 Pet. 3:21–22).[104]

Folk Muslims are established in many practices induced by fear, and they have no assurance of their destiny. By works and faithfulness, they hope Muhammad will grant them entrance to paradise. However, the Prophet himself was not sure of his eternal destiny when giving counsel on the destiny of man (Qur'an 5:266). In contrast, Jesus spoke on eternal life, salvation, and

---

104. Love, "Church Planting Muslims," 89.

human destiny with a precise assurance (Luke 23:42–43; John 5:24; 10:28); he knew exactly where he came from, where he was going, and the destiny of those who believe in him (John 14:2–3; 16:5). Such assurance can be a persuasive tool when engaging Muslims with the gospel. However, the engagement must always be in love and with great wisdom as the Scriptures have instructed. "Conduct yourselves with wisdom toward outsiders, making the most of the opportunity" (Col 4:5 NASB). Apostle Paul states, "We proclaim Him, admonishing every person and teaching every person with all wisdom, so that we may present every person complete in Christ" (Col 1:28 NASB), and James describes the practical aspect of this approach as "the wisdom that comes from heaven is first of all pure; then peace-loving, considerate, submissive, full of mercy and good fruit, impartial, and sincere. Peacemakers who sow in peace reap a harvest of righteousness" (Jas 3:17–18 NIV).[105]

Pentecostals and the Existential Needs of Folk Islam

Evangelism is not exclusively the "action of verbal communication in which the name of Jesus is central"; it is inseparable from social action and is most effective when joined with social action. The incarnation of Jesus, the Word made flesh, is the gospel. Deeds without the word is pointless, and the word without deeds results in empty rituals and an ineffective message.[106] Effective evangelism requires proclamation and practical demonstration. David Bosch rightly notes that evangelism does not only involve a verbal proclamation of Jesus but also "a deliberate proclamation of the gospel through word and deeds calling people to repentance and faith in Jesus."[107]

Muslim evangelism is the proclamation of the good news of Jesus to Muslims through practical, social actions rooted in Christ's love to win Muslims into the loving community of Christ. The aim is to lead Muslims to a new faith in Christ that is accompanied by changes in behavior and worldview. One of the factors that led to the spread of Islam in Ghana was the early Muslims' attention paid to the economic circumstances of people

---

105. Ripken, "Grace and Truth," in Woodberry, *From Seed to Fruit*, 375.

106. Newbigin, "Cross-Currents," 149, cited in Kandiah, "Lesslie Newbigin's Contribution," 53.

107. Bosch, "Evangelism," 43–63, cited in Kandiah, "Lesslie Newbigin's Contribution," 54.

in northern Ghana. Likewise, winning Muslims to Christianity in Ghana will be most effective with the church's deliberate efforts to provide for Muslims' basic needs, most of whom already live in deplorable conditions.

Sharing the gospel with folk Muslims must be supported by actions, caring deeds that turn estranged relations into ordinary encounters and present golden opportunities to share the gospel. References for the care for human needs run throughout the Bible (Matt 5–7; Luke 4:16–21; Acts 2:44–47; Jas 2:14–26),[108] proving that there is no effective gospel message without caring for needs and serving others. Jesus came "to serve and not to be served" (Mark 10:45). Thus, in sharing the gospel with folk Muslims, Christians must open their eyes to see numerous opportunities for service to Muslims. For Ghanaian Pentecostals, service to folk Muslims may include the following: helping to dig the grave during funerals, donating to bereaved families, paying tuition for the son or the daughter of a folk Muslim in the neighborhood, offering hospitality to the *kayaye* (porters of loads who migrate from north Ghana to the urban south), and responding to the call of Jesus to feed the hungry, visit the prisoners, provide water to the thirsty and clothes to the less privileged, and care for the sick (Matt 25:34–40).

Christians can close the gap between themselves and Muslims through relationship building and must avoid cultural exclusivism. The culture of hatred, abusive language, and vain theological disputes must be replaced with loving words and patience. Christians and Muslims share some common identities in Ghana. For this reason, Ghanaian Christians can adopt a communal lifestyle that builds stronger relationships during shared celebrations, such as ordinations, weddings, funerals, naming ceremonies, and political rallies, and they can extend a helping hand during Muslim religious celebrations, such as Eid al-Fitr and Eid al-Adha.

Summary

Engaging Muslims requires an attitude change toward understanding, respect, and empathetic consideration when using truth to build bridges between Muslims' understanding and the biblical understanding of the birth of Jesus, his nature and sonship, his crucifixion and death, and his return. Moreover,

---

108. Reisacher, *Joyful Witness*, 116.

the Holy Spirit constitutes Pentecostals' core element in gospel proclamation. Notably, Jesus as an ancestor is a gateway to share the gospel with Ghanaian folk Muslims in partnership with grace and love. The exemplary lifestyle of the witness is crucial to recommend the gospel to folk Muslims. The gospel can be effectively shared with folk Muslims through the discovery and application of Pentecostalism to the existential needs of folk Muslims, including the assurance of salvation. Theology or truth encounters and discovering and providing for folk Muslims' existential needs are starting points when engaging folk Muslims with the gospel. However, because Ghanaian folk Muslims are power-oriented people, they need more than the above to be receptive to the gospel.

CHAPTER 5

Pentecostals' Engagement with Folk Muslims in Ghana

Power Encounters and the Experiential Needs of Folk Muslims

The folk Muslim worldview is soaked in the consciousness of the spiritual world and powers of darkness. There is a constant struggle against beings, such as "*qarina, jinn, dews, als,* [and] *pari*" that are believed to negatively influence Muslims. To win folk Muslims to Christ, Christians must go beyond truth encounters in the proclamation of the gospel to practical power encounters through the manifestation of the works of the Holy Spirit.[1] In response to folk Muslims' quest for power to counteract that of numerous spirit beings, Jesus or Isa al-Masih (Jesus the Messiah) must be presented as the worker of miracles and the giver of the Holy Spirit who is able to address all their spiritual needs, including needs for healing. Jesus freed myriads of people from sickness, demons, and disorders, and these acts should be demonstrated to bring conviction to folk Muslims. Over the years, Muslims have testified of how God's miraculous intervention in human affairs led them to surrender their lives to follow Jesus. God's intervention in such cases usually took the form of sovereign acts, such as visions, spiritual dreams, angelic visitations, and answered prayer. At other times, followers of Jesus practically demonstrated God's power by healing the sick, casting out demons, and restoring the

---

1. Nuekpe, "Muslim Christian Encounter," 213.

physically challenged under Jesus's authority (Luke 9:1–2; 10:17–19).² Thus, Christ-centered or Jesus-centered power encounters can be an effective way of sharing the gospel with folk Muslims within the Ghanaian context, and this falls within the domain of Pentecostalism in Ghana.

The Qur'an portrays Jesus as a great healer who was able to raise even the dead (3:43–49; 5:109–110). Musk observes,

> The biblical answer to the acknowledged reality of evil spirits, including jinn, is that cure from their oppression and possession of humans is available. Such cure comes, not by magical means, nor by formulas of exorcism, but by the word of power which Jesus speaks, and which he entrusts to his disciples. It is a power derived from the victory of his death on a cross.³

With the impact of folk Islam in Ghana, evangelism must be backed by power demonstrations, as was the case after the event of Pentecost (Acts 2). Paul states that "our gospel came to you not simply with words, but also with power, with the Holy Spirit, and deep conviction" (1 Thess 1:5 NIV). Edward Rommen asserts that the Great Commission has a "proclaimed" part and a "heal[ing]" part as referenced in the Bible: "and he sent them out to proclaim the kingdom of God and to heal" (Luke 9:2 NIV).⁴ Muslims respect Jesus and are aware of his power to heal and create. Since Ghanaian folk Muslims are "power-oriented people,"⁵ they need proof of power to be won to Christ. Emphasis on the miracles of Jesus, and the manifestation of the gifts of the Holy Spirit will draw their attention and curiosity.

Understanding Power Encounters

Power encounters have occurred in the lives of the people of God in carrying out God's mission from the Old Testament to the New Testament. According to Kraft, the term power encounter was first coined by missiologist Alan Tippet, who had spent two decades as a missionary to Fiji. Tippet defined power encounters as events that often occurred among the people of Fiji;

---

2. Kim, Travis, and Travis, "Relevant Responses," in Woodberry, *From Seed to Fruit*, 245.
3. Musk, *Unseen Faces*, 44.
4. Rommen, *Spiritual Power and Missions*, 94.
5. Kraft, *Power Encounter*, 2.

when a convert fled from traditional spiritual powers to seek refuge in the Christian God, the power of God was victorious over the traditional powers.[6] Brand Howard defines power encounters as signs, wonders, miracles, and spiritual warfare, which is "the confrontation which takes place between a believer as God's agent on earth and the forces of demonic darkness."[7] Both view power encounters as the engagement of a spiritual battle between the powers of darkness and the power of God for the purpose of showing God's supremacy or authority, which is manifested through signs, wonders, and varied miracles. Herbert asserts that no single word can fully explain power encounters because they are the supernatural demonstration of God's power in an inexhaustible way.[8] They are proof of God's divine revelation, "both the official and authoritative seal of God," specially designed by the Creator to manifest his supremacy over all nature and all his creation, as well as to bear witnesses to the kingdom of God[9] and God's redemption.

A recollection of such encounters in the biblical story are the power engagements between Moses and Pharaoh (Exod 7–12) and between Elijah and the prophets of Baal (1 Kgs 18). The term power encounter in this work implies all demonstrations of God's power through the gifts of the Holy Spirit (1 Cor 12:8–11) "which manifest in healing, deliverance, exorcism, signs and wonders, and miraculous occurrences that defy natural laws."[10]

The prototype of New Testament "very strong supernatural orientation" Christianity with the demonstration of power, prophecy, healing, and exorcism generally leads to conversion and the rapid growth of Christianity, especially in Latin America and Africa.[11] Michael Pocock suggests that since Lausanne 1974, several missionaries became conscious of the fact that their lack of spiritual power to encounter the demonic world was the main factor limiting world evangelization.[12] Convinced of the fact that "the god of this age has blinded the minds of unbelievers so that they cannot see the light of the gospel of the glory of Christ" (2 Cor 4:4 HSBC), they needed the

---

6. Kraft, 1.
7. Brant, "Power Encounter," 187.
8. Lockyer, *All Miracles*, 15.
9. Lockyer, 15.
10. Nuekpe, "Muslim Christian Encounter," 213.
11. Pocock, *Changing Face*, 192.
12. Pocock, 184.

demonstration of the power of the gospel as revealed in the Scriptures. "Our gospel came to you not simply with words, but also with power, with the Holy Spirit and deep conviction" (1 Thess 1:5 NIV).[13] Thus, many missionaries and Christian workers are challenged to demonstrate power encounters to overcome satanic resistance to missions, which Pocock refers to as "binding the strong man" or "spiritual warfare."[14] Many mission thinkers[15] believe that power encounters are the center of "missiological strategy" for effective proclamation and conversion, and there is no exception when Pentecostals share the gospel with folk Muslims in Ghana.

Folk Muslims believe in the existence of a spiritual world in which dark powers are constantly seeking to destroy human beings and determining the course of events unless appeased or influenced by means of magical powers and incantations.[16] The need to engage in power encounters in missions has been a major concern for Pentecostal and charismatic mission-minded Christians all over the world. Larbi observes that the first revivalist who stepped on the soil of the Gold Coast was Liberian evangelist William Wade Harris (c. 1860–1929) whose missionary work was accompanied by signs and wonders. Wade brought the concept of a High God near to the people of Ghana through power encounters. He preached the gospel for two years and was said to have won one hundred twenty thousand converts. In contrast, Philip Quacoe (1741–1816), a British trained missionary who solely depended on the proclamation of Western theology, won only fifty-two people within the same culture after five years of missionary work. The key to Harris's success where Western missionaries had failed was his demonstration of power in missions.[17]

It is worth noting that even non-Pentecostal scholars such as Roland Anderson, an Anglican, call attention to the role of the Spirit's power and the need to do mission with both Pauline theology and the New Testament pattern of demonstrating power.[18] Peter Wagner, although not a Pentecostal, identified in his research on church growth that power encounters are the

---

13. Pocock, 185–86.
14. Pocock, 184.
15. Especially Pentecostal mission thinkers in the Southern Hemisphere.
16. Pocock, *Changing Face*, 187.
17. Larbi, *Pentecostalism*, 55.
18. Pocock, *Changing Face*, 186.

reason that Pentecostal movements are effectively and rapidly growing in missions.[19] As practical experience can change theology, missions give rise to theology. Folk Muslims may have a thousand reasons for not converting to Christianity for theological reasons, but when they are confronted with the power of the gospel, a paradigm shift occurs in thinking and action. The Christian life is a life involving power encounters between God and the hosts of demonic powers that seek to destroy the mission of God.[20] Power encounters become a hinge on which effective evangelism swings, especially in mission among power-inclined societies and religious groups like folk Muslims.

Power Encounters in the Former Scriptures

A large number of Muslims desire to read the Bible and to study about Jesus, especially because the Qur'an commends portions of the Bible – the Torah and the Injil – and holds the biblical prophets and Jesus in high regard.[21] Muslims' acceptance of the Former scriptures, the Old Testament, is one bridge by which the gospel can be shared with folk Muslims. Narratives of power encounters in the Former scriptures will appeal to folk Muslims.

The Qur'an admonishes Muslims to pay attention to the scriptures in at least four texts. It recommends the *Suhuf*, an extra-biblical book that Muslims believe was revealed through Abraham; the *Taurat*, which is the Torah of Moses; the *Zabur*, which are the Psalms of David; and the Injil transmitted through Jesus the Messiah.[22] Muslims believe that these are scriptures revealed by God: the Qur'an emphasizes that these scriptures operate as "guidance and light" to all mankind (5:44–47),[23] and says of the Taurat that "the writing of Moses is the criterion of truth" (10:64; 21:48).[24] The Qur'an also asserts that Christians are instructed not to hide the content of these books from Muslims: "Allah laid a charge on those who had received the Scripture: Ye are to expound it to mankind and not to hide it" (3:187).[25] Additionally, the

---

19. Pocock, 186.
20. Pocock, 189.
21. Gray and Gray, "Imperishable Seed," in Woodberry, *From Seed to Fruit*, 26.
22. Shenk, *Journeys*, 105.
23. Shenk, 107.
24. Shenk, 107.
25. Shenk, 105.

Qur'an commands all Muslims, and even Muhammad himself, to refer to the people of the Book if they are in doubt concerning what Allah has revealed to them (Qur'an 10:94).[26] These charges to Muslims present an opportunity to Christians to engage Muslims with the biblical scriptures, beginning first with the Torah, the Psalms, and the four Gospels. Power encounters in the Old Testament, therefore, can be used as a response to folk Muslims' quest for power. Though Muslims affirm the Torah, Prophets, and the Psalms, these texts can be a launching pad to speaking on power encounters in the entire Old Testament with emphasis that the Torah, the Prophets, and the Psalms refer to the entire message about Jesus (Luke 24:44).

The record of God's engagement in history through the Bible shows God's intention behind power encounters. God uses power encounters to reveal his truth and to inspire the loyalty and obedience of his people (Exod 3:1–12; Matt 20:29–34). Marguerite G. Kraft suggests that there is "a commitment encounter" whereby the people of God struggle to choose loyalty between God or foreign gods (Josh 24:14–15) and a "truth encounter" where God uses power encounters to distinguish his truth (Exod 3:1–12) in the midst of falsehood.[27] They affirm God's deity and the human vessel God uses to draw human beings to himself (Exod 4:5, 31; 10:2; Deut 4:34–35; 1 Kgs 17:24; 18:36). Likewise, power encounters can lead folk Muslims to commit to Jesus, and by the same means their eyes will be opened to encounter the biblical truth about Jesus.

Power encounters in the Old Testament took the form of God's compelling hand, a strong hand that obliged the enemy to accept God's reign and dominion of the world and his people (Exod 3:19–20; 6:1). Marguerite Kraft asserts that God achieved his deliverance of Israel from Egypt through power encounters (Exod 7:8–14:31) and demonstrated his power to showcase his sovereignty over all powers and rulers. God's purpose statement in Exodus 7:5 says, "the Egyptians shall know that I am the LORD, when I stretch out my hand against Egypt and bring out the people of Israel from among them."[28] Herbert Lockyer notes that the ten power encounters Moses demonstrated in Egypt (Exod 4:9; 7:14–24; Ps 78:44; 105:29) revealed a conflict between

---

26. Shenk, 105.
27. Kraft, *Understanding Spiritual Power*, 52.
28. Kraft, *Understanding Spiritual Power*, 55.

"the divine and the diabolical," proving God's power over the defiant powers of Egypt.[29]

Edwards Gross asserts that all the miracles and power encounters that follow Israel's redemption from slavery in Egypt was for the purpose of God's exaltation or glorification (Exod 9:16). The Torah/Taurat reveals that God called Israel out of the nations to be a distinct people, separated to showcase God before the eyes of other nations to see and glorify God. This responsibility included confronting paganism and abandoning idolatry (Exod 4:23; 19:3–6; Deut 4:5–8). In carrying out this responsibility effectively, they were engaged in power encounters with pagan nations and their gods who sought to destroy the promise plan of God (1 Sam 5). In 1 Kings 18:36, Elijah acknowledged miracles as the vindication of Jehovah's deity and his prophetic ministry,[30] and Jeremiah 32:20 states that these power encounters continued. Leading folk Muslims through this discovery will elicit faith in them to turn to Jesus.

Power Encounters in Jesus's Ministry

Miracles were an integral part of Jesus's earthly ministry ((Luke 7:18–23; John 9:1–12; Acts 10:38). Most often, people joined him and recognized him as the Savior after he overcame satanic powers. The power encounters of Jesus were proof that he was the perfect Elijah that was predicted (Matt 16:14; Mark 6:15; Luke 9:8). Jack Deere described the purpose of miracles in Jesus's earthly ministry as demonstrating the following:

> God is with Jesus (John 3:2); Jesus is from God (John 3:2; 9:32–33); God has sent Jesus (John 5:36); Jesus has authority on earth to forgive sins (Mark 2:10–11; Matt. 9:6–7; Luke 5:24–25); Jesus is approved by God (Acts 2:22); the Father is in Jesus and Jesus is in the Father (John 10:37–38; 14:11); in Jesus the kingdom of God has come (Matt. 12:28; Luke 11:20); and Jesus is the Messiah (Matt. 11:1–6; Luke 7:18–23) and the Son of God (Matt. 14:25–33).[31]

---

29. Lockyer, *All Miracles*, 48.
30. Gross, *Miracles, Demons*, 29.
31. Deere, *Surprised*, 103.

Mark L. Strauss asserts that Jesus was known by his exorcisms, which marked his ministry as "a spiritual assault on the rule of Satan" in all the Synoptic Gospels.[32] Jesus also taught on and affirmed the ministry of exorcism (Mark 3:22–27; 9:38–39; Luke 13:32).

Strauss points out that Jesus's power encounters with demons through exorcisms had a motif of revealing the presence and power of the kingdom of God.[33] In Capernaum Jesus encountered a demon possessed man (Mark 1:2–28; Luke 3:32–37). The exclamation of the demon possessed man revealed that it was not only one demon in the man but a host of demons. By casting them out, Jesus demonstrated the presence of the kingdom of God to destroy the kingdom of Satan: "But if it is by the Spirit of God that I cast out demons, then the kingdom of God has come upon you" (Matt 12:28). Jesus spoke of Satan as a strong man fighting to preserve his property while the power of God defeats Satan and claims back all those who are in Satan's "possession."[34] The exorcisms performed by Jesus are proof of God setting captives free (Luke 4:18–19) and fulfilling a Messianic prophecy (Isa 61:1–2).

> The Spirit of the Lord is upon me, because he has anointed me to proclaim good news to the poor. He has sent me to proclaim liberty to the captives and recovering of sight to the blind, to set at liberty those who are oppressed, to proclaim the year of the Lord's favor. (Luke 4:18–19)

Jesus also demonstrated the arrival of the kingdom of God and the power of God in healing the sick. Strauss demonstrates this motive in John the Baptist's question to Jesus (Matt 11:2–6; Luke 7:18–23) when the imprisoned John sends his own disciples to Jesus to find out if Jesus really is the "Coming One" and the Messiah. Jesus's response to John's inquiry emphasizes the significance of his healing:[35] "And he answered them, 'Go and tell John what you have seen and heard: the blind receive their sight, the lame walk, lepers are cleansed, and the deaf hear, the dead are raised up, the poor have good news preached to them'" (Luke 7:22, see also Matt 11:4–5).

---

32. Strauss, *Four Portraits*, 461.
33. Strauss, 461.
34. Strauss, 462.
35. Strauss, 462.

The healing miracles of Jesus point to the fulfillment of the Old Testament Scriptures that predicted God's salvation through Jesus the Messiah, who would come to defeat all evil and restore the fallen nature of humankind. Strauss notes that the healing miracles of Jesus point to the restoration of creation promised in the Old Testament, especially in Isaiah and other prophets (Isa 26:19; 29:18–19; Jer 30:17; Ezek 36:26–27; Joel 28). "Then the eyes of the blind shall be opened, and the ears of the deaf unstopped; then shall the lame man leap like a deer, and the tongue of the mute sing for joy. For waters break forth in the wilderness, and streams in the desert" (Isa 35:5–6). Healing miracles are conclusive evidence that the coming of Christ brought healing and life to humanity, just as the fall of Adam brought sickness and death to humanity.[36] This is the message and the demonstration folk Muslims need to turn to Christ.

Releasing Power Encounters through Prayer

Prayer is an important part of folk Muslims' devotional duty, and power encounters through the Holy Spirit are ignited through prayer and fasting. Ghanaian Muslims are attracted by prayer and fasting, which is part of their religious rituals (Qur'an 2:184). Since they revere Jesus and trust in prayer, Christians can use prayer to engage folk Muslims in evangelism. Dawn, afternoon, and evening prayers can be an effective tool to attract Muslims into the Christian faith, because that is the pattern Muslims follow. Jesus told his disciples in regard to exorcism, "This kind cannot be driven out by anything but prayer" (Mark 9:29 RSV). Through Christians' effective prayers, some Muslims are led to Christ after seeing Jesus in their dreams, and their hearts are receptive to the gospel. In such dreams, angels or Jesus himself appears to Muslims and directs them to surrender their lives to him.[37] However, care must be taken that these kinds of Pentecostal prayers be proclaimed in the name of Jesus and not "the Son of God," and the prayers should not mention the Trinity or words that provoke anger in Muslims, such as "our Lord and Savior."

---

36. Strauss, 462.
37. Musk, "Dreams and Ordinary Muslim," 168.

The prayers that address folk Muslims' needs can be split into three categories: breaking prayers, healing prayers, and deliverance prayers. Breaking prayers involve breaking specific spiritual bondage in the life of folk Muslims. Such bondage may include ancestral curses, barrenness, and other persistent predicaments believed to be caused by demons or spirit beings. During breaking prayers, folk Muslims renunciate and repent from specific acts that may have led to a spirit's permeation in their lives. Thus, portions of Scripture that deal with renunciation and repentance (Prov 28:13; Ezek 14:6; Dan 4:27; Acts 19:18–19; 2 Cor 4:2) may be used in praying with folk Muslims. This form of prayer responds to folk Muslims' occult practices, which involve:

> Invocation of spirit[s] (Deut. 18:9–14), generational bondages (Lam. 5:7; Psalm 79:8–9), ungodly "soul ties," judgement[s] of self or others (Matthew 7:1–2; James 4:11–12; Rom. 14:4), vows made outside God's will (Prov. 20:25; Matt. 5:33–37; Lev. 5:4–6), [and] curses (Psalm 62:4; 109:28; James 3:9–10, Prov. 26:2; Gal. 3:13; Romans 12:14).[38]

Healing prayer involves physical and emotional healing from painful life experiences that are buried in the memory of a folk Muslim. In prayer, the folk Muslim is assisted to pray and ask God to bring to remembrance the causes of the problem and then pour out his heart to God (Ps 38:9; 42:4; 64:1; 62:8; Lam 3:19–20; Matt 26:36–44) for inner healing and restoration. During Jesus's earthly ministry, he administered inner healing to people. For example, Kim, Travis, and Travis have noted that:

> He restored the guilt-ridden Peter (John 21:15–19), the woman at the well (John 4:4–42), the despised Zacchaeus (Luke 19:1–10), the grateful prostitute honoured by Christ (Luke 7:36–50), the rescued adulteress (John 8:2–11), the blind man emboldened by Christ (John 9:1–41), the ceremonially unclean hemorrhaging woman (Mark 5:25–34), and the man freed of myriads of demons (Luke 8:26–39).[39]

In deliverance prayer, demons are ordered to flee the territory or life of the folk Muslim by the authority of Jesus (Matt 10:8; 28:18; Eph 6:12). In

---

38. Kim, Travis, and Travis, "Relevant Responses," in Woodberry, *From Seed to Fruit*, 246.
39. Kim, Travis, and Travis, 246.

Ghana, folk Muslims engage in this type of exorcism prayer openly during their practices of healing.

Pentecostalism as Folk Christianity

Pentecostalism in Ghana, like folk Islam, is a form of folk Christianity in terms of its contextual flexibility, engagement with aspects of the African worldview, and adoption at the grass roots level without necessarily assuming a syncretistic form. Folk Christianity is a practical Christianity that blends orthodoxy with ethnic cultural elements to meet the spiritual needs of adherents. They do not necessarily adhere to principles of biblical hermeneutics but go beyond the texts and look to African cultural worldviews for acceptance and growth. Most folk Christian practices in Ghana have meshed with ATRs in ways that resonate with Ghanaian culture and spirituality. Cephas Omenyo has asserted that one cannot fully dislodge from his or her culture in order to completely embrace a foreign religion. This failure of cultural conversion arises when people convert to Christianity or Islam and yet their primal worldviews still persist.[40] For example, a Ghanaian may be a Christian but still conform to the traditional cultural understanding of death and being buried in one's homestead. When someone dies in Ghana, the place of burial is very significant. The person's house is not identical to his home. The home is the ancestral house, the ancestral land, the land of one's birth, or the town of the deceased. Thus, a Ghanaian may live in the city but must be transported to the ancestral homestead for burial, for the sake of ancestral identity. This idea of connecting with the ancestors and affirming one's kinship ties is practiced among Ghanaian Muslims and Christians, similar to the practice among folk Muslims in Kenya and most parts of west Africa.[41]

The above example portrays how the worldviews of the Ghanaian culture continuously pose questions that both Islam and Christianity attempt to answer in a way that resonates with the people, by mixing ATRs with qur'anic or biblical values. Omenyo is right to note that "the whole business of contextualization of the gospel in Africa is to a large extent, the ability of a Christian church or a movement to successfully reconcile Christianity with African

---

40. Omenyo, "Charismatic Churches in Ghana," 252–76.
41. Oseje, *African Traditions*, 16.

world-view, or using the Christian message to offer responses to the questions that are raised by the world-view of an African people."[42] In this respect, I describe Ghanaian Pentecostalism as a faith system of "folk Christianity." Similarly, William Price Payne has described Latino Pentecostalism and the Roman Catholic Charismatic Movement as "folk Christianity," because they are "indigenous faith systems that mesh with Hispanic cultures and give folk practitioners functionally equivalent alternatives to the syncretistic practices associated with popular religion," engaging "all aspects of the Latino worldview."[43]

Kwabena Darkwa Amanor has pointed out that the Ghanaian Pentecostal/charismatic faith and ATRs are soul-mates rather than antagonists who should consider each other as friends rather than foes.[44] I posit the Pentecostal faith system and ATRs are left and right hands joined to respond to the existential needs of Ghanaian Christians in the African milieu. They complement each other rather than compete for the souls of Ghanaians. Kwabena Asamoah-Gyadu has rightly noted that:

> In Africa, the Pentecostal religion is popular because it takes indigenous worldviews of mystical causalities seriously, democratizes access to the sacred, and purveys interventionist piety that helps ordinary people to cope with the fears and insecurities of life.[45]

In this sense, Pentecostalism and folk Islam share a commonality in their popularity and attempt to meet the existential needs of Africans by heavily leaning on African indigenous worldviews. Ghanaian Pentecostals' creative engagement with ATRs has led to the reconstruction of a new form of Christianity in Ghana that academic theologians do not theologically construct.[46] This form concerns a practical engagement of the Christian faith through the Ghanaian culture and its primal worldviews at a grassroots level. This new form of Christianity that responds to a grassroots people's existential needs is what I refer to as a form of "folk Christianity." Its practices do not

---

42. Omenyo, "Charismatic Churches in Ghana," 254.
43. Payne, "Folk Religion and Pentecostalism," 145.
44. Amanor, "Pentecostal and Charismatic Churches," 126.
45. Asamoah-Gyadu, "'Function to Function,'" 232.
46. Omenyo, "Charismatic Churches in Ghana," 267.

always follow the orthodoxy of Western ideology. Thus, the case in Ghana can be best understood as Christianity cooked in the pot of Ghanaian culture.

Pentecostal Practices of Healing and Deliverance

Just as folk Islam has some practices that do not conform to orthodoxy, Pentecostal spirituality in Ghana has endless variation in practices. Because of this peculiarity (the freedom from orthodoxy), Pentecostal Christians in Ghana can bridge the two faiths through practices like prayer, consultations, exorcisms, long fasts, and the nine gifts of the Holy Spirit (1 Cor 12:8–12). What folk Muslims need are solutions to everyday problems and not dogma and formulas. Because Pentecostal spirituality responds to folk Muslims' needs, it can be a means of reaching out to Muslims.

The Pentecostal concept of healing and deliverance emerged from the Spiritual Churches in Ghana. Their worship took the form of music and dancing, chanting, leaping, speaking in tongues, falling into trances (cf. Sufi Muslims), prophesying, interpreting dreams, and unveiling sources of chronic diseases. Prayer and spiritual direction and assistance use elements considered symbols of divine power, including anointing oil, holy water, cross-like amulets, ritual bathing, candles, powder, perfume, and other elements.[47]

Contemporary Pentecostals in Ghana, while they employ similar approaches to folk Muslims, consider these approaches to contextualize the Christian message in the Ghanaian cultural milieu. Some even use herbs, anointed cassettes, and porridge. Opoku Onyinah notes that emphasis on these approaches appear to be "a threat to the progress of Christianity" in Ghana.[48] However, I consider these religiomagical practices as a progressive preparation to the true message of the gospel, a point of entry into the Christian faith for the majority of people, who are less educated and whose first focus is a gospel that responds to everyday spiritual needs. Pentecostals, due to these kinds of religiomagical practices, can identify with folk Muslims and share the gospel with them. Once they are won over, discipleship can follow.

For folk Muslims in Ghana, healing and deliverance is the place where "the rubber meets the road." At the heart of all healing and deliverance practices

---

47. Onyinah, "Matthew Speaks," 125–26.
48. Onyinah, 30.

in Ghana – whether practiced within ATRs, Pentecostalism, or folk Islam – is *abisa* (the unveiling of the hidden), the concept of discovering causalities.[49] Within this context, the early revivalists that emerged in Ghana at the beginning of the twentieth century gained several converts. These prophetic figures – Sampson Oppong, John Swatson, Peter Anim, and Wade Harris, whose ministries are mentioned in chapter 1 – demonstrated the power of the gospel and drew many people to Christ.[50] They were concerned with practical salvation, much like folk Islam. Similarly, Pentecostals can meet the spiritual needs that folk Muslims experience and can, therefore, attract them. Even if a Christian does not have profound knowledge in Islamic literature and is unable to reason on the basis of the Scriptures, they can present the gospel through the power of the Holy Spirit (Acts 4:13).[51]

Most Ghanaians attribute the source of suffering, either through sickness or poverty, to spiritual realities. While I argue that Pentecostal practices of healing and deliverance from evil are suitable to bring folk Muslims to faith in Jesus, I must also emphasize that suffering, sickness, and poverty are inevitable as long as humankind remains on earth (Matt 10:28; 25:36). Thus, Jesus rebuked the people who wanted to first see signs before accepting him as an evil generation (Matt 7:38–42). The cross of Jesus cannot be taken out from the gospel that leads to true salvation. For this reason, folk Muslims must be directed to the reality of the cross and the power that is able to sustain man in the midst of all the unknown causalities in one's life. Since the mind of God is above that of human beings and he is the only all-knowing God as confirmed by both the Qur'an and the Bible, folk Muslims need to be pointed to the path of peace, which is the sustaining power of the Holy Spirit.

Power Encounters as Continuous Phenomena

The quest for the demonstration of power amidst satanic opposition has increased among mission practitioners in the majority world. However, many Western missionaries come from societies where power displayed in witchcraft, black magic, dead spirits, and demon possession are visibly absent from

---

49. Onyinah, 136.
50. Larbi, *Pentecostalism*, chap. 3.
51. Nuekpe, "Muslim Christian Encounter," 219.

everyday life. Thus, many Western thinkers doubt the phenomenon of power encounters and believe its occurrence should not be normative. Christians must recognize that there are dangerous spiritual forces that exercise control over entire nations, cities, villages, and families (Dan 10:11–13).[52] By ignoring power encounters, the evangelical world may be bound by the powers of darkness, unless they tap into the divine gifts available for believers to confront these powers.[53]

While most scholars agree about the existence of past power encounters in the Bible, many think the practice of power encounters ended with the apostles and is not for the present. Some scholars, like Charles Kraft, assert that the power encounters of Jesus's ministry are meant to be replicated by believers, because Jesus declared to his disciples that they will do greater things: "Truly, truly, I say to you, whoever believes in me will also do the works that I do; and greater works than these will he do, because I am going to the Father" (John 14:12).[54] Scripture also reveals the continuation of power encounters in missions. Jesus declared in Mark 16:17–18,

> And these signs will accompany those who believe: in my name they will cast out demons; they will speak in new tongues; they will pick up serpents with their hands; and if they drink any deadly poison, it will not hurt them; they will lay their hands on the sick, and they will recover.

By saying "those who believe in my name," Jesus was not only referring to the twelve apostles but also to those in the future who would believe in his name. All believers become candidates for the demonstration of his power. Additionally, it is evident in James 5:14–15 that the elders of the church are expected to administer healing to the sick.

In addition to Charles Kraft, other noncharismatic scholars like James Kallas, a Lutheran, admit the necessity of power encounters in missions.[55] These scholars point out that throughout his earthly ministry, Jesus cast out demons and healed the sick; thus, his followers receive his authority through the power of the Holy Spirit to cast out demons, heal the sick, and teach

---

52. Brant, "Power Encounter," 185.
53. Brant, 185.
54. Kraft, *Power Encounter*, 14.
55. Kraft, 15.

others to do the same until he returns. The disciples were not expected to go on missions without empowerment (Matt 28:20; Luke 9:1–2; Acts 1:8).[56]

Richard Gaffin, who represents the cessationist view, observes that Pentecostals affirm that everything pertaining to the operation of the Holy Spirit is traced forward or backward to the special event of Pentecost (Acts 2); thus, the outpouring of the Holy Spirit on the day of Pentecost was a model or normative case to be followed by all believers at all times after or during conversion. Scriptures used to defend this argument are often "Acts 2 (Pentecost), the Samaria experience in Acts 8, the Caesarea (Acts 10) and the Ephesus experience (Acts 19)."[57] By drawing on D. A. Carson's observation that "the essentially salvation-historical structure of the Book of Acts is too often overlooked," Gaffin argues that Pentecostals have made a doctrine out of the narrative materials in Acts, equating "Luke-Acts on the same theological foot as Paul's letters."[58] Cessationists assert that events regarding the "order of salvation" (*ordo salutis*) are applicable at all times by the believer and should be distinguished from events of "redemptive history" or the "history of salvation," which happened once and for all unto the fulfillment of salvation by Christ. With this view, they maintain that Pentecost was redemptive history based on Acts 1:5 and Luke 3:16. If so, it is not repeatable as God's finished work and the fulfillment of Messianic prophecy, just as Jesus's water baptism by John was an indicator of his entire ministry (Acts 10:37; Luke 20:4).[59]

Therefore, cessationists appeal to the historical narrative of Luke-Acts, affirming that Pentecost was "an eschatological fulfilment of Christ's historic redemptive work," a redemptive seal (Eph 1:13) without which his salvation work would not have been complete.[60] In this view, there is no salvation without Pentecost. The coming of the Spirit on Pentecost was once and for all; those who accept Christ will experience the Spirit at their conversion.[61] Cessationists, realizing the continued occurrence of power encounters in Luke-Acts, assert that the entire Luke-Acts is a record of an accomplished historical redemptive work. Even though there was enough evidence of the

---

56. Kraft, 15.
57. Gaffin, "Cessationist View," 30.
58. Gaffin, 30.
59. Gaffin, 31.
60. Gaffin, 31.
61. Gaffin, 36.

work of the Holy Spirit in Acts (Acts 8:14; 10:44–48; 11:15–18; 19:1–7), the theological motif of Luke was to reveal an eschatological fulfillment of all that had been said by the Lord (Acts 1:8). In this view, Luke-Acts should be read as a whole and not as two parts.[62] This implies that all manifestations of the Holy Spirit within the framework of 1 Corinthians 12:9–10 were marks of the apostles (2 Cor 12:12) and were not intended to continue. Thus, scholars like Robert L. Saucy argue that the apostolic period of power encounters was a foundational period that must not be considered a model of the contemporary church. To do so would go beyond what was written, which is forbidden (1 Cor 4:6).[63]

The work of the Holy Spirit is beyond human understanding. Like Peter, unless men avail themselves of God and have certain experiences with him in power encounters, divine realities would be difficult to comprehend by the inquisitive carnal mind. Thus, power encounters must be understood in light of the revealed truth in the Scriptures, so that no one can open a new canon of Scripture. However, to say categorically that power encounters have ceased with the apostles is an exaggeration or "a going beyond what is written" (1 Cor 4:6). Besides the apostles, there were other instances of power encounters that are not directly related with the fulfillment of Christ's work (Acts 15:32; 21:9; 1 Cor 14; 1 Thess 5:19).[64] For example, the prophet Agabus prophesied concerning a famine in Jerusalem (Acts 11:27–29) and was certainly not doing so regarding the redemptive accomplishment of Christ. Therefore, the argument of cessationists that power encounters have been discontinued contains a certain theological truth but is not wholly true.

Samuel C. Storm, a third wave scholar, remarks that "Luke's perspective is that Pentecost is a redemptive-historical hinge, on which both the historical once-for-all accomplishment of Christ and the future available-to-all-who-believe application to Christians swings."[65] Peter clearly explained that the gift of the Holy Spirit, including all his manifestations, are first the historic, redemptive fulfillment of the messianic prophecy of Joel (Joel 2:28; Acts 2:16). However, he also said the gifts were for both then and now: "For the promise

---

62. Gaffin, 39.
63. Saucy, "Response to Gaffin," 65.
64. Saucy, "Response to Gaffin," 65.
65. Storms, "Third Wave Response," 73–74.

is for you and for your children and for all who are far off, everyone whom the Lord our God calls to himself" (Acts 2:38–39). For this reason, we see the manifestation of miraculous events in the lives of ordinary people in the church after the apostolic period. Nowhere does the gospel say that God would not confirm his word with signs and wonders in the present and the days to come (Mark 16:17–18). Several New Testament verses point to the fact that power encounters are still available today and must not be despised based on limited experience (Acts 19:1–7; Rom 12:3–6; Gal 3:5, 1 Thess 5:19–22).

Douglas A. Oss, a Pentecostal/charismatic scholar, noted that the Holy's Spirit empowerment was repeated even within Acts (Acts 4:30–31); thus, Pentecost is not repeatable, but his power and manifestations are available today.[66] Douglas cautioned that Christians must be careful not to treat our faith with scientific rationalism, restricting our faith to theological or doctrinal confessions.[67] Douglas agrees with Deere who said:

> No one ever just picked up the Bible, started reading, and then came to the conclusion that God was not doing signs and wonders anymore and that the gifts of the Holy Spirit had passed away. The doctrine of cessationism did not originate from a careful study of the Scriptures. The doctrine of cessationism originated in experience.[68]

Deere observes that the New Testament is full of power encounters; therefore, the absence of power encounters in one's experience, like the doctrine of "election and predestination," could be ascribed to divine mystery, incapable of being exhaustively explained to human faculty.[69] The absence of experiencing miracles and God's power through the Holy Spirit's gifts should not be interpreted as evidence of cessation. Using the Bible – which is full of instances of miracles from the Old Testament, the New Testament, the time of the apostles, and the "last days" (Acts 2:17) – to disapprove power encounters today makes God a liar in a sense. Deere asserts that any attempt to despise miracles or treat them as a thing of the past follows Bultmann's rationalistic

---

66. Oss, "Pentecostal/Charismatic Response," 89.
67. Oss, 87.
68. Deere, *Surprised*, 99.
69. Deere, 99.

theology of "demythologizing" the New Testament.[70] Cessationists often claim that doctrine cannot be built on the book of Acts. However, the reformed theologians of Calvin's day used Acts 13:48 to prove their doctrine of unconditional election. Likewise, dispensationalists heavily made use of Acts to ratify dispensationalism.[71]

Saucy suggests that all evangelical scholars admit the supernatural nature of God in performing miracles. However, whether those miracles are normal for the church today is unclear. Saucy accepts the role of the Holy Spirit in the ongoing growth of the believer (Eph 5:18) but refutes the Spirit's manifestation through certain gifts of power today.[72] He refutes the occurrence of the miraculous gifts for today, citing specific miraculous instances in the Bible which are not repeatable: "Ananias and Sapphira killed for lying (Acts 5:1–11), Elymas an obstructer of the gospel was blinded (Acts 13:6–12), chains fell off and prison doors were miraculously opened (Acts 5:17–22; 16:23–26; 12:1–11), the very shadow of Peter producing healing (Acts 5:15), and the handkerchief and apron that touched Paul causing healing (Acts 19:11–12)."[73] He concluded that there is no specific teaching in the Bible that proves the discontinuity of miracles but that there is no clarity as to whether any of the miraculous events are to be continued.[74]

Brant notes that the ability to cast out demons is not linked to the possession of spiritual gifts but to the knowledge of one's position in Christ and his authority over principalities (Eph 1:19–21; 2:4–6).[75] Believers must stand in righteousness and in faith to resist Satan (1 Pet 5:8–9). Jesus has already accomplished the task of defeating Satan on the cross, disarming him and making him a public spectacle (Col 2:15). For this reason, the believer only needs to take up his position in Christ and command demons to flee in Jesus's name. Paul outlines the weapons of the believer against dark powers as having a disposition of intimacy with Christ and a righteous life (Eph 6:10–19). A sinful Christian cannot claim he possesses certain gifts of grace and is able to stand against Satan.

---

70. Deere, 111.
71. Deere, 111.
72. Saucy, "Open but Cautious View," 126.
73. Saucy, 102.
74. Saucy, 126.
75. Brant, "Power Encounter," 185.

Some scholars argue that the same disciples to whom Christ gave authority to cast out demons in Matthew 10:8 were instructed to teach others to do the same until Christ returns the second time (Matt 28:19–20).[76] The challenge of this interpretation is that, besides the command to cast out demons, Jesus gave the early disciples other instructions that are not applicable for today's disciples. For instance, the instructions to go only to the lost sheep of Israel, to not bring money, etc. (Matt 10:5–14) were certainly not meant for missionaries today. This points to the fact that not every command and power Jesus gave the disciples was intended for today's disciples. An attempt to claim all that the apostles represent and did in terms of power is a distortion of the biblical story. If the church preoccupies itself unduly with power consciousness or demon consciousness, it will eventually be distracted from its ultimate purpose for existence.[77] However, the Holy Spirit is still available and operating among Pentecostals, and they can use power manifestations as a bridge to share the gospel with folk Muslims.

Power Encounters in Missions to Folk Muslims Today

Dr. David Yonggi Cho reports that from the outset of his ministry at the Full Gospel Church in South Korea, it was power encounters of divine healing that turned hearts to God, and for many missionaries, such power encounters mean the difference between success and failure.[78] Vondey has called the practices of healing and deliverance in mission the vocalization of faith centered on the use of the nine gifts of the Holy Spirit (1 Cor 12:8–12), namely the "word of wisdom, word of knowledge, discerning of spirits (revelation gifts), faith, healings, miracles (power gifts), prophecy, diverse kinds of tongues, [and] interpretation of tongues (vocal gifts)." These pave the way for conversion in missions.[79] Julie Ma and Wonsuk Ma have remarked that within the framework of culture and religion, healing and deliverance are expectations humans have of deities and spirits. Thus, divine healing through

---

76. Brant, 188.
77. Brant, 185.
78. Cho, *Spiritual Leadership*, 55.
79. Vondey, *Pentecostal Theology*, 109.

power encounters in missions responds to a code of native religiosity and becomes a major motivation of people to draw near to God.[80] Pentecostals' emphasis on the experience of the Holy Spirit as a source of power shares commonalities with folk Muslim practices, enabling them to build bridges to share the gospel with folk Muslims. For instance, in Ghana, folk Muslims are concerned about knowing the source of causalities in their daily life. With Pentecostals' emphasis on the word of knowledge and the gift of prophecy, they can respond to folk Muslims' quest to know the present and future causalities in their lives, but this is not without its limitations.

In general, power encounters stir up faith that often leads to a form of conversion. However, whether power encounters should be used to sustain faith in God and if power encounters will help folk Muslims keep faith need to be examined. People throughout redemptive history saw the demonstration of God's power but still turned back to the very gods that God had defeated.[81] This occurs over and over in Israel's covenant relationship with God and their engagement with the nations around them. Even after Moses defeated the Egyptian gods and Elijah defeated Baal and its prophets, Israel still turned away from God (1 Kgs 22:6).[82] Power encounters in mission may lead to a change in belief and sometimes behavior, but in most cases, the worldview of the people remains the same.

Hiebert has pointed out that if a person's beliefs and behavior change while their worldview remains the same, they may pursue a "Christo-paganism."[83] Reliance on power encounters when sharing the gospel with folk Muslims, if not accompanied with the right theological understanding, may do more harm than good. Among power-oriented societies in the majority world like Ghana, power encounters are routine incidents where the adherents of weaker gods give allegiance to stronger gods while remaining loyal to their own gods. It is reminiscent of what frequently happened in the Old Testament, "So they feared the LORD but also served their own gods, after the manner of the nations from among whom they had been carried away" (2 Kgs 17:33 RSV).

---

80. Ma and Ma, *Mission in the Spirit*, 38.
81. Kraft, *Power Encounter*, 11.
82. Kraft, 11.
83. Hiebert, *Transforming Worldviews*, 11.

Folk Muslims in Ghana, due to their inclination to power, may be drawn to Jesus through power encounters. However, their worldview can only be changed if they understand the biblical principles or theology behind the power encounter, which is to point humanity to the sovereignty, supremacy, and redemptive power of God. The aim is that people might abandon all other gods and give glory to the only true God (Acts 4:12) and live according to his kingdom principles. It is the word of God that sustains faith and not miracles and signs as Paul declares, "So faith comes from hearing, and hearing through the word of Christ" (Rom 10:17). Jesus said not even the miracle of the dead coming back to life would bring people to repentance unless they listen to the word: "He said to him, 'If they do not hear Moses and the Prophets, neither will they be convinced if someone should rise from the dead'" (Luke 16:31). It is only through the genuine preaching of the word of God that people will truly follow Christ. Paul says, "For Jews demand signs and Greeks seek wisdom, but we preach Christ crucified, a stumbling block to Jews and folly to Gentiles, but to those who are called, both Jews and Greeks, Christ the power of God and the wisdom of God" (1 Cor 1:22–24). Power encounters are a means to an end but not an end in itself. They can bring folk Muslims to Jesus, but they need much more than power encounters to be retained in Jesus.

Muslims in the Postpandemic Era

The World Health Organization (WHO) on 30 January 2020, declared the COVID-19 outbreak a Public Health Emergency of International Concern, and shortly after that on 11 March 2020, the WHO declared COVID-19 a pandemic or a global outbreak expected to affect not only health but every sector of life.[84] Pandemics such as COVID-19 are catastrophes that interrogate and shake the religious worldview of a community and allow religious communities to rethink their values, perspectives, and purpose in life.

The pandemic has affected Christians and Muslims' faith expressions and responses to the enigma of evil. Social and political life were disrupted by the pandemic, and all forms of in-service gatherings were aborted, leading to the evolution of different kinds of media technologies to rescue religious

---

84. Ukah, "Prosperity, Prophecy," 447.

practices. In the midst of the deadly pandemic, all people, including folk Muslims, sought answers to life. Asamoah-Gyadu suggests that the most public response of people to the pandemic has been religious in nature.[85] The pandemic generated many political and economic conspiracy theories, which some religious leaders bought into. Some viewed the pandemic as a satanic agenda to disrupt religious activities and disrupt religious expressions of faith in various forms. Among some evangelicals and Pentecostals, the pandemic was a fulfillment of prophecy that signals the eschatological end of history, resulting from humans' evil ways in disobedience to the voice of the Creator.[86] The Christian faith promises salvation and deliverance from evil and appeals to the sustaining power of the Holy Spirit as a means of survival and comfort in the midst of trouble (John 14:16) in the context of Ghanaian Pentecostalism.

History repeats itself. In the early twentieth century, more than fifty million lives were destroyed by a worldwide influenza pandemic. People at that time searched for appropriate responses in an era when medical science was not as developed as today. In Africa, anti-medicine emerged; independent churches armed with the spiritual exercise of prayer, the "people of prayer" Aladura, responded to the pandemic with prevailing prayer.[87] In Ghana, Peter Anim, considered the father of Ghanaian Pentecostalism, was a leading figure of the anti-medicine Faith Tabernacle movement that fought the 1918–19 influenza with prayer. Even though most Pentecostals in Ghana have abandoned the anti-medicine heritage, it is worth noting that most classical Pentecostals in Ghana were hewn from Apostle Peter Anim's anti-medicine movement.[88]

With its emphasis on physical healing through the Holy Spirit and the sustaining power of the Holy Spirit in the mist of affliction, the Pentecostal community was positioned to respond effectively and innovatively to the COVID-19 pandemic.[89] COVID-19 has posed a crisis of faith to many religious communities and tests their truth claims and doctrines. Pentecostalism emphasizes healing, deliverance, and restoration, which are felt needs of

---

85. Asamoah-Gyadu, Chow, and Wild-Wood, "Covid-19 Pandemic," 213–18.
86. Asamoah-Gyadu, Chow, and Wild-Wood, 214.
87. Asamoah-Gyadu, Chow, and Wild-Wood, 214.
88. Asamoah-Gyadu, Chow, and Wild-Wood, 215.
89. Ukah, "Prosperity, Prophecy," 450.

Ghanaian Muslims in the pandemic and postpandemic period. Conceivably, Pentecostalism remains a movement that best responded to the COVID-19 pandemic; besides prosperity, healing and deliverance constitute the most essential commodities in the African Pentecostal market. Pentecostalism is "a reconstructed religion that responds to the daily needs and experiences of spiritual and physical insecurity that confront many Africans," irrespective of their religious affiliations.

Christianity was born out of "the crucibles of turmoil, epidemics, plagues and diseases"[90] and has always acted within the context of pandemics, epidemics, and lockdowns, from the Hebrew Passover to Pentecost. As early as the Antonine Plague (the plague of Galen, 165–80 CE) and the plague of Cyprian (251–66 CE), Christianity has turned pandemics into an opportunity to demonstrate credibility and gain converts.[91] Mosques in Makkah and Madina have been closed during the COVID-19 pandemic, and the Easter mass in the famous Notre Dame cathedral had only ten people in attendance. However, in Nigeria (the world capital of Pentecostalism on account of its megachurches), most Pentecostal-charismatic churches held services, thanks to the sustaining power of the Holy Spirit.[92] Christians' methods of sharing the gospel with Muslims could not remain the same during and after the pandemic. The pandemic has offered Christians, especially Pentecostals, more opportunities to share the gospel with folk Muslims because of their inclination toward divine healing by means of power encounters.

Summary

Power encounters in all forms started from the Old Testament, continued in the ministry of Jesus, and are accessible even today. Some scholars agree that power encounters continue today while others disagree. It is clear that there are numerous accounts of false prophets and counterfeit power encounters; signs and wonders are done by false prophets and Satan (Mark 14:22; Acts 8:9–24; 2 Thess 2:9; Rev 19:20). Thus, all forms of spiritual gifts must be tested. As John states, "Beloved, do not believe every spirit, but test the spirits to see

---

90. Ukah, 447.
91. Ukah, 457.
92. Ukah, 455.

whether they are from God, for many false prophets have gone out into the world" (1 John 4:1). The Bible clearly makes room for discerning all spiritual gifts in light of the written word (1 Cor 14:29; 1 Thess 5:19–22). Power encounters in the Old Testament and New Testament point to Jesus's redemptive work. However, there is some indication that these power encounters will continue until the "last days" when Christ shall come. A lack of such spiritual experiences should not cause us to arrive at a generalization that power encounters are not normative. All power encounters must be submitted and evaluated by the Scriptures. Since there is enough biblical evidence of people operating in the gifts of the Spirit even after the apostles, power encounters should not be dealt with as a thing of the past. Any willing and desiring child of God can receive such gifts based on God's will.

Since folk Muslims in Ghana are power-oriented people, power encounters are helpful in sharing the gospel with folk Muslims. Pentecostals in Ghana can certainly make use of the gifts of the Holy Spirit and power encounters to share the gospel with folk Muslims. The gifts are not in the hand and under the authority of earthly vessels to use at will; they occur as and when God sovereignly allows for the edification of the church and for his own glorification. While power encounters remain an effective means by which evangelism in mission grows, Christians must constantly rely on the written word of God for a deeper relationship with God. It is the Holy Spirit's work that sustains folk Muslims and delivers them from evil.

Christians' engagement with Muslims is an act of proclaiming the gospel to show them the worthiness and true nature of Jesus. A proclamation is an act of humans, whereas conviction and subsequent conversion into Christianity are acts of God. I, therefore, cannot sincerely propose one approach as the ultimate approach to win Ghanaian Muslims to Christ. The ways of God are different from humans' ways (Isa 55:8), and the best approach in winning one person may differ from another for various reasons, including specific cultural differences, the level of spirituality of each Muslim and Christian, and their extent of knowledge about the Qur'an and the Bible. Nonetheless, the sustaining power of the Holy Spirit to keep folk Muslims, whether they experience healing, deliverance, or lack material blessings, remains the ultimate way to preserve folk Muslims in Jesus.

Conclusion

Ghana was once known as a resistant belt to Islam in Africa. Unfortunately, this resistance has collapsed, and the presence of Islam is felt in almost every village in Ghana. While Christian-Muslim relationships in Ghana are generally cordial, there can be tension and misunderstandings that lead to religious clashes when Christians share the gospel. Thus, Christians, especially Ghanaian Pentecostals, need to have an appropriate awareness of the influence of Islam in Ghana and a clear understanding of the Qur'an. Although Pentecostal Christians once played a leading role in the growth of Christianity in Ghana, they now lack the proper understanding and approaches to engage Muslims with the gospel. To address these needs, this research aimed to highlight areas of misunderstanding/ignorance that can be reduced among Ghanaian Christians and to show how Pentecostals can engage Ghanaian Muslims with the gospel. Based on descriptive and analytic examinations of literature, it is evident that Ghanaian Muslims are folk Muslims and share a common spiritual heritage of ATR practices with Pentecostals. Thus, this work concludes that these practices can serve as bridges for Pentecostals to engage Muslims with the gospel and provide suitable approaches while preserving the two faiths' peaceful coexistence in Ghana.

Prior to the arrival of Western missionaries, the people of Ghana were influenced by the concept of a supreme being and their need for deliverance from the power of lesser gods. Although Western missionaries succeeded in providing the people of Ghana with socioeconomic development, they could not meet their need for deliverance from evil. This failure on the part of visiting missionaries led to the formation of African revival movements, from which independent and Pentecostal-charismatic churches were established. The COP emerged as the local version of African Pentecostalism, which did and does respond to the spiritual needs of the African people and Ghanaians. Islam grew in Ghana during the fourteenth century through traders and missionaries. Islam in Ghana spread through the influence of British colonialism, the adaptation and accommodation of Islam into ATRs, the influence of Ghanaian chiefs who held the traditional seats of power, and the influence of Islamic clerics who distributed charms and amulets. The encounter between Islam and ATRs produced a new form of Islam, folk Islam, which is the predominant form of Islam in Ghana.

Ghanaian Muslims' religious beliefs and practices are influenced by religiomagical practices rooted in ATRs. Though Ghanaian Muslims engage in the practice of the five pillars of Islam like all Muslims, Ghanaian Muslims have different interpretations of these religious practices and consider them to be means of liberation from evil. Ghanaian Muslims experience fear and insecurity of the unknown future and evil powers, so they seek healing, power, and blessings to overcome them. For protection, they worship saints and ancestors and rely on charms, amulets, and *malams*. Thus, Ghanaian folk Muslims are power-oriented people. This work has helped to identify the existential, experiential, and theological needs of folk Muslims to show what bridges Pentecostals can use to engage folk Muslims with the gospel.

Importantly, when sharing the gospel with folk Muslims, direct and indirect approaches that involve confrontation do not yield good results. Culturally and politically, Ghanaian Muslims and Christians live in harmony and peace influenced by their cultural community, cooperative education, and an integrative political alliance that includes adherents of both religions. Nonetheless, there are conflicts and clashes when Christians proselytize Muslims and engage them in traditional methods of polemic evangelism. However, conversational and apologetic approaches that engage folk Muslims in friendship will yield some results.

This study has shown how Pentecostals can identify and equip themselves with the theological needs of folk Muslims. These include the understanding of God's self-revelation as one God and *tawḥīd* (oneness of God) and the convergence and divergence of who Jesus is in the Qur'an and the Bible. Muslims reject Jesus as the Son of God, but they have a high regard for the person of Jesus. Therefore, an understanding of the qur'anic Jesus, his birth, and his life are crucial to engaging folk Muslims. Just as many Christians in the world misinterpret the Bible, so also many Muslims lack understanding about their own scripture. Even though Muslims deny the crucifixion and the death of Jesus, Islamic scholars have not reached a consensus regarding his crucifixion and death. The open-ended nature of the discussion provides a good opportunity for Pentecostals to engage folk Muslims with the core message of the gospel.

Nonetheless, a theological understanding of Jesus Christ can only be meaningful to folk Muslims when Jesus is presented in a way that is relevant and meaningful to the culture. Presenting Jesus to Ghanaian folk Muslims as an ancestor par excellence is one way to appeal to them, because Jesus has met all the requirements as an excellent heroic ancestor. Additionally, due to the controversial interpretation of the Spirit in the Qur'an and Muslims' shallow understanding of the Holy Spirit and his works, the Holy Spirit can be a fruitful starting point when engaging Muslims with the gospel.

The Qur'an endorses the recitation of God's revelation (Qur'an 13:39). Proclaiming the truth of the word of God verbally for the hearing of folk Muslims has the power to bring conviction: "For I am not shamed of the gospel, for it is the power of God for salvation to everyone who believes, to the Jew first and also to the Greek" (Rom 1:16). The word of God, unlike the Qur'an, is not only a revelation of God but God incarnate (John 1:1). It has the authority of God and is capable of inspiring hearers (Heb 4:12). It has been said that Saint Augustine felt God speaking to him directly through hearing and reading the word of God:

> While agonizing in his garden over his moral failure, he heard a child in a nearby house repeat[ing] in a sing-song voice the refrain, *Tolle lege* ("Pick up and read"). There was a book on the letters of Paul on a bench and Augustine picked it up and read, "Let us behave decently, as in the daytime, not in carousing and drunkenness, not in sexual immorality and debauchery, not in dissension and jealousy. Rather, clothe yourselves with the Lord Jesus, and do not think about how to gratify the desires of the flesh" (Rom 13:13–14).[1]

This led to Augustine's conversion and baptism. In the same way, proclaiming the unadulterated word of God to folk Muslims can bring conviction,

---

1. Ferguson, *Church History*, 270.

transformation, and a decision to follow Jesus. The word of God speaks, and intrinsic in the word is the power of God to save.

The lifestyle of the gospel presenter is as important as the gospel they share. For this reason, Christlike character is a necessity for those who want to share the gospel with folk Muslims. Christians must demonstrate among folk Muslims that they have the light that drives away darkness and corruption in the world. When folk Muslims see Christians living a transparent life in politics, church, business, and family, they will be attracted to the Jesus Christians profess. Additionally, biblical truth must be presented with grace and love on the basis of the Scriptures:

> But in your hearts honor Christ the Lord as holy, always being prepared to make a defense to anyone who asks you for a reason for the hope that is in you; yet do it with gentleness and respect, having a good conscience, so that, when you are slandered, those who revile your good behavior in Christ may be put to shame. (1 Pet 3:15–16)

Sharing the gospel with grace and truth involves being "all things to all people," which means identifying with the culture of folk Muslims, eating with them (Gal 2:11–16), honoring them (1 Pet 2:17), counting them better than oneself (Phil 2:3), serving them as Christ served the world (Gal 5:13), and taking no offense at them (1 Cor 10:32).[2] Becoming all things to folk Muslims (1 Cor 9:22) does not imply the abandonment of the core values of the gospel, but rather it has laid a responsibility upon the proclaimer of the gospel to demonstrate a willingness to venture into other people's lives and share their life circumstances. In the context of folk Muslims in Ghana, especially those from the north, this may imply that Pentecostals from the south who want to engage them should exchange a toothbrush for a chewing stick, a Kente cloth for a northern smock, and Coca-Cola for kola nut, which form part of folk Muslims' cultural identification.[3] It may mean declaring fasting and prayer in the month of Ramadan to seek the Lord for spiritual revival that transforms everyday encounters into power encounters.

---

2. Dretke, *Christian Approach*, 148.
3. Dretke, 148.

Providing for the existential needs of folk Muslims is another way to share the gospel with them. Christians need to identify what loving services they can provide to folk Muslims and take practical steps to meet their needs. Because Ghanaian folk Muslims are power-oriented, they should also be engaged through power encounters that can address their experiential needs. The powers of darkness pervade their world and worldview; thus, this work has provided an understanding of how power encounters can reach folk Muslims in the Ghanaian context. The Qur'an admonishes Muslims to respect the Former scriptures, including the New Testament, so the power works in the life of Jesus are ways for folk Muslims to come to the saving knowledge of Jesus. Pentecostal practices of healing, deliverance, prayer, and fasting in accordance with the Bible will meet folk Muslims' experiential needs. In a postpandemic era, power encounters for healing and deliverance can also become a suitable bridge to share the gospel with folk Muslims, because of their quest for continuous healing. However, power encounters should only serve as a launching pad to engage folk Muslims with the gospel; it is not an end but a means to an end.

Although this research aimed to find a specific approach to engage folk Muslims in Ghana with the gospel, proclamation should not be viewed as an act of humans but as the work of the Holy Spirit that leads individuals to conviction and conversion through the grace of God. The ways of God are different from human ways, and each folk Muslim has their own peculiarities; therefore, the best approach may differ from one person to another. For this reason, the ultimate way to engage folk Muslims and then preserve them in Jesus is discipleship that directs folk Muslims to rely on the sustaining power of the Holy Spirit to deliver them from evil.

Research Contributions

Ghanaian Pentecostals engage in active and persistent evangelism to share the gospel with all Ghanaians. However, through this work, I have identified that Ghanaian Pentecostals lack sufficient understanding of Muslims in the context of folk Islam to engage them in sharing the gospel. Furthermore, although some scholars, through NGOs and non-Pentecostal councils, have tried to educate Ghanaian Christians on Christian-Muslim relations, Pentecostals are not usually involved in these programs due to supposed doctrinal differences.

These findings, therefore, provide new insight to further Pentecostals' understanding of folk Muslims that can aid them in evangelism.

As a leading local version of Pentecostalism, the COP employs the local model of mission and mass evangelism in addition to numerous social interventions as mediums to share the gospel. However, there are no specific models tailored toward the needs of folk Muslims in Ghana since the Northern Outreach Ministry ceased work. Even though a few scholars have written on the COP mission, no research work has been done so far on Christian evangelism to Muslims or the COP's mission to Muslims. Thus, this research fills an important gap in the existing understanding on outreach, which may be useful to future researchers. The suggested ideas and recommendations from this research can also serve as a guide for aspiring Christian leaders seeking to effectively engage Muslims with the gospel.

In the past, Pentecostals have held negative attitudes toward Muslims that have resulted in the failure to build the right bridges by which folk Muslims can pass over from misunderstandings and anti-Christian polemics to truth encounters, and from fear to faith and hope in Jesus. This work contributes to the much-needed awareness among Ghanaian Pentecostals for constructive engagement with Muslims, proving that there are bridges in theology and everyday life. The findings highlight the crucial bond of national and tribal identity, which are primary to Ghanaian identity before their religious identity. Thus, Christians relate to Muslims first of all as brothers and sisters from Ghana. This relationship offers Pentecostal Christians a great opportunity to freely engage them, making the most of existing bridges, theological mediums, and the existential needs of folk Muslims.

This work has also demonstrated the influence of folk Islam in Ghana and called attention to the similar spiritual heritage the Ghanaian folk Muslims and Pentecostals share. This understanding of the practices of folk Islam can facilitate the effective sharing of the gospel with Ghanaian Muslims. Notably, this study not only affirms the Christology of Jesus as an ancestor to African Christians but also adds a new dimension of knowledge that Jesus qualifies to be a hero ancestor to Ghanaian folk Muslims. Jesus qualifies beyond all Ghanaian ancestors as a member of the folk Muslim clan as the universal savior. Thus, this reality is recommended as a bridge to share the gospel with folk Muslims.

Another bridge this study has identified are power encounters as a means of sharing the gospel with Ghanaian folk Muslims. However, I caution against emphasizing religiomagical practices, because folk Muslims may reinterpret Christianity as a new charm or magical power to gain more influence, which does not produce true converts. I thus affirm Hiebert's position that these practices may not lead to a genuine conversion of people who just change their symbols or fetish and give Christian names to their pagan gods and spirits.[4] In this vein, some non-Pentecostal and Pentecostal scholars assert that these approaches appear to be "a threat to the progress of Christianity" in Ghana.[5] However, I have demonstrated that these religiomagical practices can be used as progressive preparation to truth encounters in the gospel, as points of entry into the Christian faith for the majority of people who are less educated and who seek a gospel that responds to everyday spiritual needs. The Christian faith promises salvation and deliverance from evil and appeals to the sustaining power of the Holy Spirit as a means of survival and comfort in the midst of trouble (John 14:16). Therefore, in the context of Ghanaian Pentecostalism, folk Muslims must be pointed to the sustaining power of the Holy Spirit as the ultimate approach that will preserve folk Muslims in the Christian faith.

There is no one specific way of sharing the gospel with folk Muslims in Ghana. However, folk Islam is predominant in Ghana and presents bridges for Pentecostals to share the gospel. Engagement through theology in gentleness and respect, engagement through existential needs, engagement through power encounters, and engagement through the sustaining power of the Holy Spirit in discipleship are the best ways to engage folk Muslims with the gospel. Pentecostals, in their tenacity to evangelize, are branches that can bear fruit. This study offers Pentecostals in Ghana tools for self-pruning in order to bear much more fruit, as Jesus said, "Every branch that does bear fruit he prunes, that it may bear more fruit" (John 15:1–2). Pentecostals, and the COP in particular, is one branch of the vine that is producing fruit in their desire to reach out to the world. In order to bear more fruit, this research has provided an awareness and understanding of Islam that can reshape Pentecostals'

---

4. Hiebert, *Transforming Worldviews*, 11.
5. Onyinah, "Matthew Speaks," 30.

polemic approach of sharing the gospel in a more loving, respectful, and gracious engagement.

Recommendations for Further Study

This work employed descriptive and analytic research of literature sources to arrive at its findings. Thus, future researchers should use ethnographic studies to expand these findings. Because Pentecostal-charismatic churches are numerous in Ghana, researchers from different denominations or different geographic regions may further this work by analyzing and comparing different approaches to engagement with folk Muslims within their specific contexts. Additionally, while this work considered folk Muslims in Ghana, the field will benefit from research that examines orthodox Islam in Ghana and the engagement approaches of Ghanaian orthodox churches.

Bibliography

Abdul-Hamid, Mustapha. "Christian-Muslim Relationship in Ghana: A Model for World Dialogue and Peace." *Ilorin Journal of Religious Studies* 1, no. 1 (June 2011): 21–32.

Agbeti, Kofi J. *West African Church History: Christian Missions and Church Foundations: 1482–1919*. Leiden: E. J. Brill, 1986. Cited in Daniel Okyere Walker, "The Pentecost Fire Is Burning: Models of Mission Activities in the Church of Pentecost." PhD diss., University of Birmingham, March 2010.

Al-Bukhari, Sahih. *The Translation of the Meanings of Sahih Al-Bukhari*. Vol. 9. Translated and edited by Muhammad Muhsin Khan. Al Nabawiya: Dar Ahya Us-Sunnah. Cited in Caleb Chul-soo Kim. *Islam among the Swahili in East Africa*. 2nd ed. Nairobi: Acton Publishers, 2016.

Al-Ghazali, Abu Hamid. "Inner Dimensions of Islamic Worship." Translated by Muhtar Holland. Leicester: Islamic Foundation, 1983. Quoted in Carole Hillenbrand, *Introduction to Islam: Beliefs and Practices in Historical Perspective*. London: Thames and Hudson, 2015.

Al-Tabari, Abu Ja'far. *Commentaire du Coran*. Abridged and translated by M. Pierre Godé. Part 6. Quoted in J. Dudley Woodberry, "The Muslim Understanding of Jesus," *Word and Word* 16, no. 2 (Spring 1996): 173–78.

Amanor, Kwabena Darkwa. "Pentecostal and Charismatic Churches in Ghana and the African Culture: Confrontation or Compromise?" *Journal of Pentecostal Theology* 18, no. 1 (2009):123–40.

Anderson, Allan Heaton. "Diversity in the Definition of 'Pentecostal/Charismatic' and Its Ecumenical Implications." *Mission Studies* 9, no. 1 (1 January 2002): 40–55.

———. *An Introduction to Pentecostalism*. Cambridge: Cambridge University Press, 2004. Cited in Amos Jimmy Markin, "Spirit and Mission: The Church of Pentecost as a Growing African Pentecostal Denomination." PhD diss., South African Theological Seminary, 2018.

———. *To the Ends of the Earth: Pentecostalism and the Transformation of World Christianity*. New York: Oxford University Press, 2013.

Anank, Francis Kweku. "The Impact of the Northern Outreach Ministry on the Church of Pentecost." Essay submitted for BA degree, Pentecost University College, 2013. Cited in Amos Jimmy Markin, "Spirit and Mission: The Church of Pentecost as a Growing African Pentecostal Denomination." PhD diss., South African Theological Seminary, 2018.

Anim, Emmanuel. "Mission, Migration, and World Christianity: An Evaluation of the Mission Strategy of the Church of Pentecost in the Diaspora." *Pentecost Journal of Theology and Mission* 1, no. 1 (July 2016): 36–51.

Aning, Kwesi, and Mustapha Abdallah. "Islamic Radicalization and Violence in Ghana." *Conflict, Security and Development* 13, no. 2 (May 2013): 149–67.

Antoine, Mikelle. "Practice and Conversion of Asante Market Women to the Ahmadiyya Muslim Mission in the Late 20th Century." PhD diss., Michigan State University, 2010.

Arnold, Clinton E. "The Kingdom, Miracles, Satan, and Demons." In *The Kingdom of God*, edited by Christopher W. Morgan and Robert A. Peterson, 153–78. Wheaton: Crossway, 2012.

Asamoah-Gyadu, J. Kwabena. *African Charismatics: Current Developments within Independent Indigenous Pentecostalism in Ghana*. Studies of Religion in Africa 27. Leiden: Koninklijke Brill NV, 2005.

———. "'Function to Function': Reinventing the Oil of Influence in African Pentecostalism." *Journal of Pentecostal Theology* 13, no. 2 (2005): 231–56.

———. "Pentecostalism and the Missiological Significance of Religious Experience: The Case of Ghana's Church of Pentecost." *Trinity Journal of Church and Theology* 12, no. 1 (July/December 2002): 30–53.

Asamoah-Gyadu, Kwabena, Alexander Chow, and Emma Wild-Wood. "Editorial: The Covid-19 Pandemic and World Christianity." *Studies in World Christianity* 26, no. 3 (2020): 213–18. https://doi.org/10.3366/swc.2020.0306.

Asem, E. Kafui, ed. *A History of the Church of Pentecost*. Vol. 1. Accra: Pentecost Press, 2005.

Assimeng, Max. *Social Structure of Ghana: A Study in Persistence and Change*. Tema: Ghana Publishing Corporation, 1999. Cited in Daniel Okyere Walker, "The Pentecost Fire Is Burning: Models of Mission Activities in the Church of Pentecost." PhD diss., University of Birmingham, March 2010.

Ayoub, Mahmoud M. *Islam: Faith and History*. London: Oneworld Publications, 2013. Kindle.

———. *Islam: Faith and History*. Oxford: Thomson Press, 2004.

Azumah, John. "Christian Witness to Muslims: Rationale, Approaches and Strategies." *Missionalia* 34, no. 1 (April 2006): 5–21.

———. "Controversy and Restraint in Ghana." *Transformation* 17, no. 1 (January 2000): 23–26.

———. "Fault Lines in African Christian Responses to Islam." In *The African Christian and Islam*, edited by John Azumah and Lamin Sanneh, 125–46. Carlisle: Langham Monographs, 2013.

———. "Historical Survey of Islam and Christian-Muslim Relations in Africa." Lecture delivered at the Sannet Institute, Accra, Ghana, 4 November 2021.

———. *The Legacy of Arab-Islam in Africa: A Quest for Inter-Religious Dialogue*. London: Oneworld Publications, 2014.

———. "Muslim-Christian Relations in Ghana: Too Much Meat Does Not Spoil the Soup." *Current Dialogue* 36 (December 2000): 1–5.

———. *My Neighbour's Faith: Islam Explained for Christians*. Grand Rapids: Zondervan, 2008. Kindle.

Azumah, John, and Lamin Sanneh, eds. *The African Christian and Islam*. Carlisle: Langham Monographs, 2013.

Bediako, Kwame. "Christian Faith and African Culture: An Exposition of the Epistle to the Hebrews." *Journal of African Christian Thought* 13, no. 1 (June 2010): 45–57.

———. "Christianity, Islam and the Kingdom of God: Rethinking Their Relationship from an African Perspective." *Journal of African Christian Thought* 7, no. 2 (December 2004): 1–57.

———. *Jesus and the Gospel in Africa: History and Experience*. Theology in Africa. Yaounde, Cameroun: Paternoster Press, 2000.

Benyah, Francis. "Commodification of the Gospel and the Socio-Economics of Neo-Pentecostal/Charismatic Christianity in Ghana." *Legon Journal of the Humanities* 29 (2018): 116–45.

Berg, Bruce L., and Howard Lune. *Qualitative Research Methods for the Social Sciences*. 8th ed. Pearson New International Editions. Essex: Pearson Education, 2014.

Bosch, David. "Evangelism: An Holistic Approach." *Journal of Theology for Southern Africa* 36 (September 1981): 43–63. Cited in Krish Kandiah, "Lesslie Newbigin's Contribution to a Theology of Evangelism." *Transformation* 24, no. 1 (January 2007): 51–60. http://www.jstor.com/stable/43052689.

———. *Transforming Mission: Paradigm Shifts in Theology of Mission*. 20th anniversary ed. American Society of Missiology 16. Maryknoll: Orbis, 2011. Kindle.

Brant, Howard. "Power Encounter, Toward an SIM Position." *International Journal of Frontier Missions* 104 (October 1993): 185–92.

Breidenbach, Paul S. "Spatial Juxtapositions and Belief Orientations in a Ritual of a Ghanaian Healing Movement 1." *Journal of Religion in Africa* 7, no. 2 (1975): 94–110.

Broomhall, B. "The Evangelization of the World, a Missionary Band: A Record of Consecration, and an Appeal." In Woodberry, *From Seed to Fruit*, 1–14.

Cho, David Yonggi. Spiritual Leadership for the New Millennium. Seoul: Logos, 2002.

Church of Pentecost Evangelism Ministry. "The 21st Century Church: Its Evangelistic Task, Challenges and Relevance." Paper from Evacon 2021, University of Mine and Technology, Tarkwa, 13–16 June 2002, 1–96.

Clarke, Peter B. "West Africa and Christianity." London: Edward Arnold, 1986. Cited in Daniel Okyere Walker, "The Pentecost Fire Is Burning: Models of Mission Activities in the Church of Pentecost." PhD diss., University of Birmingham, March 2010.

———. West Africa and Islam: A Study of Religious Development from the 8th to the 20th Century. London: Edward Arnold, 1982.

Cragg, Kenneth. *Jesus and the Muslim: An Exploration*. Oxford: Allen and Unwin, 1985.

Crowther, Samuel Ajayi. "Experiences with Heathens and Mohammedans in West Africa." London: Society for Promoting Christian Knowledge, 1892. Quoted in Andrew F. Walls, *The Cross-Cultural Process in Christian History: Studies in the Transmission and Reception of Faith*. Maryknoll: Orbis Books, 2002.

Daswani, Girish. "(In-)Dividual Pentecostals in Ghana." *Journal of Religion in Africa* 41, no. 3 (2011): 256–79.

Deere, Jack. Surprised by the Power of the Spirit: Discovering How God Speaks and Heals Today. Grand Rapids: Zondervan, 1993.

Dovlo, Elom, and Alfred Ofosu Asante. "Reinterpreting the Straight Path: Ghanaian Muslim Converts in Mission to Muslims." *Exchange* 32, no. 3 (July 2003): 214–38.

Dretke, James P. A Christian Approach to Muslims: Reflections from West Africa. Pasadena: William Carey Library, 1979.

Effah, Yusuf K. "The Early History of the Ahmadiyya in Ghana." Accra: Ahmadiyya Muslim Mission Press, 1994. Cited in Mikelle Antoine, "Practice and Conversion of Asante Market Women to the Ahmadiyya Muslim Mission in the Late 20th Century." PhD diss., Michigan State University, 2010.

Eggen, Wiel. "Mawu Does Not Kill: On Ewe Kinship-Focused Religion." *Exchange* 31, no. 4 (October 2002): 342–61.

Ephson, Ben. "Muslim-Christian Clashes Escalate." *Christianity Today* 40, no. 2 (5 February 1996): 102. Atlas Religion Database with AtlaSerials.

Esposito, John L., ed. *The Oxford Encyclopedia of The Islamic World*. Vol. 5. Oxford: Oxford University Press, 2009.

———. What Everyone Needs to Know About Islam: Answers to Frequently Asked Questions, From One of America's Leading Experts. New York: Oxford University Press, 2002.

Evans, H. St. John T. "The Akan Doctrine of God: African Ideas of God." London: Edinburgh House Press, 1995. Quoted in Olof Petterson, "Monotheism or

Polytheism? A Study of the Ideas about Supreme Beings in African Religion." *Temenos Nordic Journal of Comparative Religion* 2 (1966): 48–67. https://doi.org/10.33356/temenos.6465.

Fairman, Walter T. "The Approach to Moslems." *MW* (July 1926): 272–74. Quoted in Sam Schlorff, *Missiological Models in Ministry to Muslims*. Upper Darby: Middle East Resources, 2006.

Falk, Peter. *The Growth of the Church in Africa*. Grand Rapids: Zondervan, 1979. Cited in Daniel Okyere Walker, "The Pentecost Fire Is Burning: Models of Mission Activities in the Church of Pentecost." PhD diss., University of Birmingham, March 2010.

Ferguson, Everett. Church History. Vol. 1. From Christ to the Pre-Reformation: The Rise and Growth of the Church in Its Cultural, Intellectual, and Political Context. 2nd ed. Grand Rapids: Zondervan, 2013.

Fredericks, Martha Th. "Let Us Understand Our Differences: Current Trends in Christian-Muslim Relations in Sub-Saharan Africa." *Transformation* 27, no. 4 (October 2010): 261–74.

Gaffin, Richard B. Jr. "A Cessationist View." In Grudem, *Miraculous Gifts*, 25–63.

Gaudeul, Jean-Marie. *Called From Islam to Christ: Why Muslims Become Christians*. Monarch Books, 1999. Quoted in Dovlo and Asante, "Reinterpreting the Straight Path," 214–38.

Geoffrey, Eric. *Introduction to Sufism: The Inner Path of Islam*. Bloomington: World Wisdom, 2010.

Ghana Evangelical Committee. "Survey of Churches in Ghana, 1989, 1991, 2010." Quoted in Amos Jimmy Markin, "Spirit and Mission: The Church of Pentecost as a Growing African Pentecostal Denomination." PhD diss., South African Theological Seminary, 2018.

Gifford, Paul Joseph. "Ghana's Charismatic Churches." *Journal of Religion in Africa* 24, no. 3 (August 1994): 241–65.

———. Ghana's New Christianity: Pentecostalism in a Globalizing African Economy. Bloomington: Indiana University Press, 2004.

Goheen, Michael W. Introducing Christian Mission Today: Scripture, History and Issues. Downers Grove: IVP Academic, 2014.

Grafton, David D. "Muslim-Christian Relations in the Midst of the COVID-19 Pandemic." *The Muslim World* 111, no. 4 (2021): 563–72.

Gray, Andrea, and Leith Gray. "The Imperishable Seed: Toward Effective Sharing of Scripture." In Woodberry, *From Seed to Fruit,* 26–37.

Green, Denis J. "Guidelines from Hebrews for Contextualization." In *Muslims and Christians on the Emmaus Road: Crucial Issues in Witness among Muslims*, edited by J. Dudley Woodberry, 233–50. Pasadena: MARC, 1989.

Gross, Edward N. Miracles, Demons and Spiritual Warfare: An Urgent Call for Discernment. Grand Rapids: Baker Books, 1990.

Grudem, Wayne A., ed. *Are Miraculous Gifts for Today?* Grand Rapids: Zondervan Academic, 1996.

Gyasi, I. K. "Ahmadiyya's Contribution to National Development." *Ghanaian Chronicle*. 8 March 2004. All Africa. https://allafrica.com/stories/200403081144.html.

Haider, Najam. *Shi'i Islam: An Introduction*. New York: Cambridge University Press, 2014.

Hakeen, Al-Hajj Maulvi Fazlur Rahman. "Ahmadiyya Movement in West Africa." *Review of Religions* 33, no. 9 & 10 (September–October 1934). Quoted in Nathan Iddrisu Samwini, "The Muslim Resurgence in Ghana Since 1950 and Its Effects upon Muslims and Muslim-Christian Relations." PhD diss., University of Birmingham, September 2003.

Haustein, Jörg. "Birmingham GloPent Conference Report." News and Events. GloPent. Last modified 30 May 2006. https://www.glopent.net/Members/webmaster/birmingham-2006/birmingham-conference-report.

Hilborn, David, and Matt Bird, eds. *God and the Generations: Youth, Age and the Church Today*. Carlisle: Paternoster, 2002. Quoted in Christian Tsekpoe, "Local Species in African Soil: The Development of James McKeown's Mission Models and the Church of Pentecost Ghana." PhD diss., Oxford Centre for Mission Studies, 2002.

Harrison, Everett F., and Donald A. Hagner. "Romans." *Romans–Galatians*. Vol. 11. Expositor's Bible Commentary. Rev. ed. Grand Rapids: Zondervan, 2008.

Hiebert, Paul G. "Power Encounter and Folk Islam." In *Muslims and Christians on the Emmaus Road: Crucial Issues in Witness among Muslims*, edited by J. Dudley Woodberry, 45–61. Monrovia: MARC, 1989.

———. Transforming Worldviews: An Anthropological Understanding of How People Change. Grand Rapids: Baker Academic, 2008.

Hillenbrand, Carole. Introduction to Islam: Beliefs and Practices in Historical Perspective. London: Thames and Hudson, 2015.

Hiskett, Mervyn. *The Development of Islam in West Africa*. Longman Studies in African History. Essex: Longman Group, 1984.

Hollenweger, Walter J. "Evangelism: A Non-Colonial Model." *Journal of Pentecostal Theology* 3, no. 7 (1995): 107–28.

Ibn Khaldun. "The Muqaddimah." Translated by Franz Rosenthal. Vol. 2. New York: Pantheon, 1958. Quoted in J. Dudley Woodberry, "The Muslim Understanding of Jesus." *Word and Word* 16, no. 2 (Spring 1996): 173–78.

Ibrahim, Mohammad Saani. "The Decline of Sufism in West Africa: Some Factors Contributing to the Political and Social Ascendancy of Wahhabist Islam in Northern Ghana." PhD diss., McGill University, Montreal, October 2011. ProQuest Dissertations & Theses Global.

———. "The Tijaniyya Order in Tamale, Ghana: Its Foundation, Organization and Role." MA thesis, McGill University, 2002.

Jawanza, Eric Clark. "Reconceiving the Doctrine of Jesus as Saviour in Terms of the African Understanding of an Ancestor: A Model for the Black Church." *Black Theology: An International Journal* 8, no 2 (2010): 140–59.

Johnson, Todd M. "Counting Pentecostals Worldwide." *Pneuma* 36 (2014): 265–88.

———. "The Demographics of Renewal." In *Spirit-Empowered Christianity in the 21st Century*, edited by Synan Vinson, 55–68. Lake Mary: Charisma House, 2011.

Johnstone, Patrick. The Future of the Global Church: History, Trends, and Possibilities. Downers Grove: IVP, 2011.

———. "Look at the Fields: Survey of the Task." In Woodberry, *From Seed to Fruit*, 1–13.

Jones, L. Bevan. *Christianity Explained to Muslims: A Manual for Christian Workers*. Calcutta: YMCA Publishing House, 1938. Cited in Sam Schlorff, *Missiological Models in Ministry to Muslims*. Upper Darby: Middle East Resources, 2006.

———. *The People of the Mosque*. London: Student Christian Movement Press, 1932. Cited in Sam Schlorff, *Missiological Models in Ministry to Muslims*. Upper Darby: Middle East Resources, 2006.

Khan, Muhammad Muhsin, and Muhammad Taqi-ud-Din Al-Hilali, trans. Interpretation of the Meanings of the Noble Qur'an in the English Language: A Summarized Version of Al-Tabari, Al-Qurtubi and Ibn Kathir with Comments from Salih Al-Bukhari. Saudi Arabia: Dar-us-Salam Publications, 1997.

Kim, Ah Young. "The Muslim Presence in Korea and Its Implications for Korean Evangelical Missiology." PhD diss., Fuller Theological Seminary, August 2003.

Kim, Caleb Chul-soo. *Islam among the Swahili in East Africa*. 2nd ed. Nairobi: Acton Publishers, 2016.

Kim, Caleb Chul-soo, John Travis, and Anna Travis. "Relevant Responses to Popular Muslim Piety." In Woodberry, *From Seed to Fruit*, 239–49.

Kobo, Ousman Murzik. "Promoting the Good and Forbidding the Evil: A Comparative Historical Study of Ahl-as-Sunna Islamic Movement in Ghana and Burkina Faso, 1950–2000." PhD diss., University of Wisconsin-Madison, 2005. ProQuest Dissertations & Theses Global.

Kraft, Charles H. *Power Encounter in Spiritual Warfare*. Eugene: Wipf and Stock, 2017.

Kraft, Marguerite G. Understanding Spiritual Power: A Forgotten Dimension of Cross-Cultural Mission and Ministry. Maryknoll: Orbis Books, 1995.

Kure, Maikudi. "Evangelism among Muslims: Notes from Nigeria." *Transformation* 17, no. 1 (January 2000): 17–19.

Lapidus, Ira M. *A History of Islamic Societies.* 2nd ed. Cambridge: Cambridge University Press, 2002.

Larbi, Emmanuel Kingsley. *Pentecostalism: The Eddies of Ghanaian Christianity.* Accra: Centre for Pentecostal and Charismatic Studies, 2015. Kindle.

Larson, Warren. "Jesus in Islam and Christianity: Discussing the Similarities and the Differences." *Missiology* 36, no. 3 (July 2008): 327–41.

Levtzion, Nehemia. Muslims and Chiefs in West Africa: Study of Islam in the Middle Volta Basin in the Pre-Colonial Period. Oxford: Clarendon Press, 1968.

Levtzion, Nehemiah, and Randall L. Pouwels, eds. *The History of Islam in Africa.* Athens: Ohio University Press, 2000.

Lewis, Bernard, and Buntzie Ellis Churchill. *Islam: The Religion and the People.* Upper Saddle River: Pearson Education, 2009.

Lipka, Michael, and Conrad Hackett. "Why Muslims Are the World's Fastest-Growing Religious Group." Pew Research Center. 6 April 2017. http://pewrsr.ch/2nOPNXY.

Liverman, Jeff. "Unplowed Ground: Engaging the Unreached." In Woodberry, *From Seed to Fruit*, 16–23.

Livingstone, Greg. "Laborer from the Global South: Partnering in the Task." In Woodberry, *From Seed to Fruit*, 39–50.

Lockyer, Herbert. *All the Miracles of the Bible.* Grand Rapids: Zondervan, 1961.

Love, Richard D. "Church Planting among Folk Muslims." *International Journal of Frontier Missions* 11, no. 2 (April 1994): 87–91.

Lull, Raymond. "Historical Paradigms of Mission." Quoted in Hyung Jin Park, "MI 9300 History of Mission and World Christianity." Lecture delivered at Torch Trinity Graduate University, Seoul, South Korea, 21 October 2020.

Ma, Wonsuk, and Julie C. Ma. *Mission in the Spirit: Towards a Pentecostal/Charismatic Missiology.* Regnum Studies in Mission. Eugene: Wipf and Stock, 2010.

Markin, Amos Jimmy. "Spirit and Mission: The Church of Pentecost as a Growing African Pentecostal Denomination." PhD diss., South African Theological Seminary, 2018.

Mbillah, Johnson. A. "African Churches and Interfaith Relations: Food for Thought." In *From the Cross to the Crescent: A PROCMURA Occasional Paper*, edited by J. Mbillah and J. Chesworth. PROCMURA, Nairobi, Kenya, 2004. Quoted in Martha Th. Fredericks, "Let Us Understand Our Differences: Current Trends in Christian-Muslim Relations in Sub-Saharan Africa." *Transformation* 27, no. 4 (October 2010): 261–74.

———. "PCG: Evangelism and the Muslim Presence." The First Evangelism Consultation of the Presbyterian Church of Ghana, 1–4 March 1994. Cited in Dovlo and Asante, "Reinterpreting the Straight Path," 214–38.

Mbiti, John S. "Challenges of Languages, Culture, and Interpretation in Translating the Greek New Testament." *Swedish Missiological Themes* 97, no. 2 (2009): 141–64.

———. *Concepts of God in Africa*. London: SPCK, 1970.

———. "The Future of Christianity in Africa (1970–2000)." *Communion Viatorum, Theological Quarterly* 13, no. 1–2 (Spring 1970): 19–38. Atla Religion Database with AtlaSerials.

McGee, Gary B. "Pentecostal Phenomena and Revivals in India: Implications for Indigenous Church Leadership." *International Bulletin of Missions Research* 20, no. 3 (1 July 1996): 112–17.

Mendonsa, Eugene L. "Etiology and Divination among the Sisala of Northern Ghana." *Journal of Religion in Africa* 9, no. 1 (1978): 33–50.

Mobley, Harris W. "The Ghanaian's Image of the Missionary: An Analysis of the Published Critiques of Christian Missionaries by Ghanaians, 1897–1965." Leiden: E. J. Brill, 1970. Cited in Daniel Okyere Walker, "The Pentecost Fire Is Burning: Models of Mission Activities in the Church of Pentecost." PhD diss., University of Birmingham, March 2010.

Musk, Bill. "Dreams and the Ordinary Muslim." *Missiology: An International Review* 16, no. 2 (April 1988): 163–71.

———. *The Unseen Faces of Islam: Sharing the Gospel with Ordinary Muslims*. Sutherland: Marc Evangelical Missionary Alliance, 1989.

Neill, Stephen. "A History of Christian Missions." London: Penguin Group, 1964. Cited in Daniel Okyere Walker, "The Pentecost Fire Is Burning: Models of Mission Activities in the Church of Pentecost." PhD diss., University of Birmingham, March 2010.

Newbigin, Lesslie. "Cross-Currents in Ecumenical and Evangelical Understandings of Mission." *International Bulletin of Missionary Research* 6, no. 4 (1982). Cited in Krish Kandiah, "Lesslie Newbigin's Contribution to a Theology of Evangelism." *Transformation* 24, no.1 (January 2007): 51–60. http://www.jstor.com/stable/43052689.

Nichols, Samuel O. "African Christian Theology and the Ancestors: Christology, Ecclesiology, Ethics and Their Implications beyond Africa." *Journal of African Christian Thought* 8, no.1 (June 2005): 27–35.

Nuamah, Sheikh Ishaak Ibrahim. *Islam, the Misunderstood Religion in Ghana: An Analytical Study of Efforts to Paint Islam Black*. Kumasi: Islamic Social Centre. Quoted in Dovlo and Asante, "Reinterpreting the Straight Path," 214–38.

Nuekpe, Dieudonne Komla. "Muslim Christian Encounter in Ghana." *Torch Trinity Center for Islamic Studies Journal* 12, no. 2 (September 2019): 193–234.

Odem, Jason. "Reviewed Work(s): Muhammad and the Qur'an, The Task and the Text by Kenneth Cragg." *Journal of Qur'anic Studies* 6, no. 2 (2004): 69–74.

Omenyo, Cephas N. "Charismatic Churches in Ghana and Contextualization." *Exchange* 31, no. 3 (2002): 252–76.

Onwubiko, K. B. C. *History of West Africa*. Book Two. Accra: Africana Publishing, 1985. Quoted in Dovlo and Asante, "Reinterpreting the Straight Path," 214–38.

Onyinah, Opoku. "Matthew Speaks to Ghanaian Healing Situations." *Journal of Pentecostal Theology* 10, no. 1 (2001): 125–26.

———. "The Movement of the Spirit around the World in Pentecostalism." *Transformation* 30, no. 4 (2 October 2013): 273–86..

Orobator, Agbonkhianmeghe E. *Theology Brewed in an African Pot*. Maryknoll: Orbis Books, 2008. Kindle.

Osborn, George, ed. "For the Turks." Poetical Words of John and Charles Wesley. Vol. 6. London: Wesleyan Methodist Conference Office, 1870. Quoted in Andrew F. Walls, The Cross-Cultural Process in Christian History: The Missionary Movement in Christian History. Maryknoll: Orbis Books, 2002.

Oseje, Lawrence. *African Traditions Meeting Islam: A Case of Luo-Muslim Funeral in Kendu Bay, Kenya*. Carlisle: Langham Monographs, 2018.

Osman, Sheikh Ahmed. *Islam: The Seal and Syntheses of Divine Revelations*. Maryland: Amana Publications, 2006.

Oss, Douglas A. "A Pentecostal/Charismatic Response to Richard B. Gaffin, Jr." In Grudem, *Miraculous Gifts*, 86–93.

Owusu Ansah, David. "Prayer, Amulets and Healing." In Levtzion and Pouwels, *The History of Islam in Africa*, 477–88.

Parrinder, Geoffrey. *Jesus in the Qur'an*. Oxford: Oneworld Publication, 1995.

Parshall, Philip L. Bridges to Islam: Christian Perspective on Folk Islam. Downers Grove: IVP, 2006.

———. *Bridges to Islam*. Grand Rapids: Baker Book House, 1983. Quoted in Sampson Kenneth Kofi Twumasi, "Understanding the Folk Islam of the Dagbani-Speaking People: A Prerequisite to Evangelism in North Ghana." PhD diss., Andrews University, 1996.

———. New Paths in Muslim Evangelism: Evangelical Approaches to Contextualization. Grand Rapids: Baker, 1992.

Payne, William Price. "Folk Religion and the Pentecostalism Surge in Latin America." *Asbury Journal* 71, no. 1 (2016): 145–74. https://place.asburyseminary.edu/asburyjournal/vol71/iss1/12.

Peskett, Howard, and Vinoth Ramachandra. *The Message of Mission*. The Bible Speaks Today. Downers Grove: IVP, 2003. Cited in Michael Goheen, *A Light to the Nations: The Missional Church and the Biblical Story*. Grand Rapids: Baker Academic, 2011.

Peterson, David. *The Apostles: PNTC*. Grand Rapids: Eerdmans, 2009. Accordance Bible Software.

Petterson, Olof. "Monotheism or Polytheism? A Study of the Ideas about Supreme Beings in African Religion." *Temenos Nordic Journal of Comparative Religion* 2 (1966): 49–67. https://doi.org/10.33356/temenos.6465.

Pew Research Center. "The Future of World Religions: Population Growth Projection 2010–2050." Washington, D.C.: Pew Research Center, 2016. Accessed 8 April 2021, https://www.pewresearch.org/religion/2015/04/02/religious-projections-2010-2050/#:~:text=Due%20to%20the%20heavy%20concentration,2050%20and%2055%25%20in%202010.

Pocock, Michael. The Changing Face of World Missions, Engaging Contemporary Issues and Trends. Grand Rapids: Baker Academic, 2005.

Pontzen, Benedikt. *Islam in a Zongo: Muslim Lifeworlds in Asante, Ghana*. Cambridge: Cambridge University Press, 2021. Kindle.

Powell, Samuel M. "The Theological Significance of the Holiness Movement." *Quarterly Review* 25, no. 2 (Summer 2005): 126–40.

Rattray, R. Sutherland. "Religion and Art in Ashanti." London: Oxford University Press, 1927. Quoted in Emmanuel Kingsley Larbi, *Pentecostalism: The Eddies of Ghanaian Christianity*. Ghana: Centre for Pentecostal and Charismatic Studies, 2015.

Reisacher, Evelyne A. Joyful Witness in the Muslim World: Sharing the Gospel in Everyday Encounters. Grand Rapids: Baker Academic, 2016.

Rheenen, Gailyn Van. *Communicating Christ in Animistic Contexts*. Grand Rapids: Baker Book House, 1991. Cited in Sampson Kenneth Kofi Twumasi, "Understanding the Folk Islam of the Dagbani-Speaking People: A Prerequisite to Evangelism in North Ghana." PhD diss., Andrews University, 1996.

Ripken, Nik. "Grace and Truth: Towards Christlike Relationships." In Woodberry, *From Seed to Fruit*, 367–79.

Rippin, Andrew. Muslims: Their Religious Beliefs and Practices. Vol. 1. The Formative Period. London: Routledge, 1991.

Robeck, Cecil M. "A Pentecostal Theology for a New Millennium." Paper presented to the twenty-sixth annual meeting of the Society for Pentecostal Studies, Oakland, California, 1997. Quoted in Allan Anderson, "Diversity in the Definition of 'Pentecostal/Charismatic' and Its Ecumenical Implications." *Mission Studies* 19, no. 1 (1 January 2002): 40–55.

Robert, Dana L. Christian Mission: How Christianity Became a World Religion. West Sussex: John Wiley & Sons, 2009.

Rommen, Edward, ed. *Spiritual Power and Missions*. Pasadena: William Carey Library, 1995.

Ryan, Patrick J. "'Arise, O God!': The Problem of 'Gods' in West Africa." *Journal of Religion in Africa* 11, no. 3 (1980): 161–71.

———. "The Mystical Theology of Tijani Sufism and Its Social Significance in West Africa." *Journal of Religion in Africa* 30, no. 2 (May 2000): 208–24.

Samwini, Nathan Iddrisu. "The Muslim Resurgence in Ghana Since 1950 and Its Effects upon Muslims and Muslim-Christian Relations." PhD diss., University of Birmingham, September 2003.

Sanneh, Lamin. *The Crown and the Turban: Muslims and West African Pluralism.* Boulder: Westview Press, 1997.

———. *Pentecostal Mission and Global Christianity.* London: Regnum Books International, 2014.

———. *West African Christianity: The Religious Impact.* London: C. Hurst, 1993.

Sarbah, Cosmas Justice Ebo. "A Critical Study of Christian-Muslim Relations in the Central Region of Ghana with Special Reference to Traditional Akan Values." PhD diss., University of Birmingham, September 2010.

Saucy, Robert L. "An Open but Cautious Response to Richard B. Gaffin, Jr." In Grudem, *Miraculous Gifts*, 65–71.

———. "An Open but Cautious View." In Grudem, *Miraculous Gifts*, 97–147.

Schimmel, Annemarie, and Abdoldjavad Falaturi, eds. "We Believe in One God: The Experience of God in Christianity and Islam." London: Seabury Press, 1979. Cited in Ah Young Kim, "The Muslim Presence in Korea and Its Implications for Korean Evangelical Missiology." PhD diss., Fuller Theological Seminary, August 2003.

Schlorff, Sam. *Missiological Models in Ministry to Muslims.* Upper Darby: Middle East Resources, 2006.

Sebunje, William. "Research Techniques." Kampala, Uganda: Centre for Statistics and Applied Research Capacity Building. Accessed 20 November 2021. https://docplayer.net/52407791-Research-techniques-researched-and-documented-by-william-sebunje.html.

Shenk, David W. "The African Christian and Islamic Mysticism: Folk Islam." Cited in Azumah and Sanneh, *African Christian and Islam*, 251–72.

———. *Journeys of the Muslim Nation and the Christian Church: Exploring the Mission of Two Communities.* Scottdale: Herald Press, 2003.

Shin, Howard. *The Dividing Worldviews of Jesus and Muhammad.* Bloomington: Bestbow Press, 2015.

Steinhaus, S. P. "The Spirit-First Approach to Muslim Evangelism." *International Journal of Frontier Missions* 17, no. 4 (Winter 2000): 23–30. https://www.ijfm.org/PDFs_IJFM/17_4_PDFs/03_Steinhaus.pdf.

Storms, C. Samuel. "A Third Wave Response to Richard B. Gaffin, Jr." In Grudem, *Miraculous Gifts*, 72–85.

Strauss, Mark L. *Four Portraits, One Jesus: A Survey of Jesus and the Gospels.* Grand Rapids: Zondervan, 2007.

Suarsana, Yan. "What is Pentecostalism? Some Historiographical Considerations." Paper submitted to the workshop, "Studying Pentecostalism in a Transcultural Perspective" at the Cluster of Excellence "Asia and Europe in a Global Context," Karl Jaspers Centre for Advanced Cultural Studies, Heidelberg University, Germany, 3–5 April 2014. https://www.glopent.net/Members/ysuarsana/suarsana_paper_workshop_2014.pdf/view. Accessed 24 November 2021.

Tasie, G. O. M. "Christian Awakening in West Africa, 1914–1918: A Study in the Significance of Native Agency in the History of Christianity in West Africa," edited by Ogbu U. Kalu. London: Longman, 1980. Quoted in Daniel Okyere Walker, "The Pentecost Fire Is Burning: Models of Mission Activities in the Church of Pentecost." PhD diss., University of Birmingham, March 2010.

Trimingham, John Spencer. "The Influence of Islam upon Africa." London: Longmans, Green & Co., 1958. Cited in Cosmas Justice Ebo Sarbah, "A Critical Study of Christian-Muslim Relations in the Central Region of Ghana with Special Reference to Traditional Akan Values." PhD diss., University of Birmingham, September 2010.

———. *Islam in West Africa*. Oxford: Oxford University Press, 1959.

———. "The Phases of Islamic Expansion and Islamic Culture Zones in Africa." In *Islam in Tropical Africa*, edited by I. M. Lewis. 2nd ed. London: International African Institute, 1980.

Tsekpoe, Christian. "Local Species in African Soil: The Development of James McKeown's Mission Models and the Church of Pentecost, Ghana." PhD diss., Oxford Centre for Mission Studies, 2002.

Twumasi, Sampson Kenneth Kofi. "Understanding the Folk Islam of the Dagbani-Speaking People: A Prerequisite to Evangelism in North Ghana." PhD diss., Andrews University, 1996.

Ukah, Asonzeh. "Prosperity, Prophecy and the COVID-19 Pandemic: The Healing Economy of African Pentecostalism." *Pneuma* 42 (2020): 430–59.

Unal, Ali. The Qur'an with Annotated Interpretation in Modern English. New Jersey: The Light, 2006.

Unluer, Sema. "Being an Insider Researcher while Conducting Case Study Research." *Qualitative Report* 17, no. 29 (2012): 1–14. https://doi.org/10.46743/2160-3715/2012.1752.

Veerman, David R. "Introduction to Hebrews." In *Life Application Study Bible, New International Version*, edited by Bruce Barton. Grand Rapids: Tyndale, 1989.

Vikor, Knut S. "Sufi Brotherhoods in Africa." In Levtzion and Pouwels, *The History of Islam in Africa*, 441–76.

Vinson, Synan. "The Charismatic Renewal After Fifty Years." In *Spirit-Empowered Christianity in the 21st Century*, edited by Synan Vinson, 7–24. Lake Mary: Charisma House, 2011.

Vondey, Wolfgang. *Pentecostal Theology: Living the Full Gospel*. New York: Bloomsbury, 2017.

Walker, Daniel Okyere. "The Pentecost Fire Is Burning: Models of Mission Activities in the Church of Pentecost." PhD diss., University of Birmingham, March 2010.

Walls, Andrew F. *The Cross-Cultural Process in Christian History: Studies in the Transmission and Appropriation of Faith*. Maryknoll: Orbis Books, 2002.

Watt, Montgomery W. "Islam and Christianity Today: A Contribution to Dialogue." London: Routledge, 1983. Quoted in Ah Young Kim, "The Muslim Presence in Korea and Its Implications for Korean Evangelical Missiology." PhD diss., Fuller Theological Seminary, August 2003.

Westerlund, D., and E. Rosander, eds. "African Islam and Islam in Africa: Encounter Between Sufis and Islamists." Athens: Ohio University Press, 1997. Cited in Mohammad Saani Ibrahim, "The Decline of Sufism in West Africa: Some Factors Contributing to the Political and Social Ascendancy of Wahhabist Islam in Northern Ghana." PhD diss., McGill University, Montreal, October 2011. ProQuest Dissertations & Theses Global.

Wilks, Ivor. "The Juula and the Expansion of Islam into the Forest." In Levtzion and Pouwels, *The History of Islam in Africa*, 93–115.

Wilson, Christy J. *The Christian Message to Islam*. New York: Fleming H. Revell, 1950. Cited in Sam Schlorff, *Missiological Models in Ministry to Muslims*. Upper Darby: Middle East Resources, 2006.

Woodberry, J. Dudley, ed. From Seed to Fruit: Global Trends, Fruitful Practices, and Emerging Issues among Muslims. 2nd ed. Pasadena: William Carey Library, 2011.

———. "The Muslim Understanding of Jesus." *Word and Word* 16, no. 2 (Spring 1996): 173–78.

———. "The View from a Refurbished Chair." In *Missiological Education for the Twenty-First Century: The Book, The Circle, and the Sandals, Essays in Honour of Paul E. Pierson*, edited by J. Dudley Woodberry, Charles Van Engen, and Edgar J. Elliston. American Society of Missiology Series 23. Eugene: Wipf and Stock, 2005.

World Council of Churches Central Committee. "Towards Common Witness." Resources. World Council of Churches. 19 September 1997. https://www.oikoumene.org/resources/documents/towards-common-witness.

Wright, Christopher J. H. The Mission of God's People: A Biblical Theology of the Church's Mission. Grand Rapids: Zondervan, 2010.

Wyllie, Robert W. "Pioneers of Ghanaian Pentecostalism: Peter Anim and James McKeown." *Journal of Religion in Africa* 6, no. 2 (1974): 109–22.

Yakubu, Rahman. "Ghana." In *The African Christian and Islam*, edited by John Azumah and Lamin Sanneh, 303–16. Carlisle: Langham Monographs, 2013.

Yung, Hwa. "Pentecostalism and the Asian Church." In *The Charismatic Face of Christianity in Asia*, edited by Allan Anderson and Edmond Tang, 30–45. 2nd ed. Regnum Studies in Mission. Oxford: Regnum, 2005.

Zwemer, Samuel. *The Influence of Animism on Islam*. New York: McMillan, 1920. Quoted in Sampson Kenneth Kofi Twumasi, "Understanding the Folk Islam of the Dagbani-Speaking People: A Prerequisite to Evangelism in North Ghana." PhD diss., Andrews University, 1996.

Langham Literature, with its publishing work, is a ministry of Langham Partnership.

Langham Partnership is a global fellowship working in pursuit of the vision God entrusted to its founder John Stott –

> *to facilitate the growth of the church in maturity and Christ-likeness through raising the standards of biblical preaching and teaching.*

Our vision is to see churches in the Majority World equipped for mission and growing to maturity in Christ through the ministry of pastors and leaders who believe, teach and live by the word of God.

Our mission is to strengthen the ministry of the word of God through:
- nurturing national movements for biblical preaching
- fostering the creation and distribution of evangelical literature
- enhancing evangelical theological education

especially in countries where churches are under-resourced.

Our ministry

Langham Preaching partners with national leaders to nurture indigenous biblical preaching movements for pastors and lay preachers all around the world. With the support of a team of trainers from many countries, a multi-level programme of seminars provides practical training, and is followed by a programme for training local facilitators. Local preachers' groups and national and regional networks ensure continuity and ongoing development, seeking to build vigorous movements committed to Bible exposition.

Langham Literature provides Majority World preachers, scholars and seminary libraries with evangelical books and electronic resources through publishing and distribution, grants and discounts. The programme also fosters the creation of indigenous evangelical books in many languages, through writer's grants, strengthening local evangelical publishing houses, and investment in major regional literature projects, such as one volume Bible commentaries like the *Africa Bible Commentary* and the *South Asia Bible Commentary*.

Langham Scholars provides financial support for evangelical doctoral students from the Majority World so that, when they return home, they may train pastors and other Christian leaders with sound, biblical and theological teaching. This programme equips those who equip others. Langham Scholars also works in partnership with Majority World seminaries in strengthening evangelical theological education. A growing number of Langham Scholars study in high quality doctoral programmes in the Majority World itself. As well as teaching the next generation of pastors, graduated Langham Scholars exercise significant influence through their writing and leadership.

To learn more about Langham Partnership and the work we do visit **langham.org**

www.ingramcontent.com/pod-product-compliance
Lightning Source LLC
Chambersburg PA
CBHW052056230426
43662CB00037B/1959